The Work-at-Home Sourcebook

The Work-at-Home Sourcebook

How to Find "at Home" Work That's Right For You

Lynie Arden

Live Oak Publications
Boulder, Colorado

Note: If you are in a position to hire home-based workers and you want your company to be listed in future editions, please send your name, address and phone number to Lynie Arden, c/o Live Oak Publications, at the address below.

Published by **Live Oak Publications**
>   6003 N. 51st Street, #105
>   P.O. Box 2193
>   Boulder, CO 80306

Library of Congress Cataloging-in-Publication Data
Arden, Lynie, 1949-

The work-at-home sourcebook.

Includes index.
1. Home labor--United States--Directories. 2. Home-based businesses--
   United States--Directories.
3. Business enterprises--United States--Directories.
I. Title.
HD2336.U5A73   1988   338.7'4'02573   87-35699
ISBN 0-911781-07-2

Disclaimer

Every attempt has been made to make this book as accurate and complete as possible. There may be mistakes of content or typography, however, and the author and publisher make no guarantees, warranties, or representations of any kind. This book is designed as a general guide to the subject. The reader is urged to investigate and verify information and its applicability under any particular situation or circumstances.

The author and publisher shall have no liability or responsibility to anyone with respect to contacts, negotiations, or agreements that may result from information in this book, or for any loss or damage caused or alleged to have been caused directly or indirectly by such information. If legal advice or other expert assistance is required, the services of a competent professional person should be sought.

Table of Contents

Chapter 1
How To Go To Work From Your Home

"This is our lifestyle; it's called freedom."
—Janice Katz, Sacramento Professional Typists Network

Personnel manager Pat Mahy wasn't looking for a job at home, but when Escrow Overload asked her to give it a try a couple of years ago, she said okay.

"Starting out I had my doubts. I couldn't imagine being without the stimulation of other people at work. It had some appeal, though. I figured my time might be better spent if I wasn't wasting it commuting. Well, I was thrilled within a week!"

Pat is one of the 25 million Americans who currently work at home, a number the U.S. Department of Labor predicts will double in the next decade. Some government studies have indicated that as much as 75% of the work done in this country could eventually be moved home.

Not everyone would be happy working at home, of course, and many people are simply not interested in moving their work home. Still, more and more people are having the same experience as Pat Mahy, who says "I'm still finding more hidden benefits to working at home the longer I do it."

Using This Book

If you want to give working at home at try, this book can be a good place to start. It won't show you how to start a home business and it won't duplicate certain other work-at-home topics that are well covered in other books.* As far as we know, though, nowhere else can you find as many specific opportunities for working at home—involving so many diverse options—already assembled for you into one neat package.

For an unusually good selection of home-business books see the catalog available from The New Careers Center, listed in the Resource Guide at the back of this book.

A Wide Range of Possibilities

You'll quickly notice that there are a variety of work styles represented in this book. Once you leave the confines of the traditional nine-to-five centralized work mode, a colorful rainbow of employment options appear. There is freelancing, independent contracting, working on commission, salaried positions, co-oping, and various combinations of these and other ways of working. You can get paid by the hour, by the piece, by the sale, by the project, or by the year.

You'll want to consider your needs carefully. Do you need the security of a salary? If so, freelancing is not for you. Have you always wished you could get paid for what you produce because you do it faster and better than almost everybody else? Then you may be able to boost your income by opting for piece rates. Alternately, you might want to be able to depend on a set salary, yet have lots of opportunities for earning more than the base rate by earning commissions, bonuses or other incentives. Telemarketing and market research positions, for example, often offer this type of compensation package.

One other point needs to be made about salaries. In comparing the salaries (and other forms of compensation) offered for working at home to those of conventional employment, be sure to take into consideration the many savings you'll enjoy by working at home. The money you'll save on clothing, commuting, parking, lunches and other items may make it worthwhile for you to take a home-based job that, on the surface at least, offers less money than you would make going into an office every day.

Opportunities Everywhere

You'll find over 1,000 companies in this book which have work-at-home arrangements, but it's important to keep in mind that these listings represent only a small sample of the work-at-home opportunities actually available today. This book will be most valuable to you if you use it as an idea generator.

Suppose, for example, that in skimming through the company listings you notice there are a number of jobs for processing insurance claims at home. You worked in an insurance office for several years and feel confident you could do the work, but for one reason or another none of the specific jobs in the listings are exactly right for your situation.

By all means don't be discouraged. Study the job listings carefully, noting the names of the companies, their pay structure, how many home workers they employ and other pertinent information. Then go talk to each insurance company in your town. They may never have considered hiring home workers before but if you can explain how other insurance companies have organized their home work programs—and the benefits they are getting from their programs—you'll have a good chance at getting exactly the work you want.

Some of the benefits you'll want to mention are the following (and they're not limited to insurance companies):

Increased Productivity
A 20% increase in productivity is average, with some employers reporting substantially more than that. Some dedicated telecommuters have reported up to an 80% increase over their office-bound counterparts.

Lower Turnover
Once settled into a home-based job, would you give it up? Turnover among home-working employees is so low, some companies have waiting lists up to a year long for new applicants.

Near Zero Absenteeism
Flexiplace usually means flexitime, too. Work schedules can be manipulated to accomodate child-care needs, fevers and sniffles, and yes, an occasional case of playing hookey on a beautiful spring day. As long as the work gets done within the overall time limits of the job, everyone's happy.

Improved Recruiting
In areas with low unemployment, flexiplace is often used as an added inducement to potential employees. This is especially true for fields like computer programming where demand for highly qualified workers often exceeds supply. Several years ago, Continental Illinois Bank had a problem finding qualified secretaries in the Chicago area. They reasoned that many competent women were at home with children and were therefore unable to participate in the job market. The bank started Project HomeWork to solve the problem.

Lower Costs
Many companies start home work programs when they run out of room for expansion and don't want to tie up additional capital in office space. Insurance, utilities, training, maintenance and other costs often go down when workers go home.

The important thing to remember is that home work programs benefit businesses as well as employees. In asking for a job at home, you're not asking for any favors; you're asking for an arrangement that will be beneficial to all .

Getting a Home-Based Job, Step-by-Step

The first step in getting the home-based job of your choice is to define exactly what it is you want. You should ask yourself what kind of a commitment you are willing to make. Are you looking for a long-term career or just a short-term job? Do you need to support yourself or do you just need some extra income? Do you want to work in the same industry where you've always worked or try something new?

A wide range of occupations are covered in this book. Do you see something you like? If not, back up and give some thought to the type of jobs that can be done at home. While opportunities for home work span a wide spectrum of employment possibilities, not all work can effectively be moved home.

First of all, home work is work which can be easily measured. Why? Because you and your employer need to know what to expect, such as when the work will begin and when it will be completed. If you are paid a piece rate, which is very common, this factor is crucial. Besides that, your employer wants to know that he's getting his money's worth. Along these same lines, the work should require minimal supervision after initial training.

It is also important to know whether there are physical barriers to doing a particular type of work at home. Work which requires minimal space and no large and/or expensive equipment is ideal. In some cases, the type of equipment and the amount of space used for home work is restricted by local zoning ordinances. More on that later.

Where The Work Is

In general, home work tends to be available at very large corporations and at very small companies. Mid-sized firms often lack the management expertise available at large companies and may be less willing to take risks than small companies. There are many exceptions to this, however, especially among companies originally started using home workers.

Information-intensive industries such as the banking industry, the insurance industry and the computer software industry are prime candidates for home work because so much of their work is done via computer and telephone.

All types of sales organizations have traditionally been open to working at home. Real estate, publishing, insurance, pharmaceuticals, apparel, cosmetics, and printing are just a few of the businesses that typically use home-based representatives.

Home businesses are often forced by zoning ordinances to use home workers or else move out of their original home base. Such businesses may need secretaries, sales reps, bookkeepers, assemblers, shipping clerks, artists, copy writers, public relations consultants, programmers, lawyers, and accountants.

Any rapidly growing company may also be a good bet. Whenever a company suddenly outgrows its available space, the option of having additional workers provide their own space can be very appealing. Besides, if the growth is temporary, the money spent on additional facilities would be wasted. It is normally far cheaper for a company to pay for extra phone lines, computer terminals, or other equipment for employee's homes than to build new office space.

Moving Your Work Home

Now that you have zeroed in on the job you would like to have at home, you have two options. You can either start from scratch and find a new job starting at home or you can move your present (or future) job from its current location to your home.

Large corporations are most likely to accept the latter option. There are presently several hundred major corporations in the U.S. that have home workers on the payroll. Very few, however, hire home workers from the outside. As a rule, they want to develop confidence in their employees before allowing them to take their work home. Therefore, the very first thing to do is make sure you are known for being a valuable and trustworthy employee.

Next, develop a plan of action. Define the job tasks which are feasible for home work. Don't ignore problems that could arise later and undermine your position. Consider all of the possible problems and devise a "worst case" scenario and alternative solutions for dealing with each of them. That way, you will be prepared and can confidently assure your company there will be no unpleasant surprises.

You will need to sell your home work idea to your employer, focusing on the ways moving your work home will benefit the company. Remember, your employer is in business to make a profit, and while he/she probably prefers happy employees, the bottom line is ultimately the highest priority. You can take comfort in the fact that the benefits employers gain from work-at-home arrangements are well documented. If you want to refer to some success stories, see the company profiles scattered throughout this book. In addition, the following information is likely to grab your employer's attention.

The number one benefit to employers is increased productivity. The best documented cases are from Blue Cross/Blue Shield of South Carolina, which reported productivity gains of 50%, and from Control Data Corp., which showed gains of 35%. Employees at home tend to work at their individual peak hours, don't get paid for long lunch hours and time spent at the water cooler, and often continue to work while feeling slightly under the weather rather than take time off.

The second greatest benefit to employers is the cost savings from not spending money on additional office space, utilities, parking space, etc. This is especially helpful for growing companies and also for home-based businesses that need to expand, but want to limit the costs of doing so. Some companies have even sent employees home and rented out the unoccupied space to compatible firms. As a direct result of its home work program, Pacific Bell closed three offices last year, saving $40,000 in rent alone.

Another advantage to employers is a far lower turnover rate among employees allowed to work at home. In some industries, rapid turnover is a serious problem. The insurance industry, for instance, has a turnover rate between 30% and 45%. As you would expect, recruiting and training costs are very high in such industries.

All of this should give you ample ammunition to convince your manager(s) to let you try working at home. It's usually best not to try for an immediate move to full-time home work, though. Start slowly, asking to take your work home a couple of times in the afternoon, and then proposing a two-day project. While you're testing the waters, make sure you check in by phone to see if anything has come up at the office that you need to take care of. After a few months of occasional home work, you'll be ready to go to your manager and point out that you get a more accomplished when you're not distracted by office routines and don't have to waste valuable time commuting.

Remember, you're not asking for favors. You are simply offering what every employer wants—a motivated, efficient worker interested in increasing productivity.

Starting From Scratch

If you're presently not working and need to find a job you can do at home right from the start, there is a good chance the type of work you're looking for is secondary to your need to be at home. (This has proven to be true about 75% of the time.)

The first thing you should do is examine your skills and match them up with possible job types. If you don't see anything here that you're already trained in, consider what you would like to learn. Many jobs offer training at a central location or right in your home.

Preparing a Resume

It's time to prepare a resume that stresses skills needed to work at home. In other words, you should emphasize anything that demonstrates your ability to work well without supervision. Because your employer won't see you very often (or ever, in some cases), your reliability is extremely important. For every job you apply for, you should write a cover letter openly stressing your desire and ability to work efficiently and effectively at home.

There are basically two kinds of resumes—chronological and functional. Both include identifying information, work history, and educational background. Neither is necessarily better than the other, but generally speaking, employers prefer the chronological style because its format is quick and easy to read.

The functional resume presents essentially the same information, but in a different order. The purpose of this type of resume is to emphasize your skills. Instead of starting with dates, you head each descriptive paragraph with a job title.

Regardless of the style of resume you choose, the following rules apply.

• Include only information that is directly relevant to the job for which you are applying. While it is great to have many skills and accomplishments, employers are only interested in what you can offer them in particular.

• Limit your resume to two pages. A ten page resume may look impressive, but what employer has time to read it? It will be easier to keep your resume brief if you carefully follow the rule above.

• Present a professional image. Your resume should be typed or typeset in a neat and orderly fashion. Leave sufficient margins and double space between paragraphs. Proofread carefully. Grammatical errors and typos could cost you a highly desirable job.

The Cover Letter

A cover letter is a personalized letter stating your interest in a job in clear, concise terms. You should indicate which job you are applying for and point out a few good reasons why you should be considered. There is no need to repeat any of the information included in the resume.

Letter of Interest

In some cases an employer is more interested in your aptitude and enthusiasm than in your background. This is often the situation when a training course will be provided, or for "people jobs" such as sales, customer service, and market research positions. The basic requirement here is an ability to relate to people and communicate effectively. How do you prove that ability with a resume? You can't, really, so you use a letter of interest.

A letter of interest is similar to a cover letter except that you (briefly) describe any background or personality traits that are applicable to the position and then request an application or an interview, or both.

Phone Interviews

Prospective home workers are often interviewed over the phone; many are hired without ever meeting their new employers.

After sending in an application, you can normally expect to be called within a week or two if you are going to be considered for an opening in the near future. Of course, you won't know exactly when to expect the call, but you should be prepared right from the start.

• Find out as much as you can about the company ahead of time. Then, make a list of questions you want to ask about the job. Keep the list and a copy of your application near the phone. Don't forget to keep a pen or pencil and paper handy, too.

• Try to use a phone in a quiet part of the house where you will not be interrupted.

• Listen carefully, take your time and answer all questions in a clear, steady voice. Don't mumble. Speak with confidence and honesty.

• Be polite and friendly, but not "chummy."

• Be enthusiastic even if you're not sure you want the job. You can always change your mind later.

• Be prepared to give references if asked.

Most important, you want to present yourself as the right candidate for the job. Ask yourself one question: "Why should this company hire me?" This is, after all, what they are calling to find out.

Don't Expect Too Much

Looking for a job that you can do from home is essentially no different, and definitely no easier, than looking for a job in a "traditional" work place. You cannot assume that because an employer uses home workers, that somehow means the employer is desperate for help and getting the job is going to be easy. On the contrary, employers often offer the work-at-home option as an incentive in order to have a larger pool of applicants to choose from. A single small ad in a local newspaper mentioning a job that can be done at home typically elicits hundreds of responses. That means competition, and lots of it, for you. It's up to you, and you alone, to convince any prospective employer that you're a cut above the rest and that you will handle the job professionally with a minimal amount of supervision.

Most home worker employers never advertise at all (like most of the ones in this book). They don't need to because the jobs are so sought after, word-of-mouth alone often creates a waiting list of eager applicants. If you should apply to any of these firms and don't receive a reply, understand that they don't have the manpower or the time to do so and your name has been placed on file for possible future openings. Rather than sit around waiting for a response that may not come for quite a while, your time would be better spent seeking out new opportunities in your field that nobody else knows about yet.

Home Work and the Law

There are two areas of the law that directly affect home workers; labor laws and zoning ordinances.

Labor Laws

Only a handful of states have labor laws specifically regarding working at home. In each case, their purpose is to govern "industrial home work" (work which would normally be done in a factory such as product assembly). Industrial home work is usually low skilled, low pay work in which there has been a history of worker exploitation. The purpose of the state labor laws is to insure worker safety and insure that minimum wage requirements are met.

States without labor laws specifically relating to home work fall under the jurisdiction of the U.S. Dept. of Labor and its Fair Labor Standards Act of 1938 (FLSA).

The FLSA initially prohibited seven industries from using home workers. In 1938, this was a good idea since sweatshop conditions were the established norm. In December, 1984, after years of see-sawing through the courts, the ban on knitted outerwear was lifted. The remaining prohibited industries are: gloves and mittens, belts and buckles, jewelry, women's apparel, embroidery, and handkerchiefs.

There are currently bills in both the House and the Senate that are intended to do away with any and all restrictions on home work at the federal level.

Senator Orrin Hatch introduced the Freedom of the Workplace bill (S.665) soon after the ban on knitted outerwear was lifted. It calls for the complete reversal of the FLSA restrictions on home work. As written, workers' rights would be protected by the same certification process that is required for home knitters.

Congresswoman Olympia Snowe of Maine introduced a similar bill, the Home Employment Enterprise Act (HR2815) in the House of Representatives. It is virtually the House twin of Hatch's bill. Congresswoman Snowe told the House, "Cottage industries play a vital role in the economy of the state of Maine, large parts of New England, and other areas of the nation. The independent nature of home work and the unavailability of alternative employment opportunities make working at home ideal. It is time to safeguard the freedom to choose to work at home."

Both bills are supported by the Reagan Administration and several industry associations are actively lobbying for passage of both bills before the next presidential election.

Aside from the prohibitions mentioned here, there are no other occupations covered by labor laws. Furthermore, these laws only pertain to employees, not independent contractors, independent business people, or otherwise self-employed workers.

Zoning

Before working at home in any capacity, you should find out what your local zoning ordinance has to say about it. If you live in a rural area, chances are good that you have nothing to worry about. In populated areas, however, there are often specific provisions in the zoning laws pertaining to home occupations.

Zoning laws tend to focus on the impact of a given activity. Sometimes called "nuisance laws," they are designed to protect neighborhoods from disruptive noise, traffic, odors, etc.

Chicago is an extreme example. Within the city limits, it is illegal to use electrical equipment in a home occupation. That means no calculators, no type-writers, no computers. The laws are outdated in Chicago and are too often outdated elsewhere around the country. The city council in Chicago is working on a new ordinance that will be more accomodating to home work, and it's possible for you to initiate zoning changes in your city, too.

Zoning boards are made up of your neighbors and local business people, and it is likely they are unaware of problems caused by outdated zoning ordinances. If you are frustrated by your city's zoning code, get to know these people, attend some meetings, and propose that the laws be changed.

You may find approaching local zoning or planning boards easier with a copy of the "Model Zoning Ordinances Set" in hand. The set was prepared by the National Alliance of Homebased Businesswomen and consists of a model zoning ordinance and two brochures, "Planning for Homebased Businesses" and "Zoning for Homebased Businesses." The set is available for $2 from NAHB, P.O. Box 306, Midland Park, NJ 07432.

Independent Contractor Status and Tax Savings

More often than not, home workers are paid as independent contractors. In essence, this means you are totally responsible for your own work. While different government agencies don't necessarily agree on the definition of independent contractor, generally speaking, there are two major factors affecting how home workers are classified. They are the "degree of control which the employer exercises over the manner in which the work is performed," and "opportunities for profit and loss."

It should be noted that no government agency will take you on your word that you are an independent contractor. Even if you have a written contract with a company declaring that you both agree to an employer/independent contractor relationship, the legitimacy of that relationship must be proven.

The issue here is not whether being an employee is better or worse than being an independent contractor. There are advantages and disadvantages in every situation. Rather, the issue is whether the term "independent contractor" is being applied consistantly and correctly. If you meet all I.R.S. criteria for independent contractor status, you'll be responsible for your own taxes, most notably Social Security tax, which is renamed "Self-Employment Tax" for this purpose.

The present rate of self-employment tax is 12.3% for any income over $400 and under $40,000 annually. To a new independent contractor, this may sound totally outrageous. After all, wasn't it bad enough when the boss deducted 6%? Acutally, the independent contractor is at a real advantage because the 12.3% is based on net income—that is, your profit after all your business deductions have been taken.

Notice the word "profit." This may be new to you, but being an independent contractor means being self-employed—and that means being in business. If you're in business, that means you're making a profit (hopefully) after paying your business expenses.

Business expenses will help you at tax time, so you need to keep records right from the start of any and all expenditures. Business expenses generally fall into two categories: direct and indirect.

Direct expenses are those which occur in the day-to-day operation of your business. Costs for office supplies, phone service, advertising, bookkeeping, equipment, books, trade publications and seminars related to your work, and insurance are all examples of direct, fully deductible expenses.

You shouldn't forget the more subtle types of deductions, either. Entertainment in the course of your work, whether in your own home or not, is ordinarily deductible if you discuss or conduct business while you're entertaining and keep a record of what went on and with whom.

The same thing is true for vacations. You can generally write off a portion of your vacation expenses if you spend some time along the way looking for new business. Remember, the government expects you to try to expand your business.

Indirect expenses are those that are a part of your usual domestic bills— utilities, rent or mortgage payments, maintenance and housecleaning, property insurance, etc. Indirect expenses come under the heading of the Home Office Deduction.

The Home Office Deduction is the most common and significant way for home workers to reduce their federal tax. In order to claim the deduction, you must show that your home work space is used regularly and exclusively as your principal place of business and meeting place. (If you are a salaried employee, you may also be eligible if you can prove that your employer requires you to keep a home office as a condition of employment. In this case, you should consult an expert to determine if you meet the requirements.)

Home office expenses are deductible at the rate of whatever percentage of square footage your work space takes up. If your home is 1,000 square feet and you use 200 square feet exclusively for work space, you can normally deduct 20% of those receipts. A word of caution: if you use your work space for any other purpose than work, you can not deduct any of these expenses. Therefore, working on the kitchen table is a bad idea unless you really don't have any choice.

At last count, there were some 23 possible deductions for a home office. To make sure you don't miss any, get a copy of I.R.S. Publication 587, "Business Use of the Home." It is available free from any I.R.S. office and is updated annually.

Making the Most of Working at Home

If you perservere in your efforts to land a home job, in time you're likely to succeed. Your home work space is where you will be spending a large portion of your life—in fact, you will most likely spend more time there than any other place. The consideration you give to its design could have a tremendous impact on the success of your home work experience.

Wouldn't it be wonderful to have a work place all your own, some private space free from distractions? A beautiful office maybe, with a separate entrance, big windows facing out onto a garden, with elegant furniture and the latest equipment modern technology has to offer. Fortunately, dreaming is free.

You may have to start out on the kitchen table or in a corner of the living room. Millions have started the same way and that's okay—for a while. To make the most out of working at home, though, you'll need to begin planning ways to make your working space more comfortable, efficient and permanent.

Five elements directly affect mental attitude and productivity in every work space: light, sound, furniture, air quality, and color.

Proper lighting is essential to the good health of any worker. It has been conclusively demonstrated that improper or inadequate light has varying degrees of negative effects on people. At the very least, it can cause significant decreases in productivity. Some people have more serious reactions, including long term bouts with depression.

Adequate overall lighting is not necessarily optimal lighting. Care should be taken to reduce glare from both direct and indirect sources. Whether light is reflected from a bright window or from a video display terminal (VDT), glare can cause eyestrain and headaches. You can usually solve glare problems by moving your furniture around, changing the type and strength of your lightbulbs, or installing screens over windows and VDTs.

Sound doesn't usually have the same impact on the work place as light, but it is an important factor to consider. Noise can come from traffic, children and lawnmowers outside and appliances, children, pets and your own work equipment inside, causing distraction and lower productivity. You can install sound absorbing material to reduce noise or you can attempt to mask the noise with neutral sounds (white noise) or with music. Most electronics stores sell white noise generators.

The right furniture can also make a difference in your work performance and satisfaction. The type of work surface you need depends on the type of work you're doing, but in any case it doesn't have to be fancy or expensive. What is important is that the surface be large enough to suit the task, that the height is right for you, and that it is sturdy enough to hold your equipment without wobbling.

A good chair is definitely worth the investment. It should provide ample back support, thereby reducing fatigue and backaches. Features such as adjustable back tension, an easily-adjusted height mechanism and rollers will make your life easier, too. If you work with a keyboard, even for short periods of time, don't get a chair with armrests. Armrests can prevent you from getting close enough to the edge, with resulting aches and pains in your back, neck and shoulders.

Air quality and temperature can also have a major impact on your physical comfort. Ideally, you want fresh, clean air no warmer than 75 degrees or cooler than 68 degrees. Indoor pollution can be caused by lack of ventilation, especially with highly weatherized homes. Pollution sources include carpets, upholstery, stoves, aerosols and cleaning fluids, to name only a few. In addition, there are few jobs that don't involve their own polluting substances. Correction fluid, hobby and craft supplies, paint, glue and lint are examples.

The best way to clean up your indoor air is with ventilation. Plants help, too. Certain common houseplants, such as Spider Plants, gobble up indoor toxins. Electric air filters can help, too. They cost more than plants, but require less care. Negative ion generators are especially helpful in the presence of electronic equipment such as computers.

Color is the final factor which you should consider. It can set the overall tone of your work space and make it a place you want to be—or a place you'd rather avoid.

White and very light colors aren't stimulating, but do reflect the most light, making a space appear larger than it is. Blacks, browns, and greys make a space appear smaller than it is, absorbing light and creating feelings of fatigue.

Blues and greens are relaxing, feel cool, and reduce blood pressure. Reds, oranges, and yellows are bright, stimulating, cheerful and warm. In too strong a contrast, however, they can cause irritability and increased blood pressure.

Carefully choosing the color scheme and other aspects of your work space can make a big difference in your productivity as well as how you feel about your work. It's usually not necessary to spend a lot of money to make your work place pleasant; just use some imagination and take the time to think through how you can make the most of the space that's available to you.

Chapter 2
Opportunities in Arts

Artists of all kinds have been working at home since the beginning. An artist is a special breed of worker, with a need for freedom that may be stronger than the need for security. To be able to work when the flash of inspiration strikes is important to the artist; not being forced to work when there is no inspiration is equally important.

Included in the following pages are freelance opportunities for graphic artists, illustrators, designers, calligraphers, photographers, writers, and editors. To get work in any artistic field, the primary requirement is proof of talent, skill, and dependability. Some prospective employers may require evidence of previous publication; others are on the lookout for new talent and will take a look at samples.

Graphic art is a growing field that has traditionally accepted the work-at-home option. Currently, about 75% of all graphic artists work in their own studios as independent contractors. They design, by hand or computer, the visuals for commercials, brochures, corporate reports, books, record covers, posters, logos, packaging, and more. Their major clients are ad agencies, publishers, broadcast companies, textile manufacturers, and printers.

Illustrators and calligraphers may find that work is more sporadic. Illustrators often work for publishers, but both illustrators and calligraphers will find the most opportunities among ad agencies and greeting card publishers. Both of these are huge industries. The greeting card industry has grown rapidly over the past five years, and it is now worth $3.8 billion a year. Photographers, writers, and poets will also find this to be fertile ground for home work.

The biggest field for photographers is still advertising. Agencies large and small are in constant need of professional photographers who can deliver high quality work according to the concept developed by the agency. Rarely will an agency use an inexperienced photographer; the business is too fast-paced to risk losing time on a photographer who may not work out. A freelance photographer looking for any kind of work should be prepared with a professional portfolio of his/her best work, tearsheets of previously published photos if possible, a resume, business cards, and samples that can be left on file.

AARDVARK PRESS, 562 Boston Avenue, Bridgeport, CT 06610.
Positions: Aardvark Press is very unusual in that it hires full-time novelists to write multi-generational sagas according to company-provided outlines.
Requirements: Writers need personal computers with modems. Must be previously published. Inquiries are welcome. Local people are preferred.

LESLIE AARON ASSOCIATES, 520 Westfield Avenue, Elizabeth, NJ 07208.
Positions: Freelance photographers work on assignment basis only for this advertising agency. Agency's clients are in heavy industry.
Requirements: Must be local and experienced in the advertising business. Submit resume, samples, and business card.
Provisions: Pay methods vary.

ABBEY PRESS, St. Meinrad, IN 47577.
Positions: Freelance artists, poets, and photographers. Abbey Press produces greeting cards, gift wrap, and greeting cards for all occasions; gift wrap is for Christmas only.
Requirements: Prefers long poetic verses; poets send samples. Artists should submit several sketches. Photographers submit tear sheets.

ADELE'S INC., 17300 Ventura Boulevard, Encino, CA 91316.
Positions: This producer of high quality personalized giftware uses freelance artists for product design.
Requirements: Submit resume along with photographs of work samples.

AIRLINE PROMOTIONS, Valley Studio, 13246 Weidner Street, Pacoima, CA 91331.
Positions: Freelance artists are used to produce materials for promoting airlines for this public relations firm.
Requirements: Must be local resident. Experienced artists only. Send letter of interest along with work samples and tear sheets (or resume).
Provisions: Pay methods vary.

ALBION CARDS, Box 102, Albion, MI 49224.
Positions: Artists are used in the production of greeting cards and related products. Albion uses a very special style of high contrast line art accented with calligraphy. Interested artists should send for guidelines first; include SASE with request.
Requirements: Only serious artists that can produce very high quality work should inquire. After studying the guidelines, send a letter of interest with samples.
Provisions: Pays a royalty.

ALFA COLOR LAB INC., 535 West 135th Street, Gardena, CA 90248.
Positions: Company produces customized products for interior designers. Freelance photographers are used to produce wall decor of all kinds.
Requirements: Submit sample slides that best represent matter and quality of work. Include business card.
Provisions: Pays a percentage.

ALLIED ADVERTISING AGENCY, INC., 800 Statler Building, Boston, MA 02116.
Positions: Photographers are assigned to all sorts of work connected with advertising: direct mail, magazines, packaging, etc. All subject matter is covered.

Requirements: Works only with experienced local photographers. Submit several sample transparencies that represent your best work. Include resume and request interview.

ALOYSIUS, BUTLER, & CLARK, Bancroft Mills, 30 Hill Road, Wilmington, DE 19806.
Positions: Freelance artists for the design and illustration of all kinds of advertising materials.
Requirements: Only local experienced artists will be considered for assignments. Send resume, work samples, and business card to be kept on file.
Provisions: Pay varies with project.

AMBERLEY GREETING CARD COMPANY, Box 36519, Cincinnati, OH 45236.
Positions: Freelance writers and illustrators for studio style cards.
Requirements: Writers can live anywhere, but artists work on assignment and must be local. Both writers and artists can send for market guidelines before submitting work samples.

AMERICAN CRAFTS, 13010 Woodland, Cleveland, OH 44120.
Positions: Contemporary fiber arts are accepted on consignment.
Requirements: Submit slides (only) and prices you want. Include SASE.
Provisions: Pays 50/50 split.

AMERICAN GREETINGS CORPORATION, 10500 American Road, Cleveland, OH 44102.
Positions: Artists, writers, and photographers. Company makes cards, wrapping paper, posters, calendars, stationary, and post cards. Work is on a freelance basis; some is assigned, some is bought.
Requirements: To be considered, send samples of work with letter of interest. If appropriate, ask to arrange for a personal interview to show portfolio.

ARDREY INC., Suite 314, 100 Menlo Park, Edison, NJ 08837.
Positions: Photographers on assignment basis only. This is a public relations firm that works exclusively with industrial clients.
Requirements: Submit resume, business card, and tear sheets to be kept on file. Work will be conducted on industrial locations, so be sure to indicate how far you can travel.
Provisions: Pays day rates.

ARGONAUT PRESS, RR 1, #142, Fairfield, IA 52556.
Positions: Photographers. Company produces postcards with contemporary themes.
Requirements: Submit transparencies along with resume. A guideline sheet is available upon request.
Provisions: Pays for photos outright or in royalties.

ARGUS COMMUNICATIONS, One DLM Park, Allen, TX 75002.
Positions: Argus publishes humorous, quality greeting cards. Freelance assignments are available for artists, photographers, and writers.
Requirements: To be considered, send six samples of your work in any form (originals, copies, slides, etc.) along with SASE for their safe return. Resume is also required; include a list of credits and a business card to be kept on file.

ARMSTRONG'S, 150 East Third Street, Pomona, CA 91766.
Positions: Freelance designers and illustrators. Company manufactures collectibles: lithographs, plates, and figurines.
Requirements: Prefers to work with local artists. Must have experience working with these kinds of collectibles. Send letter of interest with tear sheets.

ARTFORMS CARD CORPORATION, 725 County Line Road, Dearfield, IL 60015.
Positions: Artists and writers.
Requirements: Artists, send sketches only for consideration. Writers, send batches of 10 samples. All work must have a Jewish theme suitable for the greeting card market. Send for market list and include SASE.
Provisions: Artists' rates vary according to assignment. Writers are paid per verse. 50% of work is freelance.

ATTENZIONE, THE ITALIAN LIFESTYLE MAGAZINE, Adam Publications, Inc., 152 Madison Avenue, New York, NY 10019.
Positions: Freelance writers work on assignment.
Requirements: Must be previously published and have creative ideas on the subject of Italian lifestyles. Submit proposal with published clips and SASE.

AUTOMATIC MAIL SERVICES, INC., 30-02 48th Avenue, Long Island City, NY 11101.
Positions: Freelance artists work on assignment basis to design and illustrate catalogs and brochures used in the direct mail industry.
Requirements: Prefers local artists. Submit samples or tear sheets and business card.
Provisions: Pays by the project.

CAROLYN BEAN PUBLISHING, 120 Second Street, San Francisco, CA 94105.
Positions: Writers, artists, and photographers for contemporary greeting card company.
Requirements: To be considered, writers should send SASE with 54c postage for guidelines. Artists send samples of work (any medium okay) along with SASE. Do not send originals. Photographers should arrange personal interview to show portfolio. Bring slides only, tear sheets and business card; the two latter items will be kept on file. "About 90% of our work is done by freelancers."

BEAUTYWAY, Box 340, Flagstaff, AZ 86002.
Positions: Photographers. Company produces postcards, calendars, and posters. Interested mostly in scenics and animals.
Requirements: Submit any size transparencies. Guidelines are available. Include SASE with request. Prefers to work with previously published photographers.
Provisions: Pays one-time fee for each photo used.

BENTLY HOUSE, P.O. Box 5551, Art Sources Department, Walnut Creek, CA 94596.
Positions: Bentley House has been a major national publisher of art for over eight years. They sell to major accounts, print shops, and distributors at the rate of 100,000 pieces per month. For the first time, new artists are being sought. Preferred subject matter includes anything of interest to "Middle America"; nostalgia, country, scapes, local folk arts, people, animals, etc. Can be any medium; oils, water color, acrylics, etc. Original art will be reproduced for mass sale.
Requirements: No prior publishing is required. Bentley House is most interested in

long term working relationships. To be considered, send slides (only) of your work plus a cover letter to introduce yourself. Be sure to number your slides and keep a file of them at home for later reference. Bentley house requires no investment of any kind (and suggests strongly that any artist should beware of buyers of any kind asking for money up front).

Provisions: Reproduced prints sell in the $15 to $60 range. Different arrangements are worked out with different artists; buys outright, on commission, and other ways. A new line is introduced every four to five months.

BEST RESUME SERVICE, 625 Stanwix Street, Pittsburgh, PA 15222.
Positions: Freelance and permanent part-time writers used to write business correspondence, reports, and client's resumes.
Requirements: Excellent communication skills necessary. Good typewriter needed. Send resume or letter of interest. Must live in Pittsburgh area.

> "We're always looking for responsible people, especially full-timers."
>
> --Gallup Poll

B.M. ENTERPRISES, Box 421, Farrell, PA 16121.
Positions: Freelance artists. Company is a clip art service bureau. Assigns line drawings and cartoons to previously published artists only.
Requirements: Write first for market guide. Then submit letter of interest with tear sheets.
Provisions: Payment is a 50/50 split.

BOZELL & JACOBS ADVERTISING & PUBLIC RELATIONS, 2000 Two Allen Center, Houston, TX 77002.
Positions: Uses freelance photographers on assignment basis for newspapers, magazines, brochures, flyers and some TV.
Requirements: Professional experience required. Need to provide samples of work. Especially interested in people pictures, food layouts, and underwater shots. Arrange for personal interview to show portfolio of work. Prefers to work with photographers in Houston area.
Provisions: Payment varies according to the job. Offers assignments to more than 100 freelance photographers annually.

BRADFORD EXCHANGE, 9333 Milwaukee, Chicago, IL 60648.
Positions: Bradford is a manufacturer of collectible plates. Freelance professional artists are used to design landscapes and portraits that will be reproduced on the plates.
Requirements: Submit resume, samples that can be kept on file, and references or tear sheets.

BRETT-FORER GREETINGS, INC., 105 East 73rd Street, New York, NY 10021.
Positions: Freelance artists and writers. Brett-Forer cards are whimsical; mostly Christmas and everyday, with a few other occasions. Writers can submit verse for consideration. Artists are usually assigned.
Requirements: Writers should send batches of 10 verses. Artists submit samples and business card.
Provisions: Pays flat fee.

BRUMFIELD-GALLAGHER, 3401 West End Avenue, Nashville, TN 37203.
Positions: Photographers are used for assignments in public relations work. Photos are usually products to be featured in all types of ads.
Requirements: Works only with experienced local photographers. Send resume and tear sheet; request personal interview to show portfolio.
Provisions: Pay methods vary; usually day rates, sometimes hourly.

BUCKBOARD ANTIQUES, 1411 N. May, Oklahoma City, OK 73107.
Positions: Folk art and other traditional country crafts like rag dolls and quilted items will be considered.
Requirements: Send photos and prices you want along with an SASE.

SIDNEY J. BURGOYNE & SONS, INC., 2030 East Byberry Road, Philadelphia, PA 19116.
Positions: Company produces greeting cards and calendars with Christmas theme only. Uses freelance artists for design, illustration, and calligraphy.
Requirements: Experienced artists only. Submit letter of interest with work samples and business card.

BURTON ADVERTISING, 1400 City National Bank Building, Detroit, MI 48226.
Positions: Photographers are assigned to various advertising media: newspapers, brochures, magazines, and direct mail.
Requirements: Experience is necessary. Send letter of interest and ask to arrange for an interview in order to show portfolio of work samples. Prefers to work with photographers in Detroit only.
Provisions: Payment is negotiable. All work is done on a freelance basis. Uses 10 freelancers on assignment per year.

CALIFORNIA DREAMERS, 331 West Superior, Chicago, IL 60610.
Positions: Photographers and writers. California Dreamers is a greeting card company which has replaced illustrative cartoons with photo "cartoons."
Requirements: Study the company's line very carefully first; then send for guidelines. All ideas must be innovative, contemporary, and above all, have a sense of humor about what's happening socially. "You should be on the mark for today; if it hits home or makes you laugh, let us see it. We're looking for what people are really talking about today. The number-one rule is clarity of concept." This advice is mostly for writers, who should send sample copy and concepts with SASE. Photographers are encouraged to send transparencies as samples of style and skill.
Provisions: All work is done on a freelance basis. Photographers are paid $400 and up per assignment. Writers are paid $100 to $150 per line. If a writer is "hot", company will ofer a royalty deal tied to sales goals.

Jim Lienhart, Tom White and Herb Murrie (from left to right), founders of California Dreamers

It was only five years ago that California Dreamers started by offering 81 card designs at the West Coast Gift and Stationery Show. Only 16 of the cards drew any interest at the time, but that was enough to grow on. Today, they have over 1,200 items in their line and *Forbes Magazine* called them the number one company in the alternative card market. Founders Jim Lienhart, Tom White, and Herb Murrie will introduce gift wrap, calendars, new greeting card lines, post cards, and invitations this year. The Chicago-based company is recognized for its attention grabbing non-occasion photographs and illustrative cards.

"We replaced illustrative cartoons with photo cartoons," says president Herb Murrie. "They stuck out like a sore thumb. What we've got going for us is creativity."

If you're a copy writer or photographer with a contemporary vision, you might want to send some samples of your work to California Dreamers. "We only want to see work that is on the mark for today. You've got to be up-to-date and professional. It's a war out there!"

CANTERBURY DESIGNS, INC., Box 4060, Martinez, GA 30907.
Positions: Freelance artists are used to produce new designs for needlework design books.
Requirements: Send photographs of your work samples. Include letter of interest that indicates professional background.
Provisions: Pay methods vary.

CAPE SHORE PAPER PRODUCTS, INC., 42A North Elm Street, Box 537, Yarmouth, ME 04096.
Positions: Freelance artists for design and illustration of giftwrap and stationery products. Company uses primarily nautical theme with some Americana, Christmas, and other traditional themes such as floral, birds, and animals.
Requirements: Send for quidelines first. Then submit letter of interest with samples.
Provisions: Pays flat fee.

CHESAPEAKE BAY MAGAZINE, 1819 Bay Ridge Avenue, Suite 200, Annapolis, MD 21403.
Positions: Freelance writers and photographers.
Requirements: Any material about the Chesapeake region will be considered. Photographers submit color photos only. Writers can submit either proposal or complete manuscript.
Provisions: Pays on acceptance.

CMP PUBLICATIONS, 600 Community Drive, Manhasset, NY 11030.
Positions: Editors, associate editors, reporters, and writers are all outfitted with computers and modems in order to transmit material from the field. Freelance stringers are hired to cover business news from all over the country.
Requirements: Hard news reporting experience a must. Must feel comfortable going to top industrial companies looking for stories and information. Apply with resume and previously published clips.
Provisions: Payment varies. Some reporters are salaried, some are paid by individual contract. Phone charges are reimbursed.

COMMUNICATIONS DYNAMICS CORPORATION, Box 3060, Glen Ellyn, IL 60137.
Positions: Freelance copy writers and technical writers.
Requirements: Must be reliable and experienced. Send resume and work samples. Must be local resident.
Provisions: Pays by the job.

COMMUNICATIONS ELECTRONICS, Box 1045, Ann Arbor, MI 48106.
Positions: Freelance artists for advertising work.
Requirements: Send resume and samples or tear sheets to be kept on file. Request an appointment to show portfolio. Only local artists will be considered.
Provisions: Pays by the project.

COMMUNICATION SKILL BUILDERS, INC., Box 42050, Tucson, AZ 85733.
Positions: Freelance artists are used in a variety of ways by this educational publisher. Most work consists of illustration and layout for books as well as some advertising work.
Requirements: Prefers local artists, but will consider highly skilled artists from out of the area. Must be very experienced in this field. Submit resume and photographs of work

samples.
Provisions: Pays by the project.

CRYSTAL GREETINGS INC., 53 Noll Street, Waukegan, IL 6085.
Positions: Writers and artists. Company produces humorous everyday cards as well as Christmas cards and gift wrap.
Requirements: Send work samples with letter of interest.

CUSTOM STUDIOS, The Custom Building, South Hackensack, NJ 07606.
Positions: Freelance photographers on assignment basis only for Christmas card department. Offer over 100 assignments annually.
Requirements: To be considered, Send letter of interest with SASE requesting "Photo Guidelines." Include busines card.
Provisions: Pays by the job; $50 minimum.

DEADY ADVERTISING, 17 East Cary Street, Richmond, VA 23236.
Positions: Freelance illustrators.
Requirements: Must be very experienced in the advertising field. Local artists only. Submit resume and work samples.
Provisions: Pay methods vary from project to project.

DISPLAYCO, 2055 McCarter Highway, Newark, NJ 07104.
Positions: Freelance artists. Company manufacturers advertising display fixtures.
Requirements: Must have experience working in the advertising field and, in particular, with display fixtures. Submit work samples or photos of work and resume. Prefers local artists.
Provisions: Pays by the project.

DORSEY ADVERTISING AGENCY, Box 270942, Dallas, TX 75227.
Positions: Photographers used for production of all types of advertising media. All subject matter is covered.
Requirements: Works exclusively with experienced local photographers on assignment basis. Submit letter of interest along with samples of high quality work. Be sure to include SASE for reply and/or return of samples.
Provisions: Pay methods vary according to assignment.

DRAWING BOARD GREETING CARDS, INC., 8200 Carpenter Freeway, Dallas, TX 75247.
Positions: Artist, writers, and photographers design cards and calendars.
Requirements: Artists should submit sketches; photographers submit color transparencies. Send sample portfolio with return postage included.
Writers should submit ideas on 3x5 index cards. Be sure name and address is on the back of each card submitted.
Provisions: Payment depends on individual situation. Sometimes ideas are purchased outright; sometimes work is assigned and paid for by the project. New talent is actively solicited.

EHRIG & ASSOCIATES, 4th and Vine Building, Seattle, WA 98121.
Positions: Freelance artists used in the production of all kinds of advertising materials.
Requirements: Works only with experienced local artists. Submit resume and request appointment to show portfolio.

Provisions: Pays by the project.

ELVING JOHNSON ADVERTISING, INC., 7800 West College Drive, Palos Heights, IL 60463.
Positions: Freelance photographers. Company's clients are in heavy industry.
Requirements: Works only with experienced local photographers. Submit resume and request appointment to show portfolio.
Provisions: Pays for each photograph.

EMBOSSOGRAPH DISPLAY MANUFACTURING COMPANY, 1430 West Wrightwood, Chicago, IL 60614.
Positions: Freelance artists design and illustrate custom advertising display fixtures.
Requirements: Local artists preferred. Must be previously published in this field. Submit resume with samples of published work only.
Provisions: Pays by the hour.

ENESCO IMPORTS CORPORATION, 1 Enesco Plaza, Elk Grove Village, IL 60007.
Positions: Artists, designers, and sample makers for giftware line.
Requirements: Artists and designers must have exceptional creativity and the work samples to prove it. Sample makers must have all necessary tools to produce samples from artists' renderings. Must be local resident.
Provisions: Artwork is often bought outright. Others are paid by the project or by the hour.

THE EVERGREEN PRESS, INC., 3380 Vincent Road, Pleasant Hill, CA 94523.
Positions: Artists for design and illustrations of cards, gift wrap, children's picture books, and bookmarks. Cards are generally produced in a series with a common theme. Especially in need of Christmas Card designs. Gift wrap is also for Christmas; prefers country or folk art theme.
Requirements: Send for guidelines first. To be considered for assignment, send a group of samples and resume.
Provisions: Generally pays royalty.

FABER SHERVEY ADVERTISING, 160 West 79th Street, Minneapolis, MN 55420.
Positions: Freelance illustrators.
Requirements: Must be local resident. Experience in the advertising field is required. Send letter of interest and business card. Request an appointment to show portfolio.
Provisions: Pays hourly rate.

FANTUS PAPER PRODUCTS, 4459 West Division Street, Chicago, IL 60651.
Positions: Photographers are used by this producer of greeting cards and gift wrap. All subject matters. Buys some photos outright for stock; also hires on assignment.
Requirements: Send for guidelines before submitting anything; include SASE with request. Then submit sample transparencies, resume, business card, and tearsheets to be kept on file.
Provisions: Payment varies with different situations.

FELLERS LACY GADDIS, 2203 Saratoga, Austin, TX 78741.
Positions: Freelance photographers are used by this advertising agency. Photos are used

Dana Cassell, President
Writer Data Bank

"To make it as a writer, you've got to be competitive. Start by making your manuscript look better. The look of it has a lot to do with whether you get the assignment. It's just like you look and talk, it's the image that sticks.

"If you have no specific field, try a little bit of everything until you find your niche. Look for the field where you are getting the highest ratio of return from query letters, then sales, and so on. A full-time writer can work into $20,000 and more. One writer I know makes $50,000 a year in the medical field.

in consumer publications.

Requirements: Prefers to work only with local photographers. Must be experienced and have professional portfolio. Write letter of interest requesting appointment.

Provisions: Pays photographers regular rates.

FIBERWORKS GALLERY, 1940 Bonita Avenue, Berkeley, CA 94704.

Positions: This nonprofit gallery is interested in quality ceramics, glassware, jewelry, textiles, and fiber arts.

Requirements: Submit slides (only), written description, and prices you want. Include SASE.

Provisions: Items accepted on consignment only --30% commission.

FILLMAN ADVERTISING, INC., 304 West Hill Street, Champaign, IL 61820.

Positions: Freelance illustrators for the production of direct mail packages and brochures.

Requirements: Must be local and experienced. Send resume and sample line drawings. Include business card to be kept on file.

Provisions: Pay methods vary with different projects.

FRANKLIN & ASSOCIATES, 600 B Street, San Diego, CA 92101.

Positions: Freelance artists are used in the production of advertising materials. There is also some photography done for the same purpose.

Requirements: Local artists only. Must be experienced in the advertising field. Submit resume and photos of samples or tear sheets for the files.

Provisions: Pays hourly rates.

FREEDOM GREETING CARD COMPANY, P.O. Box 715, Bristol, PA 19007.

Positions: Writers and artists. Writers sell verses outright. Artists work on assignment only.

Requirements: Sample of work, letter of interest, and SASE required for either type of work.

FREMERMAN, ROSENFIELD, & LANE, 106 West 14th Street, Suite 2102, Kansas City, MO 64105.
Positions: Freelance illustrators work on various types of advertising materials.
Requirements: Must be local and experienced. Submit resume and photos of work samples.
Provisions: Pays by the project.

G.A.I. AND ASSOCIATES, INC., Box 30309, Indianapolis, IN 46203.
Positions: G.A.I. is a licensing agent in the collectibles industry. Freelance artists that seek representation are encouraged to submit samples of people-type art in any medium. There is no fee; G.A.I. takes a commission for successfully completed projects.
Requirements: Send resume and color photographs of work samples. Include SASE for reply.
Provisions: Artists are generally paid a royalty.

GARDNER ADVERTISING, 10 South Broadway, St. Louis, MO 63102.
Positions: Freelance illustrators for advertising and packaging materials.
Requirements: Works only with experienced local artists. Submit resume only. Request appointment to show portfolio.

GERBIG, SNELL, WEISHEIMER & ASSOCIATES, 8000 Ravine's Edge Court, Worthington, OH 43085.
Positions: Freelance illustrators and photographers used for the production of advertising materials.
Requirements: Works only with local experienced people. Submit resume, tear sheets, and business card.

C.R. GIBSON, COMPANY, Knight Street, Norwalk, CT 06856.
Positions: Freelance artists. Company produces stationery products and buys new designs.
Requirements: Only previously established artists are considered. Submit samples and resume.
Provisions: Pays flat rate for each design accepted.

GLENCOE PUBLISHING COMPANY, 17337 Ventura Boulevard, Encino, CA 91316.
Positions: Freelance artists illustrate textbooks.
Requirements: Work must be top notch. Submit resume and tear sheets. Will consider only previously published illustrators.
Provisions: Pays by the project.

GREETING CARD MASTERS, INC., 2990 Griffin Road, Ft. Lauderdale, FL 33312.
Positions: Freelance artists and photographers for the design of seasonal and everyday greeting cards.
Requirements: Artists send actual samples with letter of interest. Photographers send transparencies and business card.

HALLMARK GREETING CARDS, P.O. Box 419580, Kansas City, MO 64108.
Positions: Hallmark, the largest greeting card company in the country, is also the biggest employer of artists. Writers and artists of all kinds design greeting cards, other paper

products, and gift items, and do public relations and advertising work. Currently has hundreds in home work pool. "We have so many, the total number is uncertain at any given moment."

Requirements: Start by sending for guidelines. Follow up with samples of work and letter of interest. Although Hallmark is constantly on the lookout for new talent, only the most outstanding creative people can expect to get in.

Provisions: Positions include all types of situations from freelance to full-time, regular employees (at home). Workers are found through submissions, word-of-mouth, referrals, and in-house employees.

THE HAMILTON GROUP, 9550 Regency Square Boulevard, Jacksonville, FL 32211.

Positions: Photographers are commissioned for photos to be used in the manufacture of collectibles; uses mostly scenics and some clients' products.

Requirements: Must be local resident. Only experienced photographers with resume and references are considered. Include business card and tearsheets to be kept on file.

Provisions: Pays varying fees.

HARCOURT BRACE JOVANOVICH PUBLICATIONS, 7500 Old Oak Boulevard, Cleveland, OH 44130.

Positions: Freelance writing assignments are available from this major business publisher.

Requirements: Only very experienced writers will be considered. Apply with resume and writing samples along with letter of interest.

HEALTH & RACQUET CLUB MEMBERS, 15 Bank Street, #400, Stamford, CT 06901.

Positions: Freelance writers and photographers. Magazine contains material on upscale travel and leisure.

Requirements: Submit samples and proposal.

HERFF JONES, Box 6500, Providence RI, 02940.

Positions: Freelance illustrators and designers. Company makes medals, trophies, and class rings.

Requirements: Several years of experience is required. Submit resume and samples.

Provisions: Pays by the project.

HIAWATHA, INC., 6100 N Keystone Avenue, Suite 627, Indianapolis, IN 46220.

Positions: Lyrical-style poetry is used by this greeting card company.

Requirements: Submit ideas and/or samples of your work on 3x5 cards; include SASE.

Provisions: Pays on acceptance.

IN TOUCH, The International Tours Travel Magazine, Go Publishing, Inc., 110 Broad Street, Boston, MA 10010.

Positions: Freelance writers and photographers. All material is travel related.

Requirements: Both writers and photographers should send for guidelines first; include SASE.

THE INQUISITIVE TRAVELER, Travel Quest, 20103 La Roda Court, Cupertino, CA 95014.

Positions: Freelance writers and photographers for quarterly travel magazine.

Requirements: Writers should send for guidelines first; include SASE with request. Photographers send samples of travel photos.

INTERCONTINENTAL GREETINGS, LTD., 176 Madison Avenue, New York, NY 10016.
Positions: Freelance artists for greeting cards, gift wrap, calendars, posters, and stationery. Prefers very graphic designs with some cartoon style illustrations.
Requirements: Works only with professionals. Send resume, work samples, and include SASE.
Provisions: Generally pays royalties.

HENRY J. KAUFMAN & ASSOCIATES, 2233 Wisconsin Avenue, Washington, DC 20007.
Positions: Freelance artists and photographers for the production of advertising materials.
Requirements: Local residents only. Submit resume and work samples.
Provisions: Pays by the project.

KERSTEN BROTHERS, P.O. Box 5510, Scottsdale, AZ 85261.
Positions: Writers and artists for greeting cards. All cards are humorous and seasonal; Christmas, Thanksgiving, Halloween, Mother's Day, Father's Day, Graduation, Easter, Valentine's Day, and St. Patrick's Day.
Requirements: Writers submit batches of short verses for consideration. Artists send skeches or photocopies of finished originals.

KLITZNER INDUSTRIES, 44 Warren Street, Providence, RI 02901.
Positions: Freelance designers and illustrators for advertising specialty products.
Requirements: Must have experience in the advertising field and the proven ability to follow through on assignments. Submit resume and tear sheets. Prefers local artists.
Provisions: Pays by the project.

LAFF MASTERS, INC., 557 Oak Street, Copiague, NY 11726.
Positions: Illustrators work on assignment only for this greeting card publisher. Style is very contemporary and sophisticated.
Requirements: Only previously published artists experienced in the greeting card industry are considered for assignments. Must be local artist. Submit resume and tear sheets.
Provisions: Pays by the project.

LASER CRAFT, 3300 Coffey Lane, Santa Rosa, CA 95401.
Positions: Established greeting card company always on the lookout for artists with new ideas for greeting card designs. Company prefers humorous themes, but anything innovative (and good) will be considered.
Requirements: Submit ideas/designs in card format and send with SASE.
Provisions: Pays for each design.

LIFE BEAT MAGAZINE, R.R. 2, Box 64a, Blanchardville, WI 53516.
Positions: Freelance writers work on assignment for this monthly magazine about dynamic lifestyles.
Requirements: Send for guidelines; include SASE.

LIGHT IMAGES, 207 Miller Avenue, Mill Valley, CA 94941.
Positions: Light Images is a stock photo agency that occasionally takes on new freelance photographers.
Requirements: Must be highly professional photographer; only top-notch work will be considered. Must have experience shooting for advertising. Send resume and request interview in order to show protfolio. Prefers Bay area photographers only.

LILLIAN VERNON CORPORATION, 510 South Fulton Avenue, Mount Vernon, NY 10550.
Positions: Lillian Vernon is one of those rare "kitchen table" success stories. The company is one of the most successful of all direct mail catalog marketers. Products include all kinds of paper products, textiles, housewares, etc. Freelance artists design and illustrate on assignment only.
Requirements: Only regional artists are used. Prefers artists with experience, but is willing to look at someone with exceptional talent. Send letter of interest with tear sheets or samples that can be kept on file.
Provisions: Pays flat fee.

LOS ANGELES REVIEW OF BOOKS, 10005 Pruitt Drive, Redondo Beach, CA 90278.
Positions: Stringers and staff writers for reviews, features, and interviews with writers and others in the publishing industry.
Requirements: At least one sample of previously published work. Knowledge of the publishing industry is preferred.
Provisions: Staff members are salaried employees. Stringers are paid per assignment.

ROB MACINTOSH COMMUNICATIONS, INC., 92 Massachusetts Avenue, Boston, MA 02115.
Positions: Graphic artists work on assignment for this ad agency.
Requirements: Submit resume and work samples or tear sheets. Submissions should indicate the particular skills of the artist and the level of experience.

THE MAIN EVENT, P.O. Box 64, Glen Rock, NJ 07452.

Positions: Freelance sports writers work as stringers from several major cities.
Requirements: Solid knowledge of sports in general is necessary with additional knowledge of medicine preferred. Resume and published clips required.

MAINE LINE COMPANY, Box 418, Rockport, ME 04856.
Positions: Writers, artists, and photographers. Company produces greeting cards, postcards, plaques, books, T-shirts, buttons, mugs, and stickers with a humorous theme.
Requirements: Start by sending a #10 envelope with three stamps for a current market list and creative guidelines. Format instructions will be included. Photographers send sample slides, no snaps, with SASE. Artists design cartoons, graphics, and illustrations. Send sketches of work. Writers send ideas/samples with SASE. Company prefers multi-talented people.

MANGAN, RAINS, GINNAVEN, HOLCOMB, 911 Savers Federal Building, Little Rock, AR 72201.
Positions: Freelance artists work on a variety of advertising materials.
Requirements: Prefers experienced local artists. Submit letter of interest and business card. Request appointment to show portfolio.
Provisions: Pays hourly rates.

MARTIN-WILLIAMS ADVERTISING, INC., 10 South Fifth Street, Minneapolis, MN 55402.
Positions: Freelance photographers work on assignment.
Requirements: Works with experienced local photographers only. Submit resume and tear sheets. Request appointment to show portfolio.

MASTERPIECE STUDIOS, 5400 West 35th Street, Chicago, IL 60650.
Positions: Freelance artists for seasonal greeting cards. Especially needs highly stylized designs for Christmas cards.
Requirements: Send for guidelines first. Submit full color sketches or finished art. Samples will not be returned.
Provisions: Pays flat fee for each design. Pays higher fees for assigned illustration.

MCCANN-ERICKSON, 1469 South Fourth, Louisville, KY 40208.
Positions: Freelance artists. Assignments include all kinds of advertising medium.
Requirements: Local artists prefferred. Submit resume and work samples. Request appointment to show portfolio.
Provisions: Pays by the project.

MCDONALD DAVIS & ASSOCIATES, 250 West Coventry Court, Glendale, WI 53217.
Positions: Freelance photographers for advertising materials.
Requirements: Only local photographers with advertising experience will be considered. Send resume with tear sheets. Include SASE with all correspondence.
Provisions: Pays day rates.

MCGRAW-HILL, School Division, 1200 N.W. 63rd Street, Oklahoma City, OK 73116.
Positions: Freelance illustrators work on educational books.
Requirements: Only highly experienced, previously published artists are considered. Submit letter of interest with tear sheets.

MERION PUBLICATIONS, INC. 636 School Line Drive, King of Prussia, PA 19406.
Positions: Freelance staff writers for newspaper read by health professionals.
Requirements: Must live in the area. Need experience and resume with samples.
Provisions: Story leads are provided for features.

METRO ASSOCIATED SERVICES, INC., 33 West 34th Street, 4th Floor, New York, NY 10005.
Positions: Freelance illustrators. Metro is a clip art dealer that works with dozens of artists.
Requirements: Must apply with resume and request personal interview to show portfolio of professional work samples. Prefers New York artists, but will consider anyone with real talent.
Provisions: Pay worked out on an individual basis.

MIDWEST LIVING, 1912 Grand Avenue, Des Moines, IA 50336.
Positions: Freelance writers work on assignment for this monthly travel and leisure magazine.
Requirements: Send proposal along with clips of previously published material.
Provisions: Pays excellent rates upon acceptance.

MORNING STAR, INC., 6680 Shady Oak Road, Eden Prairie, MN 55344.
Positions: Freelance artists for the design and illustration of greeting cards, giftware, stationery, and associated products. All products have a Christian theme. Also assigns artists for bordering and calligraphy.
Requirements: Send letter of interest with work samples.
Provisions: Pays flat fee.

ERIC MOWER & ASSOCIATES, 101 South Salina Street, Syracuse, NY 13202.
Positions: Graphic artists for advertisements and illustrators for catalogs.
Requirements: Send resume, business card, and work samples that represent top notch skills and professionalism.

STANLEY H. MURRAY ADVERTISING, Box 4876, Greenwich, CT 06830.
Positions: Freelance designers and illustrators work on direct mail packages, brochures, and print media ads.
Requirements: Must be experienced in the advertising field. Local artists preferred. Submit resume and work samples.
Provisions: Pays hourly rate.

NATIONAL HARDWOOD MAGAZINE, P.O. BOX 34808, Memphis, TN 38184.
Positions: Freelance writers work on assignment basis in various metropolitan areas around the country. Publication is a wood industry trade journal.
Requirements: Send resume and writing samples.

THOMAS NELSON PUBLISHERS, Box 141000, Elm Hill Pike, Nashville, TN 37284.
Positions: Freelance artists illustrate religious publications and design advertising materials.

Requirements: Only local experienced artists are considered. Submit letter of interest and tear sheets.

NEW DOMINION, P.O. Box 19714, Alexandria, VA 22320.
Positions: Freelance writers write most of this quarterly magazine for northern Virginia.
Requirements: Must be regional writer. Send for guidelines and sample issue first.
Provisions: Pays by the word.

NU-ART, INC., Box 2002, Bedford, IL 60499.
Positions: Writers and artists for greeting cards, wedding invitations and accessories, and boxed stationery. Cards are for Christmas only.
Requirements: Writers submit verse along with design ideas for total concept. Artists submit color roughs or finished art.

OATMEAL STUDIOS, Box 138, Rochester, VT 05767.
Positions: Writers and illustrators for greeting card design.
Requirements: The first step for both positions is to send for Oatmeal's guidelines and current market list. Include SASE with your request. Then send several samples with a letter of interest.
Provisions: Writers are paid for each idea that is accepted. Pay for artists depends on the situation. 90%of Oatmeal's work is done by freelancers.

PAMCO SECURITIES AND INSURANCE SERVICES, 16030 Ventura Boulevard #500, Encino, CA 91436.
Positions: Freelance writers for composing banking training manuals.
Requirements: Must be local resident. Minimum five years experience in this type of writing is required. Must have thorough knowledge of banking industry. Must own IBM compatible word processor. Submit resume and references.

PAPEL, Box 9879, North Holywood, CA 91609.
Positions: Freelance illustrators, designers, and calligraphers work on greeting cards and ceramic souvenir items.
Requirements: Several years experience is required. Submit resume and tear sheets.
Provisions: Pays by the project.

PARAMOUNT CARDS INC., 400 Pine Street, Box 1225, Pawtucket, RI 02863
Positions: Writers, artists, and photographers for greeting card production and promotional work. Cards are seasonal and everyday with a humorous theme (studio style).
Requirements: First send for instruction sheet, including SASE with request. Then send samples with letter of interest. Be sure to include SASE with any samples.
Provisions: Specific art assignments and purchase agreements are given to freelance artists/designers. Pay methods vary.

PARLAY INTERNATIONAL, 417 - 24th Street, Suite 35, San Francisco, CA 94114.
Positions: Freelance illustrators and graphic artists are used by this publisher of instructional materials.
Requirements: Resume and samples of previously published work are required. Only San Francisco residents will be considered.
Provisions: Payment varies.

PENDLETON HAND WEAVERS, P.O. Box 233, Sedona, AZ 86336.

Positions: Will consider hand woven and other fabric art pieces for inclusion in regular retail line.
Requirements: Send either slides or photos along with written description and prices of your offerings. Include SASE.

PORTAL PUBLICATIONS, 21 Tamal Vista Boulevard, Corte Madera, CA 94925,
Positions: Freelance writers. Company produces greeting cards especially for young adult working women.
Requirements: Study the line first and send for market guidelines. Then submit verses on index cards in small batches with SASE.

THE PRODUCERS, 1095 East Indian School Road, Phoenix, AZ 85014.
Positions: Illustrators, photographers, and calligraphers for work involved in advertising.
Requirements: Prefers local talent. Send letter of interest and samples that can be kept for future reference.
Provisions: Pays hourly wage.

PROFESSIONAL MARINER, 55 John Street, New York, NY 10038.
Positions: Freelance writers/stringers produce most of the articles on marine subjects for this magazine.
Requirements: Send sample ideas along with clips of previously published work. Must have some particular knowledge of marine subjects

PSYCH IT, 6507 Bimini Court, Apollo Beach, FL 33570.
Positions: Freelance writers, poets, artists, and cartoonists produce all of the material in this quarterly publication.
Requirements: Need not be previously published to be considered. Must first send for sample issue; $1.50 plus SASE.

RAINBOW ARTS, 488 Main Stret, Fitchburg, MA 01420.
Positions: Freelance designers and illustrators for contemporary greeting cards.
Requirements: Send for market guidelines first. Then send samples along with resume.

RAINFALL GREETINGS, INC., 90 Market S.W., P.O. Box 7321, Grand Rapids, MI 49510.
Positions: Writers, artists, and photographers for greeting cards, stationery, and stickers.
Requirements: Writers should submit poetry or humor.

RAYMOND, KOWAL & WICKS, 1 Broadway, Cambridge, MA 02142.
Positions: Freelance photographers work on assignment for ads that will go in trade magazines and brochures.
Requirements: Send samples of high quality work along with business card.

READER SEARCH COMMITTEE, 12224 Victory Boulevard, North Hollywood, CA 91606.
Positions: Freelance writers work as stringers for this weekly arts publication.
Requirements: Must be local resident. Resume and three previously published clips with byline required.

RECYCLED PAPER PRODUCTS, INC., 3636 North Broadway, Chicago, IL 60613.

Positions: Freelance artists and calligraphers. Company produces greeting cards and other stationery items.
Requirements: Submit samples and letter of interest. Guidelines are available for SASE.

RED FARM STUDIO, P.O. Box 347, 334 Pleasant Street, Pawtucket, RI 02862.
Positions: Writers and artists. Company produces greeting cards, gift wrap, and note papers.
Requirements: Send for a current market list; include a business size SASE. Then send letter of interest with work samples.
Provisions: Writers are paid by the line. Artists' pay varies, depending on the situation.

REED STARLINE CARD COMPANY, 3331 Sunset Boulevard, Los Angeles, CA 90026.
Positions: Artists and writers for work involved in the production and promotion of greeting cards. 100% of all work is done by freelancers on assignment basis only.
Requirements: To be considered for any of the hundreds of project assignments each year, start by sending for company guidelines and market list; include SASE with request. Then send samples of your style with SASE. Include business card which will be kept on file for future assignments.

RENAISSANCE GREETING CARDS, P.O. Box 126, Springvale, ME 04083.
Positions: Writers and artists for all occasion and Christmas cards.
Requirements: Writers send verse ideas; especially likes humorous verse. Include ideas for design. Artists send samples of full color work in batches of a dozen; include resume. Prefers bright cartoons.

RESOURCE MARKETING, 8434 North Waukegan Road, Morton Grove, IL 60053.
Positions: Freelance illustrators, designers, photographers and account executives.
Requirements: Must be local resident. Send resume with work samples.
Provisions: Pay methods vary depending on situation.

ROUSANA CARDS, 28 Sager Place, Hillside, NJ 07205.
Positions: Writers and artists for everyday and seasonal cards.
Requirements: Works only with established greeting card designers. Submit work samples with resume and/or tear sheets.

LOWE RUNKLE COMPANY, 6801 North Broadway, Oklahoma City, OK 73116.
Positions: Freelance graphic artists, designers, and illustrators work on assignment for this ad agency.
Requirements: Prefers experienced local artists. Submit resume and tear sheets.
Provisions: Pay methods vary.

SAN FRANCISCO BAY GUARDIAN, 2700 19th ST, San Francisco, CA 94110.
Positions: Freelance writers produce over half of the contents of this alternative newsweekly.
Requirements: Only previously published Bay Area writers will be considered. Especially interested in investigative reporters. Send query with clips of previously published work.

SANGAMON COMPANY, Route 48 West, Taylorville, IL 62558.

Positions: Writers and artists for greeting card and gift wrap design.
Requirements: Writers should submit verses with SASE included. Artists submit finished art or color sketches.

SAWYER CAMERA & INSTRUMENT COMPANY, 1208 Isabel Street, Burbank, CA 91506.
Positions: Freelance photographers work on assignment for this multimedia ad agency.
Requirements: Local photographers only. Must have experience in multimedia production. Submit resume, business card, and tear sheets.
Provisions: Pays by the project.

> "The beauty of our company is we have no quotas, set territories, or anyone looking over our shoulders."   --The Creative Circle

SEEDS OF PEACE MAGAZINE, P.O. Box 37021, Denver, CO 80237.
Positions: Freelance writers and photographers produce over half of this bimonthly publication of self-awareness and new age philosophy.
Requirements: Send clips, samples, and proposal.

SEYBOLD CONSULTING GROUP, INC., 148 State Street, Suite 612, Boston, MA 02109.
Positions: Independent writers are contracted by the year to write stories from evaluation reports of automated office systems and software. Company publishes 35 to 40 reports each month on UNIX and Office systems.
Requirements: Experience and references are required. Send letter of interest with work samples. Prefers to work with writers in Boston.
Provisions: Pay is worked out on an individual contract basis.

SHEEHY & KOPF, INC., 10400 Linn Station Road, Louisville, KY 40223.
Positions: Freelance artists handle illustrations and lettering for advertisments.
Requirements: Submit resume and work samples.
Provisions: Pay methods vary.

SHOSS & ASSOCIATES, INC., 1750 South Brentwood Boulevard, Suite 259, St Louis, MO 63144.
Positions: Freelance local photographers work on assignment for this ad agency.
Requirements: Submit work samples that include product shots. Include resume and request appointment to show portfolio.

SHULSINGER SALES, INC., 50 Washington Street, Brooklyn, NY 11201.
Positions: Freelance artists design greeting cards and gift wrap with Jewish themes.

Requirements: Submit work samples and resume.

SINGER COMMUNICATIONS, 3164 Tyler Avenue, Anaheim, CA 92801.
Positions: Freelance cartoonists. Singer is a large syndicate that buys thousands of cartoons for distribution worldwide each year.
Requirements: Must be previously published. Submit copies of published work.
Provisions: Pays a percentage split.

SKILL BUILDERS, Box 42050, Tucson, AZ 85733.
Positions: Freelance artists. Company produces specialty educational products.
Requirements: Must be experienced illustrator. Submit letter of interest and tear sheets.

SSC&B, INC., 1 Dag Hammarskjold Plaza, New York, NY 10017.
Positions: Freelance graphic artists, photographers and illustrators work on a variety of assignments in the advertising field.
Requirements: Submit letter of interest, business card, and tear sheets.

SUNRISE PUBLICATIONS, INC., P.O. Box 2699, Bloomington, IN 47402.
Positions: Writers and artists for production of greeting cards.
Requirements: First, send for Sunrise's Creative Guidelines and current market list. Then send letter of interest with work samples. Include SASE.
Provisions: Payment varies..

SUPERMARKET BUSINESS MAGAZINE, 25 West 43rd Street, New York, NY 10036.
Positions: Freelance correspondents write about the food and grocery industry within their assigned areas.
Requirements: Send letter of interest with writing samples. Must be familiar with the industry.

SYNDICATION ASSOCIATES, INC., P.O. Box 1000, Bixby, OK 74008.
Positions: This company sells patterns and plans for fabric, craft, and woodworking projects through newspaper syndication which amounts to a potential readership base of a whopping 34 million. Submissions of new, original, and unpublished designes are accepted.
Requirements: Send for submission instructions.
Provisions: Payment for accepted material is worked out on an individual basis for either lump sum payment in advance and/or royalties.

TAVERNON PHOTO ENGRAVING COMPANY, 27 First Avenue, Paterson, NJ 07514.
Positions: Campany makes silk screens for wallpaper and fabric. Hand work consists of color separation of textile designs. Freelance artists do all the design work.
Requirements: Must live in Paterson in order to pick up and deliver supplies and finished work. Experience is required.
Provisions: Pay depends on the colors and intricacy of the design.

TRAVEL PAGES, 213 West Institute Place #604, Chicago, IL 60610.
Positions: Freelance writers produce color travel guides that are distributed to state travel offices.
Requirements: For the coming year, only writers in California and the Carolinas will

be considered. Send for guidelines first, then send proposal.

TURNROTH SIGN COMPANY, 1207 East Rock Falls Road, Rock Falls, IL 61071.
Positions: Freelance artists design billboards and other kinds of signs on assignment.
Requirements: Submit letter of interest with sketches or finished work samples.
Include SASE with all correspondence.
Provisions: Pays flat rates for each project.

UNIVERSITY OF NEW HAVEN, 300 Orange Avenue, Public Relations Department,
West Haven, CT 06516.
Positions: Freelance photographers take shots of campus life, working on assignment
basis only. Work is used in all sorts of PR presentations.
Requirements: Send letter of interest along with resume and at least one sample shot
to be kept on file. Include SASE and business card. You will be contacted for an
interview. Be ready with a portfolio. Local photographers only.
Provisions: Pays by the hour at a minmum of $20.

UNIX, MULTIUSER, MULTITASKING SYSTEM, Tech Valley Publishing, 444
Castro Street, Mountain View, CA 94041.
Positions: Freelance writers work on assignment for this monthly magazine.
Requirements: Must have thorough knowledge of this end of the computer industry.
Send query along with clips of previously published work.
Provisions: Pays for articles on acceptance. Sometimes pays expenses.

USA, INC., P.O. Box 2984, Canoga Park, CA 91306.
Positions: Freelance artists work on assignment for this national advertising service.
Requirements: Ability to produce high quality figure drawings on assignment. Submit
copies of work samples and resume.

VON WEST, 103 Smokey Street, Ft. Collins, CO 80525.
Positions: Freelance artists provide line drawings for wall hangings.
Requirements: Send for market guidelines first. Submit letter of interest and samples
in pen and ink.

WARNER PRESS, INC., Box 2499, Anderson, IN 46018.
Positions: Writers and artists for work on greeting cards, calendars, posters, postcards,
and plaques. Artists work on assignment. Writers are freelance.
Requirements: Before applying, write for current market list and guidelines. Include
SASE. Be sure to study company's style before sending samples. Talented new artists
are especially sought.
Provisions: Pay varies.

WILDER LIMITED, P.O. Box 46212, Los Angeles, CA 90046.
Positions: Silkscreen artists, calligraphers, and translators. Company produces
children's wallhangings.
Requirements: Experience is required. Send letter of interest; state fee desired.
Provisions: Pays by the job.

WILLIAMHOUSE-REGENCY, INC., 28 West 23rd Street, New York, NY 10010.
Positions: Freelance artists design wedding invitations and related stationery pieces.
Requirements: Submit sketches or finished samples.

WILLITTS DESIGNS, 1327 Clegg Street, Box 178, Petaluma, CA 94953.
Positions: Designers and illustrators for porcelain and earthware giftware. Some calligraphy. All designs are three-dimensional and range from the light and whimsical to the detailed and serious.
Requirements: Submit full color design samples with resume.
Provisions: Pay methods vary from outright purchase to royalties.

WOMEN'S CIRCLE HOME COOKING, Box 198, Henniker, NY 03242.
Positions: Freelance writers and photographers produce all of the material in this monthly magazine.
Requirements: Send for guidelines first; include SASE.

WORLDLING DESIGNS/NYC CARD COMPANY, INC., P.O. Box 1935, Madison Square Station, New York, NY 10159.
Positions: Writers and artists for contemporary style greeting cards and related paper products. All products have a strong New York City look. Also assigns some calligraphy work.
Requirements: Send resume or letter of interest with work samples showing highest quality work. Writers send only short verses that are upbeat. Writers guidelines are available upon request. Be sure to include SASE with all correspondence. Artists send resume and samples of bold, stylistic work in any medium. Artists guidelines are also available. Request appointment to show portfolio.
Provisions: Pays flat rate.

WRITER DATA BANK, Cassell Communicaitons, Inc., P.O. Box 9844, Fort Lauderdale, FL 33310.
Positions: The Writer Data Bank is a national computerized listing of freelance writers categorized according to experience, areas of expertise, subject specialties, and geographic locations. Editors, PR firms/departments, and other clients who need the services of a writer call the Data Bank toll free (and without a search fee) and a writer with the appropriate expertise will be referred to them.
Requirements: Writers can be listed for an annual processing/update fee of $25. Then, when the writer receives payment from any assignment resulting from the Data Bank listing, he or she remits 5% of that fee back to Cassell Communications, Inc. Send for the "Writer Data Bank Info Form."
Provisions: Contracts are worked out by the writers and clients.

WRITER'S EXCHANGE, 1738 North Las Palmas, Hollywood, CA 90028.
Positions: Writer's Exchange is a membership organization designed to expand the opportunities for creative writers. The organization recently relocated from New York to Los Angeles, but can help anyone, anywhere, find more work as a writer. Presents workships regularly in various areas of writing; also acts as an agency to place articles, books, and screenplays.
Requirements: Charges a 10% fee for placements. Annual membership dues are $25. Apply with clips of (commercially) published material or work samples.

Chapter 3
Opportunities in Crafts

A craft is any occupation that requires manual dexterity or artistic skill. In this section, you'll find quite a few crafts represented—jewelry making, macrame, knitting, embroidery and merrowing, sewing, and silkscreen among others.

Knitting is one of the original seven industries that was banned from using home workers in 1938 under the Fair Labor Standards Act. The ban was lifted on knitting alone in December of 1985, after many years of struggling in the courts. Now there are dozens of companies that are certified by the U.S. Dept. of Labor to hire home workers. Most of these companies are based in New England, where home knitting has been a traditional occupation for generations.

Most knitting is still done by hand, but knitting machines are being used in increasing numbers. As you can imagine, using a knitting machine speeds up the process and allows the knitter to make more clothing and therefore more money. A new development has just arrived on the scene, which could revolutionize the entire home knitting industry. A computerized knitting machine has been introduced that will make it possible for a home knitter to custom design and produce a completed sweater in under two-and-a-half hours. And that's an inexperienced knitter! Best of all, the complete set-up only costs $250, including the computer.

Sewing is among the remaining six industries that are still banned from using home workers. Actually, only certain types of sewing are banned and most have to do with women's and children's apparel. That doesn't mean there isn't any home sewing going on. There are tens of thousands of home sewers across the country, but most are working "underground." The companies listed here are all located in states with labor laws that allow home sewing under specific certification procedures. (State labor laws supercede federal laws.)

Sewing is a skill that most women learn to some extent, but that doesn't mean that every woman is qualified to be a professional home sewer. Most home sewing is specialized so that each sewer works on a particular type of garment or, in many cases, a particular piece of garment. Employers have indicated that it isn't easy finding workers who are capable of doing quality work.

No matter what kind of craft you want to do, in order to get a job you will have to show samples of your work in order to prove that you have the necessary skills. There are a few situations mentioned in the following pages that offer training to inexperienced people, but these are the exceptions to the rule.

ADLAWN ENTERPRISES, LTD., 39 West 32nd Street, New York, NY 10001.
Positions: 50 year old company makes men's neckties by hand. Work includes sewing and folding.
Requirements: "This is highly skilled work, more than just sewing. You must have an understanding of the lay of the fabric, for instance. People come to us knowing the art already." Must live in Manhattan.
Provisions: "We pay very well." The number of home workers varies, but generally the company has more work than people.

> "The best thing about working at home is the 30 second commute down the hall--it can also be the worst."
> --John Everett, home worker

ALERT EMBROIDERY, INC., 775 Main Avenue, Passaic, NJ 07055.
Positions: Trimming threads, merrowing, and pressing of place mats. Hand work only, no machinery is used. Mostly rush work and overflow.
Requirements: No experience is required. Must live in Passaic.
Provisions: Company will pick up and deliver supplies and finished work, usually in the evening, every day. Pays piece rates.

ALMIA, INC., 1110 - 13th Street, North Bergen, NJ 07047.
Positions: Sewing sections of ladies' blouses including cuffs, collars, and pockets. Occasionally sewing entire T-shirts.
Requirements: Experience is necessary. Must be local resident, since workers must pick up and deliver their own supplies and finished work. Must own sewing machine.
Provisions: Pays piece rates.

ALORNA COAT CORPORATION, 1515 Willow Avenue, Hoboken, NJ 07030.
Positions: Sewing of coat pieces and linings. Work is distributed only to contractors licensed by the state of New Jersey Department of Labor to distribute home work. Contractors are then responsible for farming the work out to their own home workers.

ALPO COAT COMPANY, INC., 351 - 8th Street, Hoboken, NJ 07030.
Positions: Sewing of linings for ladies' coats.
Requirements: Experience is necessary. Must own sewing machine. Must be local resident in order to pick up and deliver supplies and finished work.
Provisions: Pays piece rates.

AMSTER NOVELTY CO., 75-13 - 71ST Avenue, Middle Village, NY 11375.
Positions: Sewing, trimming, stringing, and other hand work involved in the manufacture of soft tote bags, pouches for cosmetics, and decorations (bows and appliques) for little girls' dresses. Currently has about 100 home workers.
Requirements: No experience is necessary. Must be local resident.
Provisions: Pays piece rates.

ART EMBROIDERY CORP., 5821 Adams Street, West New York, NJ 07093
Positions: Sewing, mending, cutting, and merrowing of emblems and patches.

Requirements: Must be local resident since home workers must pick up and deliver their supplies and finished work. Experience is preferred. In some cases, a sewing machine is required.
Provisions: Pays piece rates. Currently has several home workers, with some of the cutters also having several more home workers working for each of them.

AVANTE FASHIONS, INC., 321 Newark Street, Hoboken, NJ 07030.
Positions: Sewing linings for ladies' coats and toppers.
Requirements: Must be local resident. Experience and sewing machine are required.
Provisions: Piece rates paid. Most of the work assigned is overflow from the factory.

BABBIDGE PATCH, 31 Babbidge Road, Falmouth, ME 04105.
Positions: Sewing of sweater sleeves. Currently has 20 home workers.
Requirements: Sewing machine is required. Must be local resident.
Provisions: Some training is provided. Pays piece rates.

BARRY MANUFACTURING COMPANY, INC., Bubier Street, Lynn, MA 01901.
Positions: Stitching and hand assembly of infant and children's shoe parts.
Requirements: Experience is required. Must be local resident.
Provisions: Some of the work requires machinery, which is supplied by the employer. Pays piece rates equal to minimum wage, which is what in-house workers are paid for the same work.

BERGEN COUNTY ELDER CRAFTSMEN GUILD, 12 North Dean Street, Englewood, NJ 07631
Positions: This nine-year old non-profit organization operates the "Golden Ladder," a "beautiful boutique in an upper middle class neighborhood." Currently there are 150 active members and new members are encouraged to join. Must be local resident.
Provisions: Handcrafts are sold for participants with 60% of the retail price being returned to the producer. Projects and services include various training programs such as the "Quilt In a Day" workshop. Training for upgrading skills also provided. Especially in the case of handicapped workers, help is provided to make the products as saleable as possible. The Guild also works at getting materials for the workers at wholesale prices. "We are a very active group. Over 600 have been involved in the past nine years."

BLUEBERRY WOOLENS, P.O. Box 318, Randall Street, Anson, ME 04911.
Positions: Machine knitting of whole sweaters for wholesaler.
This is an established and growing company with close to $1 million in annual sales. Currently has a pool of 60 knitters.
Requirements: Enrollment in company's training classes and submission of acceptable samples is required. Must own a knitting machine or purchase one from the company. Must be local in order to pick up and deliver supplies and finished sweaters.
Provisions: Pays per finished sweater. Hours can be full time or part time. Workers are independent contractors. Inquiries are welcome, as company continues to grow.

BORDEAUX, INC., 102 East Washington Street, Clarinda, IA 51632
Bordeaux has over 150 home workers sewing appliques onto ladies' sportswear, mostly sweatsuits. The company was started by Bertha Turner and her two partners six years ago. Since then, the company has grown to a $3.5 million a year business. Clarinda

Janet Nagel sews at her home for Boston-based Rocking Horse clothing store for children. Photo courtesy of *The Salt Lake Tribune.*

is an economically depressed farm community. All of the home workers are farm wives (or ex-farm wives). Each day, a van delivers work to farmhouses up to 50 miles away from headquarters. Each seamstress is considered by Bordeaux to be an independent contractor and is paid piece rates. This independent contractor status is being challenged in court by the U.S. Department of Labor at the insistence of the Ladies'Garment Workers Union. This is unfortunate because if Bordeaux loses, all work will have to be moved to a factory. Not only is the idea of working in a factory dismal, but most of the workers will not be able to commute and will simply lose their jobs. Bertha Turner says all applications for home work are on hold until the matter is resolved.

ABRAHAM BOXER & SONS, 110 West 26th street, New York, NY 10001
Positions: Sewing and assembly of suspenders and garters.
Requirements: Experience is required. Must be local.
Provisions: Pays piece rates.

BRUDER NECKWEAR COMPANY, INC., 1 East 33rd Street, New York, NY 10016.
Positions: Sewing, cutting and folding of men's neckties.
Requirements: Must be local and have a minimum five years experience making men's neckties.
Provisions: Pays piece rates.

C.D.C. FASHIONS, 533 - 61st Street, Union City, NJ 07087
Positions: Sewing ladies' blouses.
Requirements: Must own sewing machine. Professional level experience is required. Must be local resident.
Provisions: Pays piece rates.

COMET INDUSTRIES CORPORATION, 3630 South Iron Street, Chicago, IL 60609.
Positions: Comet manufactures model airplane kits and crafts. Part-time home workers paint craft samples for buyers.
Requirements: Must be local resident. Only referrals are considered. Must obtain home worker certificate from Illinois State Department of Labor.
Provisions: Pays piece rates.

JOSEPH P CONROY, INC., 110 South Market Street, Johnstown, NY 12095.
Positions: Sewing and assembly of gloves and glove parts.
Requirements: Must be local resident. Must have proven need to work at home.
Provisions: Pick up and delivery provided. Workers have full employee status with same benefits as in-house workers.

CORVI FASHIONS, INC., 195 New York Avenue, Jersey City, NJ 07307.
Positions: Sewing linings for ladies coats and other garments.
Requirements: Need sewing machine and professional level experience.
Provisions: Pays piece rates.

COTTON TIME, 22436 Abordo Drive, Saugus, CA 91350.
Positions: Sewing for design work with cotton (only) fashions. Company makes ladies' slips, gowns, pajamas, some men's apparel, and special clothing for nursing mothers.
Requirements: Must be local to pick up and deliver materials and finished work. Ordinary sewing machine needed. Independent contractors only.
Provisions: Training provided for qualified people. Pays piece rates.
Inquiries from local workers are welcome.

COUNTRY CURTAINS, INC., Main Street, Stockbridge, MA 01262.
Positions: Sewing trim on basic curtains. Currently has about 25 home workers.
Requirements: Need sewing machine. Must be local resident.
Provisions: Pick up and delivery provided. Pays piece rates equal to minimum wage.

THE CREATIVE CIRCLE, 9243 Cody Street, Overland Park, KS 66214.
Positions: Party plan sales of needlework kits. Work involves conducting classes in needlework.
Requirements: $40 investment buys $90 worth of merchandise and paperwork supplies for three classes.
Provisions: Pays 25% commission plus incentives. Also provides thank you gifts for hostesses and premiums used during parties. Managerial opportunities available. "The beauty of our company is we have no quotas, set territories, or anyone looking over our shoulders."

CREATIVE TREASURES, 6836 Duckling Way, Sacramento, CA 95842.
Positions: Creative Treasures is a home party business that markets quality handcrafts of all kinds. Crafter can submit any item for approval. If an item is approved, it is included in the company's regular line and sold one of three ways. Consignment orders: Company receives 40% of retail price. Party orders: Items are ordered from a sample that is provided by the crafter. Company receives 45% of retail price. Delivery for these items is 15 days from order date. Wholesale orders: These items will be stocked and paid for by Creative Treasures for wholesaling. Company receives 50% of retail price. Send good photo of item, or a sample, with letter of interest including suggested retail price for

consideration. Home party demonstrators and their supervisors also used. Write letter of interest.

DAINTY MAID MANUFACTURING COMPANY, 12 North Street, Fitchburg,MA 10420.
Positions: Sewing aprons.
Requirements: Must be local resident and own a sewing machine. Experience is required.
Provisions: Material is supplied. Pays piece rates equal to approximately $4 an hour.

DANTE FASHIONS, INC., 721 Grand Street, Hoboken, NJ 07030.
Positions: Sewing of linings in ladies' coats.
Requirements: Must be local resident and own a sewing machine. Experience preferred.
Provisions: Pays piece rates.

DESIGN SOURCE, Box 158, Greenleaf, ID 83626.
Positions: Crafting of soft sculptured wall hangings, holiday table ornaments, patterns, kits and "craft packs". Company sells these products through hospital gift shops, catalogs, and other wholesale outlets. Workers are independent contractors. Design Source contracts by the week, determining how many items will be produced and when they are due. Currently has 30 regulars, with number increasing in the fall to about 60.
Requirements: Must have sewing machine and must live nearby. Some kind of sewing experience is necessary.
Provisions: Specific training, such as tricks for working with felt and other difficult fabrics, is provided. Pays piece rates.

DESIGNS-IN-YARN, INC., Children's Division, 212 Center Street, Auburn, ME 04210.
Positions: Knitting of children's outerwear.
Requirements: Knitting machine and experience is required. Must be local resident.

DEVA CLOTHING COMPANY, a Cottage Industry, Box C, 303 East Main Street, Burkittsville, MD 21718.
Positions: DEVA has been using the cottage industry method for producing unisex, natural fiber apparel for 10 years. About two dozen local stitchers work as true independent contractors; they work on their own equipment, set their own prices, set their own production schedules, etc. Since the company's philosophy is based upon quality, only quality workers remain. "More of our stitchers wash out for not being businesslike. It is hard for them to get organized working at home. They need discipline and they have to find it for themselves without the structure of the factory."

D'GIACOMO ORIGINALS, INC., 715 Grand Street, Hoboken, NJ 07030.
Positions: Sewing linings of ladies' coats and other garments.
Requirements: Must be local and experienced. Need own sewing machine.
Provisions: Pays piece rates. Unlikely to expand home work force due to limitations imposed by law.

EAST ORANGE MILL END SHOPS, INC., 30 Broad Street, Bloomfield, NJ 07003.
Positions: Sewing draperies.
Requirements: Must own sewing machine and have experience sewing draperies in

particular. Must be local resident.
Provisions: Pays piece rates. Number of home workers limited by law.

LEE ENGLAND, 27 Alta Street, San Francisco, CA 94133.
Positions: Sewing, bead stringers and hand knotters for jewelry designer. All positions
are on an independent contractor basis. Number of workers depends upon orders, season,
etc. Averages more than 10. Company was much larger in the past, but it has been
reduced to "a more manageable size with creativity the primary emphasis."
Requirements: Sewing requires experience with fine and antique fabrics and trims for
high-fashion evening jackets. Sewing machine required. Stringers need no experience.
Knotters do need experience. Must be local resident.
Provisions: Limited training available. Pick up and delivery provided only if necessary.
Pay rates per production based upon difficulty of project.

ESP EXCLUSIVE FASHIONS, 4515 New York Avenue, Union City, NJ 07087.
Positions: Sewing of ladies' blouses, both parts and whole garments.
Requirements: Must be local resident and have professional experience.
Need sewing machine.
Provisions: Pays piece rates. Number of home workers limited by law.

ET PUIS, INC., 101-3 Church Street, Matawan, NJ 07747.
Positions: Sewing and finished fabric promotions and decorative items such as pillows.
Company was originally started as a home business.
Requirements: Must be experienced and own sewing machine. Must live in Matawan.
Provisions: Pays piece rates.

EVERETT ASSOCIATES, INC., dba LIVING EARTH CRAFTS, 429 Olive Street,
Santa Rosa, CA 95407.
Positions: Production of several types of crafts. Most work consists of sewing bags,
vinyl pieces, sheets, blankets and pad covers.
Requirements: Must own sewing machine. Must live in Santa Rosa. Experience is
required.
Provisions: Materials are supplied. Workers are considered regular employees with

medical and dental insurance, paid holidays and sick leave. Pays piece rates equal to an average of $8 an hour. Applications are kept on file indefinitely.

EVITA ORIGINALS, INC., 611-613 Jefferson Street, Hoboken, NJ 07030.
Positions: Sewing parts for ladies' coats; linings, pockets, and belts.
Requirements: Experience required. Must be local resident. Sewing machine necessary.

FENTON SHOE CORPORATION, 129 Franklin Street, Cambridge, MA 02139
Positions: Stitching and assembling of pre-cut shoe parts provided by Fenton Shoe.
Requirements: Must have some experience. Local residents only.
Provisions: All necessary machinery and tools are supplied. Pays piece rates equal to minimum wage.

FLAME APPAREL, 171 Avenel Street, Avenel, NJ 07001
Positions: Sewing and pasting of novelty headwear and outerwear.
Requirements: Must be experienced and live nearby.
Provisions: Daily pick-up and delivery is provided. All supplies and machinery are provided. Pays piece rates.
"The laws here in New Jersey work well for everyone concerned. It's a good balance between what's good for the people and what's good for the manufacturer.

FLIGHT APPAREL INDUSTRIES, INC., Columbia Road, Box 166, Hammonton, NJ 08037.
Positions: Cutting, sewing and assembly into finished garments for men and women. Mostly skirts, vests, slacks, coats, and zippered jackets in small quantities. Home workers fill in on special orders such as samples for designers or stores, when quantities are too small for full-scale factory production runs.
Requirements: Must be local resident and own sewing machine. Prefers experienced people.
Provisions: Home workers are regular employees with all benefits paid. Pays piece rates equal to $8 to $12 an hour.
"Cottage industry should be encouraged; it plays a very important part in America. It adds to the gross national product and makes the country stronger. Cottage workers are more skilled, versatile, adaptive and have a better attitude. Generally, they are self-sufficient people and what could be better than that?"

FRENCH CREEK SHEEP AND WOOL COMPANY, INC, Route 345, R.D. #1, Elverson, PA 19520.
Positions: Knitting sweaters on hand operated machines. Currently has about 40 workers.
Requirements: Must be local resident in order to pick up and deliver supplies and finished sweaters.
Provisions: Some training, specific to the work here, is provided. Pays production rate, which is "well above minimum wage."

GATER SPORTS, 3565 SW Temple, Suite 5, Salt Lake City, UT 84115
Positions: Sewing cold weather sports accessories, socks, face protectors, eyeglass cases, etc. Currently uses 25 to 50 home workers.
Requirements: Need some sewing experience and own sewing machine. Must be local resident in order to pick up and deliver supplies and finished work.

Provisions: Will train for specifics of the job. Pays piece rates. Workers are independent contractors. At this time, most of the available work fluctuates seasonally but the company is growing and hopes to be able to offer full-time, year-round work in the near future.

GATES-MILLS, INC., 30 North Market Street, Johnstown, NY 12095.
Positions: Sewing of gloves and glove parts.
Requirements: Must be local resident. Must own sewing machine and have sewing experience.
Provisions: Pays piece rates.

GELBERG BRAID COMPANY, INC., 249 West 39th Street, New York, NY 10018.
Positions: Hand sewing. Work consists of finishing covered buttons, sewing buckles onto belts, and sewing embroidery onto dress parts.
Requirements: Must be local resident. Some experience preferred, but not really required.
Provisions: Pays piece rates.

GELLES NECKWEAR LTD., 76 Essex Street, Boston, MA 02111.
Positions: Stitching neckties.
Requirements: Must have specific experience in making neckties and be a local resident.
Provisions: Sewing machines are provided. Pays hourly wage up to $5 an hour.

GOLDEN ENTERPRISES, HACAP, P.O. Box 789, Cedar Rapids, IA 52406.
Positions: Handcrafting of gifts and keepsake type items: baby things, dolls, wall signs, hangings, quilts, and comforters. Program is designed to provide income for home-based senior citizens by marketing handcrafts through retail and catalog orders. Currently has over 100 active participants, but the organization is expanding rapidly. Inquiries are welcome from senior citizens in Cedar Rapids.
Provisions: Buys some items outright; others are accepted on consignment.

ESTELLE GRACER, INC., 950 West Hatcher Road, Phoenix, AZ 85021.
Positions: Knitting and croqueting jackets and sweaters. Work has previously been done by hand only, but company is now going into machine knitting. Currently has over 50 home workers; that number fluctuates up to 200. "Inquiries are always welcome."
Requirements: Must be experienced. Phoenix residents only.
Provisions: Specific training is provided. Home workers are full employees. Pays for production.

HAIRITAGE, INC., 16909 Parthenia Street, Suite 202, Sepulveda, CA 91343.
Positions: Sewing hairpieces.
Requirements: Specific experience is necessary. "This is very intricate work. Our home workers were Max Factor employees before they came to us." Must be local residents.
Provisions: Pick up and delivery of supplies and finished work is provided. Pays piece rates.

HEADLINER HAIRPIECES, INC., 1448 North Sierra Bonita, Los Angeles, CA 90046.
Positions: Hand sewing and assembly of hairpieces.

Requirements: Must live nearby and have specific experience with this kind of work.
Provisions: Pays piece rates equal to about $5 an hour.

H.O.M.E., INC., Route 1, Orland, ME 04472.
Positions: H.O.M.E. stands for Homeworkers Organized for More Positions. It is a non-profit cooperative founded in 1970 for the purpose of marketing handcrafted products from this economically depressed area. H.O.M.E. operates a country store, many types of craft and trade workshops, a child-care center, The Learning Center for adult education, a saw mill, a shingle mill, a woodlot and two hospitality houses. It also publishes a quarterly newspaper ("This Time") and a crafts catalog, and builds homes for otherwise homeless neighbors. Currently has 3,500 members. Anyone living in the area is encouraged to participate.

HOMESTEAD HANDCRAFTS, North 1301 Pines Road, Spokane, WA 92206.
Positions: Company markets quality handcrafts with a country theme such as tole painting. Different situations are worked out on an individual basis.
Requirements: Must live in Spokane.

HOUSTON METROPOLITAN MINISTRIES, 3217 Montrose Boulevard, Houston, TX 77006.
Positions: Manufacturer of sewn goods, appliqued textiles, and decorative products with a Texas motif. Produces high quality goods with a quick turnaround for major department store lines. Purpose of the program is to solve the problems of those that may be homebound for a variety of reasons — child-care, transportation, illness, etc. Especially proud that several "welfare mothers" have been able to get off the system and take care of themselves. Currently has 30 home workers and is trying to expand both the product line and work force. Houston residents only.
 Provisions: Complete training is provided, along with all supplies, tools, and equipment. Pick up and delivery is provided every Tuesday and Thursday. Pays piece rates. Quality control people go over finished goods and offer assistance where necessary. Program's advisory committee includes a member of the Union. "We have a great concern for the workers and are very responsive to social pressure."

JERSEY MADE FASHIONS, INC., 130 Washington Street, Hoboken, NJ 07030.
Positions: Sewing parts of ladies' coats.
Requirements: Experience is necessary. Must be local resident and own sewing machine.
Provisions: Pays piece rates.

J'MAR GLOVES COMPANY, 66 East Fulton Street, Gloversville, NY 12078.
Positions: Sewing inseams of gloves.
Requirements: Must be local resident and have some professional sewing experience.
Provisions: Machine is provided if necessary. Pays piece rates. Number of workers fluctuates seasonally.

J. S. & COMPANY, 20045 Northwind Square, Cupertino, CA 95014.
Positions: Handcrafters produce quality items for home show presentations.
Requirements: Send sample or photo of craft item for consideration.
Provisions: Some items are bought outright, some are accepted on consignment.

KAY COMPANY, 17309 Burbank Boulevard, Encino, CA 91316.
Positions: Kay Company is a jewelry "manufacturer" that retails both from a storefront and through craft shows in Los Angeles. Uses bead workers.
Requirements: Prefers someone who is dependable and willing to make a minimum committment of six months. About $50 worth of small tools will be required. Prefers someone with some kind of handcraft experience. Must live in the West Valley in order to pick up and deliver inventory and supplies.
Provisions: Training will be provided and owner Kim Bovino says the training is very valuable and can be transferred to other companies upon leaving Kay Company. The work is part-time, on-call as orders come in. Pays piece rates.

KIPI OF MAINE, P.O. Box 311, Bingham, ME 04920.
Positions: Knitting, sewing, and blocking sweaters, pants, and other sportswear. Handcrafting of gift items for retail store and wholesale orders for catalog companies. Currently has around 50 home workers. "We have several knitters we have never seen." Number fluctuates seasonally.
Inquiries are welcome.
Requirements: Must live within 200 mile radius of company. Must submit a sample of work.
Provisions: Training is provided, particularly on Singer and Studio knitting machines for which the patterns are made. Pick up and delivery is provided. UPS is used for workers outside local area, but for these people only repetitive, larger orders are available so the work may not be steady. All workers are regular employees with full benefits provided by law. Quotas and tests are conducted to insure income meets D.O.L. requirements. Pays piece rates.

LACE -TRENDS, INC., 324 -61st Street, West New York, NJ 07093.
Positions: Hand cutting, trimming and merrowing of embroidery, appliques, and fabric pieces.
Requirements: Must be local resident.
Provisions: Pick up and delivery of supplies and finished work is provided daily. Workers are independent contractors and are paid piece rates bi-weekly. "We treat our home workers with respect. We invite them to our Christmas parties, for instance, to keep them involved with the rest of the company. We don't cheat them, either. If someone makes a mistake, the company absorbs the loss."

THE LANCE CORPORATION, 321 Central Street, Hudson, MA 01749.
Positions: Lance is a manufacturer of pewter ceramic-like figurines. About a dozen home workers paint the unfinished figurines.
Requirements: Must be local residents.
Provisions: Pick up and delivery is provided. Pays piece rates.

LEHUA HAWAII, INC., 1001 Dillingham, Suite 319, Honolulu, HI 96817.
Positions: Production sewing of mu-mus, dresses, bras, and shirts.
Requirements: Must be experienced and own interlocking sewing machine. Must be an in-house employee prior to moving work home. Local residents only.
Provisions: Pays hourly wages.

LENOX KITES, 98 Main Street, Lenox, MA 01240.
Positions: Sewing of appliques, designs, and pockets onto kites.
Requirements: Must own sewing machine and have experience working with fine

A Closer Look: **H.O.M.E.**

No one ever said it is easy to live in Maine. The weather is harsh, the land rocky and hard to till, and jobs are not easy to come by.

Nonetheless, Mainers have always stuck together, not just for survival, but to defend their way of life in their staunch New England style.

It was in 1970 when the first Bangor shoe factory stopped providing work for home stitchers. In this mostly rural area, employees, almost all of them women, were faced with little hope beyond welfare and poverty. Oe of those women was Sister Lucy Poulin, a Carmelite nun living in a convent in nearby Orland. Sister Lucy was determined not to let unemployment destroy her or her neighbors. She set about organizing a cooperative of crafts people and called it H.O.M.E., or Homeworkers Organized for More Employment. The original purpose was to provide a marketing outlet for homemade products.

H.O.M.E. may well go down in history as the classic community effort. Since those fragile beginnings, it has grown into a comprehensive organization "engaged in rural economic development and social reconstruction." Today it boasts 3,500 members.

Local handcrafts are sold at the H.O.M.E. crafts store and through a mail-order catalog that is published annually.

The facilities include much more than that, though. The Learning Center has child-care, an accredicted high school and adult education courses. Farming skills are taught and four craft workshops teach woodworking, pottery, weaving, leatherwork and more. There are two hospitality houses for those in extreme need. Seven 1,200 sq. ft. homes have been built for what would otherwise have been homeless families. Each is located on 10 acres, complete with a greenhouse.

H.O.M.E. set out early to build a stable economy based on the area's only natural resources, wood and land. It owns an extensive wood lot which provides firewood to the elderly and poor. There is also a sawmill which provides lumber for the building projects and, in the process, a number of jobs too.

There are 65 families involved in the Down Home Farms Project, which helps members improve their farming skills and supplies animals to poor farm families. Since 1983, the Project has operated a year-around market to sell local produce, dried fruit and nuts, and grains and seeds both to the co-op members and the general public.

It took 13 years but H.O.M.E. now operates in the black. 1983 was the year when the co-op began breaking even in all departments. Considering the recession of 1981 and 1982, when the remaining shoe factories either closed their doors or sent their work to cheap labor markets abroad, becoming self-supporting was a major victory.

Hard work and persistance have paid off for thousands of Mainers in a community literally made up of home workers.

fabics. Must be local resident in order to pick up and deliver supplies and finished work.
Provisions: Pays piece rates equal to a minimum of $4 an hour.

LOGOS NECKWEAR, INC. 126 Gill Avenue, Paulsboro, NJ 08066.
Positions: Hand sewing of 10" bands, hand sewing and tying of clips onto boys' redities, and putting linings to points on ties.
Requirements: Must be local resident.
Provisions: Pays piece rates. Would like to hire more home workers, but state laws limit expansion of home work pool.

LUCY ANN ORIGINALS, INC., 55 Park Avenue, Hoboken, NJ 07030.
Positions: Sewing linings for ladies' coats.
Requirements: Must be experienced with production work and own a sewing machine. Must be local resident.
Provisions: Pays piece rates.

MANDALA DESIGNS, RFD #1, Box 480, Starks, ME 04911.
Positions: Machine knitting of woolen outerwear including sweaters, jackets, socks, scarves, and hats.
Requirements: Prefers local knitters. Must be experienced and own knitting machine.
Provisions: Provides supplies and patterns. Pays piece rates.

MANHATTAN FASHIONS, INC., 1620 Manhattan Avenue, Union City, NJ 07087.
Positions: Sewing linings for ladies' coats.
Requirements: Must be experienced at a production level and own sewing machine. Must be local resident.
Provisions: Pays piece rates.

MARIA FASHIONS, INC., 315 First Street, Hoboken, NJ 07030.
Positions: Setting of coat sleeves on ladies' coats.
Requirements: Must be licensed by the state of New Jersey to be a home-based subcontractor. Inquiries from local residents only.
Provisions: Pays production rates.

MARILENA FASHIONS, INC., 1105 Summit Avenue, Jersey City, NJ 07307.
Positions: Sewing parts of ladies' coats.
Requirements: Must be experienced and own sewing machine. Must be local resident.
Provisions: Pick up and delivery of supplies and finished work provided daily or weekly. Pays piece rates.

MAYFLOWER TEXTILE COMPANY, INC., 305 Union Street, Franklin, MA 00551.
Positions: Sewing of draperies for this wholesale/retail fabric store.
Requirements: Must be local resident. Must be experienced in sewing draperies and own an industrial sewing machine.
Provisions: Supplies and customer specifications are provided. Pays $5 an hour.

MC DESIGNS, 115 Altura Way, Greenbrae, CA 94904.
Positions: Hand knitters are used by sweater designer.
Requirements: Must be local resident. Professional level experience required. Apply with resume only.

Provisions: Pays piece rates.

MERMAID WOOLENS, Leighton Point Road, West Pembroke, ME 04666.
Positions: Knitting of outerwear.
Requirements: Knitting machine and experience are required. Must be local resident.
Provisions: Pays piece rates.

MICHEL COAT COMPANY, INC., 102 Cambridge Avenue, Jersey City, NJ 07307.

"We treat our home workers with respect. We invite them to our Christmas parties, for instance, to keep them involved with the rest of the company. We don't cheat them either. If someone makes a mistake, the company absorbs the loss."   --Lace-Trends, Inc.

Positions: Sewing ladies' coats and belts.
Requirements: Must be local resident. Production experience and industrial sewing machine are required.
Provisions: Pays piece rates.

MISSION MILL MUSEUM ASSOCIATION, Northwest Textile Center, 1313 Mill Street S.E., Salem, OR 97301.
Positions: Handcrafters produce handwoven products and needlework kits.
Requirements: Must live in Salem.
Provisions: Pays piece rates.

MORIARTIE'S HATS AND SWEATERS, Mountain Road, Stowe, VT 05672.
Positions: Mrs. Moriartie started this company in the late '50's when she handknitted a hat for her son and almost single-handedly launched the New England home knitting industry as it is today. Moriartie's has a reputation for being the best hat and sweater store in the world. Home knitters make hats, Christmas stockings, ornaments, and sweaters. Work is done on hand-operated machines. Company sells products wholesale as well as retail. Currently has 30 permanent home workers.
Requirements: Must be local resident in order to come in once a week to get supplies. Must own machine.
Provisions: Knitters can select designs, patterns and yarns from stock and make as many or as few items as they like. Can accept custom orders, too. "Each knitter has something they like to do especially and they usually stick to it. Some prefer to knit hats that only take 25 minutes to complete. Others prefer sweaters that take much longer. It's up to them." Pays piece rates.

MOUNTAIN LADIES & EWE, INC., Box 391 Route 7, Manchester Village, VT 05254.
Positions: Knitters make ski hats and sweaters. Products are sold both retail and wholesale. Currently has 25 permanent home workers.

Requirements: Prefers workers that live within a 60-mile radius of Manchester Village. Must own knitting machine. Pick up and delivery of supplies and finished work is required of each knitter.
Provisions: Specific training is provided. All supplies are provided.
Pays production rates, but workers are considered regular employees and receive basic benefits provided by law. Inquiries are welcome from qualified applicants.

MOUNTAIN WOMEN'S EXCHANGE, P.O. Box 204, Jellico, TN 37762.
Positions: Mountain Women's Exchange is a community effort run by women in rural mountain communities on the Kentucky-Tennessee border. One of its programs is the Mountain Way Herbs and Arts which is a cottage industry designed to provide supplemental family income. It combines traditional skills in gardening and food preservation with new efforts to learn enterprise development and marketing. Centralized gardens in communities in both Kentucky and Tennessee are prepared in "double-dug" bed fashion. Women and men hired as gardeners tend these beds, planting them in spring with seedlings raised in local greenhouses. In 1985 over 30,000 plants were set in and thousands of straw flowers, globe amaranth, ornamental peppers, and statice flowers were gathered. Flowers are hung in a barn in Emlyn, Kentucky to dry, then gathered and stored in a warehouse in Newcomb, Tennessee. Women come to the warehouse to get materials and to receive training in making decorative wreaths and herbal products. They produce all the items in their homes and return them to the warehouse to be stored and shipped out as mail orders dictate. The women are paid at a rate above minimum wage for their labors. Women living in the rural communities surrounding Williamsburg, Kentucky, and Jellico, Tennessee are encouraged to participate.

NEUMA AGINS DESIGN, INC., Main Street, Southfield, MA 01105.
Positions: Embroidery of sweaters according to custom orders. Decorations may also be applied. Currently has over 200 home workers.
Requirements: Must have experience and do quality work. Local residents only.
Provisions: Pays about $3.65 an hour.

NEW ENGLAND MANUFACTURING COMPANY, INC., 250 Canal Street, Lawrence, MA 01840.
Positions: Sewing of pocket linings for wool coats.
Requirements: Experience and industrial sewing machine are necessary. Must be local resident.
Provisions: Pays piece rates equal to about $5.50 an hour.

NEW JERSEY CASKET COMPANY, INC., 1350 Clinton Street, Hoboken, NJ 07030.
Positions: Hand sewing of velvet material for caskets.
Requirements: Must have experience doing quality work. Must be local resident.
Provisions: Pays piece rates.

NORDIC NOMADS, P.O. Box 389, Norwich, VT 05055.
Positions: Knitting of specialty sweaters.
Requirements: Must own knitting machine and must be experienced. Worker is responsible for pick and delivery of supplies and finished work. Some workers are local; others depend on mail service.
Provisions: Pays piece rates.

NORTH COUNTRY GLOVES, INC., P.O. Box 65, Johnstown, NY 12095.
Positions: Sewing of leather gloves and linings. Work is part-time and seasonal.
Requirements: Must own sewing machine and live nearby.
Provisions: Pays piece rates.

NORTH OF BOSTON, P.O. Box 1308, Stowe, VT 05672.
Positions: Knitting sweaters for wholesale orders. Currently has 30 home workers.
Requirements: Must own knitting machine and live in the area. Workers are required to pick up and deliver supplies and finished work or use the mail for that purpose.
Provisions: Some training is provided. Pays piece rates.

NORWELL GLOVES, INC., 110 South Market Street, Johnstown, NY 12095.
Positions: Sewing of glove parts. Work is seasonal.
Requirements: Must own sewing machine and be local resident.
Provisions: Pays piece rates.

ODDSTITCH EMBROIDERY COMPANY OF NEW BEDFORD, INC. 61 Wamsutta Street, New Bedford, MA 02740.
Positions: Embroidery of bathroom, bedroom, and dining room linens.
Requirements: Experience is required. Must be local resident.
Provisions: Bonnaz embroidery machine is provided. Pays piece rates equal to about $6 an hour.

OSCAR DESIGNS, INC., 1152 - 51st Street, North Bergen, NJ 07047.
Positions: Sewing of ladies' blouses.
Requirements: Sewing machine with interlock features is required as well as production level experience. Must be local resident.
Provisions: Pays piece rates.

OUR WAY ENTERPRISES, INC., 1552 West 6th Drive, Mesa, AZ
Positions: Sewing and assembly of various products such as wall clocks and small lamps. All work is performed by handicapped persons. The company's Research & Development team invented and subsequently manufactured a device that enables paraplegics to sew by controlling the machinery with their foreheads.
Requirements: Work is for handicapped individuals of Mesa only.
Provisions: Complete training is provided since the objective of Our Way is "to train handicapped persons in a marketable skill, and then help to place these persons in industry where they could make as much money in wages as anyone else."

PATTY ANNE, 1212 Crespi Drive, Pacifica, CA 94044.
Positions: This well-established retailer/wholesaler of children's apparel and gifts uses home-based seamstresses. There are different jobs for different types of machines; appliques, blind hems, etc.
Requirements: Industrial overlock machine is necessary. Experience is required. Must live within reasonable proximity to Pacifica.
Provisions: Pick up and delivery provided. Pays piece rates equal to about $7.50 an hour for an average part-time income of $75 to $100 a week. Work tends to be seasonal.

PEPPI SPINA COAT AND SUIT COMPANY, 323 - 56th Street, West New York, NJ 07093
Positions: Sewing linings of ladies' jackets.

Requirements: Must be experienced in production work of this kind and own sewing machine. Must be local resident.
Provisions: Pays piece rates.

PERIWINKLE, 3928 17th Street, San Francisco, CA 94114.
Positions: Hand knitting of high fashion sweaters that match dresses, jackets, and coats. No finishing involved.
Requirements: Must be experienced, especially with all types of special yarns. Only local residents will be considered.
Provisions: Supplies and patterns are provided. For knitters that live too far away to come in regularly, supplies will be sent UPS. Pays by the piece, ranging from $30 to $55 each.

PERELLA GLOVES, INC., 39 Union Street, Gloversville, NY 12078.
Positions: Stitching of gloves and glove parts.
Requirements: Must be local resident with own sewing machine. Prefers experience in this kind of work.
Provisions: Pays by the piece.

PRINTEX LABELS, INC., Wanaque Avenue, Pompton Lakes, NJ 07442.
Positions: Inspection of woven and printed labels and hand pinking/cutting.
Requirements: Must be local resident in order to pick up and deliver supplies and finished work. Experience is necessary.
Provisions: Pays hourly wage.

P.R.W. DESIGNS, P.O. Box 684, Union Town, OH 44685.
Positions: Knitting and sewing of outerwear.
Requirements: Must be experienced and local resident.
Provisions: Pays piece rates.

REGIANA FASHIONS, 65th Street, Union City, NJ 07087.
Positions: Sewing linings for ladies' Coats.
Requirements: Must be local resident. Experience and sewing machine are necessary.
Provisions: Pays piece rates.

ROCKING HORSE, 1265 West Illinois Avenue, Salt Lake City, UT 84104.
Positions: Sewing, knitting, and crafting of elite children's wear and heirlooms. Rocking Horse is a chain of children's stores based in Boston. There are four stores now and the company is rapidly expanding coast to coast. All sewing of children's apparel is done by home workers in Utah. Other items (cloth dolls, quilts, toys and heirlooms) can be done elsewhere only upon approval.
Requirements: Ability and proper machinery is required. Especially wants quilters and smockers. Knitters must have knitting machine.
Provisions: Patterns, supplies, and training are provided. Pays piece rates. "We have lots of work coming up. In addition to our established line, we are open to any new ideas. Be prepared to send samples."

RUBIN GLOVES, INC., 51 East Fulton Street, P.O. Box 631, Gloversville, NY 12078.
Positions: Sewing glove parts.
Requirements: Must own knitting machine. Must be local resident in order to pick up and deliver supplies and finished work.

Provisions: Some training is provided. Number of home workers is diminishing.

SALT AIR OF MARBLEHEAD, 63A Atlantic Avenue, Marblehead, MA 01945.
Positions: Knitting of sweaters.
Requirements: Must own knitting machine. Must be local resident in order to pick up and deliver supplies and finished work.
Provisions: Some training is provided. Number of home workers is diminishing.

"Talented new writers are especially sought."

--Warner Press, Inc.

SEA GULL, P.O. Box 147, Wharton, TX 77488.
Positions: Sewing of garments especially designed for easy dressing of hospitalized people, nursing home residents, and handicapped people. Garments are sold through hospital gift shops.
Requirements: Must own sewing machine with interlock features and be experienced. Local residents only.
Provisions: Patterns and supplies are provided. Pays piece rates. Company is small and is not likely to grow for a while.

SIENA ORIGINALS, INC., 715 Grand Street, Hoboken, NJ 07030.
Positions: Sewing of linings for ladies' coats and other garments.
Requirements: Must be experienced in production work and have the right machine. Local residents only. Pays piece rates.

SNOB FASHIONS, INC., 300 Observer Highway, Hoboken, NJ 07030
Positions: Sewing of belts and other pieces for ladies' coats.
Requirements: Must be experienced and own sewing machine. Local residents only.
Provisions: Pays piece rates.

SOHO CREATIONS, a Division of Aldegrino, Inc., 1133 Broadway, Room 430, New York, NY 10010.
Positions: Part-time sewing of sweat bands.
Requirements: Professional experience required. Must live nearby.
Provisions: Pays piece rates. Currently has a waiting list.

ST. MARYS WOOLENS, Bruce Mountain, St. Marys, IA 50241.
Positions: Knitting and hand stitching of outerwear; sweaters, hats, and scarves. Company is described as "vertically integrated" since it does everything from raising special sheep for the color and texture of their wool to marketing the finished products through retail outlets and catalogs. Currently has 19 home knitters.
Requirements: Must live nearby and provide samples of quality work.
Provisions: Training and supplies are provided. Knitting machine will be rented to worker if necessary. Knitters are independent contractors so there are no benefits. Pays

piece rates. Work is part-time: average annual income is $7,000. "Inquiries are okay, but we have a very low turnover rate and a waiting list."

ST. THOMAS, INC., St. Thomas Place, Gloversville, NY 12078.
Positions: Machine sewing and hand pasting of small leather goods; wallets, eyeglass cases, cosmetics cases, etc.
Requirements: Must be local resident.
Provisions: Training is provided. Sewing machine is available for loan if necessary. Work is very seasonal with fall being the busiest time.

STEIN-TOBLER EMBROIDERY COMPANY, 2714 Kennedy Boulevard, Union City, NJ 07087.
Positions: Hand cutting of yokes and collars for use on lingerie.
Requirements: Experience is necessary. Work is done by hand so only a pair of scissors is needed. Must live in Union City.
Provisions: Pays production rates. In addition to the work given to Stein-Tobler home workers, contracts are given to home work contractors who then subcontract to more home workers.

STITCHES 'N STENCILS, 17 Star Road, Cape Elizabeth, ME 04107.
Positions: Knitting and sewing of sweaters, Christmas ornaments, hats, scarves, placemats, and potholders. Currently has about a dozen home workers.
Requirements: Must be local and own appropriate machinery.
Provisions: Pays production rates for knitting and hourly wage for sewing. Inquiries are welcome.

STOWE WOOLENS, RR 1, Box 1420, Stowe, VT 05672.
Positions: Knitting of outerwear; sweaters, hats, and scarves. Currently has 40 to 50 home knitters.
Requirements: Must be experienced and have own knitting machine. Must live within an hour's drive from Stowe.
Provisions: Pays piece rates.

STREAMLINE INDUSTRIES, 845 Stuart Avenue, Garden City, NY 11530.
Positions: Hand sewing cloth onto buttons and buckles.
Requirements: Must live nearby.
Provisions: Pays piece rates.

SUITCASE BOUTIQUE, 12228 Spring Place Court, Maryland Heights, MO 63043.
Positions: Suitcase Boutique is a home party business. Company buys many types of handcrafted items including stuffed animals, wood crafts, toys, soft sculpture, framed pictures, and cross-stitch.
Requirements: Crafters should send photo of product and description.

F. T. SUTTON COMPANY, INC., 14 North Perry Street, Johnstown, NY 12095.
Positions: Stitching leather gloves and mittens.
Requirements: Must be experienced and live in the area.
Provisions: Pays piece rates. Work is part-time only.

SWISS MAID EMBLEMS, INC., 26 Industrial Avenue, Fairview, NJ 07022.

Positions: Manual trimming and merrowing of embroidered appliques and emblems. Also bagging and counting of emblems. Currently has about a dozen home workers.
Requirements: Must be local resident.
Provisions: Training is provided. Pick up and delivery of supplies and finished work will be provided if necessary. Workers are considered regular employees and are paid hourly wages plus benefits. Inquiries are welcome.

T & S APPAREL, 813 Main Avenue, Passaic, NJ 07055.
Positions: Machine sewing of pre-cut linings of ladies' coats and jackets.
Requirements: Sewing machine and experience are required. Must be local resident.
Provisions: Pays piece rates.

TAVERNON PHOTO ENGRAVING COMPANY, 27 First Avenue, Paterson, NJ 07514.
Positions: Company makes silk screen for wallpaper and fabric. Hand work consists of coloring of textile designs. Freelance artists do all the design work.
Requirements: Must be local in order to pick up and deliver supplies and finished work. Experience is required.
Provisions: Pay depends on the colors and intricacy of the design.

JOSEPH TITONE & SONS, INC., Jacksonville Road, Burlington, NJ 08016.
Positions: Cutting, tying, and packing of hair nets. Currently has 10 home workers.
Requirements: Must be local resident.
Provisions: Training and appropriate equipment is provided. Pick up and delivery of supplies and finished work is provided weekly. Home workers are considered regular employees and are given basic benefits in addition to being paid piece rates equal to about $3.40 and hour.

TOMORROW TODAY CORPORATION, P.O. Box 612, Westfield, MA 01086.
Positions: Hand work consists of tying bows and working with flowers to make decorations.
Requirements: Must live in Westfield.
Provisions: Pays minimum wage.

TOP NOTCH KNITS, 12840 N.E. 88th, Kirkland, WA 98033.
Positions: Knitting and sewing of complete garments. Currently has 50 home workers.
Requirements: Must own knitting machine (any type is okay). Will only accept applications from experienced local residents.
Provisions: Pick up and delivery of supplies and finished work is provided. Pays production rates.

TOTSY MANUFACTURING COMPANY, INC., Cabot & Bigelow Streets, Holyoke, MA 10140.
Positions: Sewing of doll clothes and accessories. Currently has about 50 home workers.
Requirements: Must be local resident. Experience and sewing machine are required.
Provisions: Pick up and delivery is provided. Pays minimum wage.

TRIUMPH FASHIONS, INC., 1110 - 13th Street, North Bergen, NJ 07047.
Positions: Sewing and assembly of ladies' blouses and sections.
Requirements: Sewing machine with interlock features and experience are necessary. Must be local resident in order to pick up and deliver supplies and finished work.

Provisions: Pays piece rates.

UNCOMMON TOUCH EMBROIDERIES, INC., 429 - 62nd Street, West New York, NJ 07093.
Positions: Hand mending of embroidery samples. Currently has up to 30 home workers.
Requirements: Must be local resident.
Provisions: Pays piece rates.

UNDERWOOD'S FURNITURE GALLERIES, 2417 North University Street, Peoria, IL 61605.
Positions: About half a dozen home workers sew draperies and accessories for this retail interior design and furniture store.
Requirements: Must have machinery and experience. Local residents only.
Provisions: Pays piece rates.

UNION DOLL MANUFACTURING, 95 Edward Street, Fitchburg, MA 01429.
Positions: Sub-contract sewing of women's and children's apparel.
Requirements: Must be experienced and own appropriate sewing machine. Local residents only.
Provisions: Pays piece rates equal to $4 an hour.

UNIQUE 1, P.O. Box 744, 2 Bayview Street, Camden, ME 04843.
Positions: Knitting of sweaters using both wool and cotton yarn for retail shop. Currently has 14 home workers.
Requirements: Must be experienced and be a local resident.
Provisions: Training is provided. If home worker doesn't own a knitting machine, Unique 1 will lease one. Pays piece rates. "Camden is a tourist town, so the summer is the best time for us, especially for custom orders."

UNITED STATES PROVIDENCE CORPORATION, 20 Alden Drive, P.O. Box 3010, North Attleboro, MA 02761.
Positions: Sewing, trimming, lacing, and inspecting of display packaging products.
Requirements: Must be experienced. Must be local resident.
Provisions: Training is provided. Machinery is provided when necessary for the job. Pick up and delivery of supplies and finished work is provided. Pays piece rates equal to $4 an hour.

THE VILLAGE OF THE SMOKY HILLS, Osage, MN 56570.
Positions: Crafts of all kinds made by local home-based craftspeople are sold at the Village. Currently has over 350 home workers.

B.T. WAGNER, INC., 99 Hawthorne Avenue, Pittsfield, MA 01201.
Positions: Sewing braid trim onto curtains.
Requirements: Must own sewing machine and be experienced. Local residents only.
Provisions: Pays piece rates equal to about $4.50 and hour.

WAIN MANUFACTURING CORPORATION, 589 Essex Street, Lynn, MA 01901.
Positions: Stitching and thread trimming of eye glass cases.
Requirements: Must be local resident with experience.
Provisions: Training and machinery are provided. Pays $4 and hour.

WASHINGTON GARTER CORPORATON, 13 Laight Street, New York, NY 10013.
Positions: Sewing and hand assembly of garters and suspenders.
Requirements: Must live locally and be experienced.
Provisions: Pays piece rates.

BARBARA WEST, 495 - 17th Avenue, San Francisco, CA 94122.
Positions: Hand knitting of high fashion sweaters. Most designs are for women, but a men's line is a new addition. Patterns are for hand knitting, but machine knitting is okay.
Requirements: Ability and quality work are most important. Must be local.
Provisions: Patterns, material, and pick up and delivery servies are provided. Pays about $50 per piece depending upon the difficulty of the design.

WEST HILL WEAVERS, Box 108, Stowe, VT 05672.
Positions: Knitting and sewing of outerwear. Also some handwoven clothing and crafts. Currently has about 30 home workers located all over the state.
Requirements: Must own and have full knowledge of proper machinery. Pick up and delivery of supplies and finished work is the responsibility of the home worker; therefore must be local.
Provisions: Training for particular designs is provided. Pays piece rates. Inquiries are welcome. "When we're hiring, we're hiring. Otherwise we will keep your name on file for future work."

WOMAN'S EXCHANGE, INC., 3 Village Street, Heritage Village, Southbury, CT 06488.
Positions: Woman's Exchange is a non-profit national organization with 41 centers. Handcrafted items of all kinds are marketed at a very small markup through storefront operations. Most needed are children's clothing, quilts, and fine hand sewing. Several thousand women are participants nationwide. Look the the white pages of your phone book for the center nearest you. If you don't find a listing, write to the headquarters.

WOODSTOCK NEEDLEWERKX, a Division of Green Mountain Showcase Ltd., 8 Central Street, Woodstock, VT 05091.
Positions: Knitting of outerwear for retail and wholesale.
Requirements: Kitting machine and experience is required. Must be local.

THE YARN BARREL, 426 U.S. Route One, P.O. Box 2368, Scarborough, ME 04074.
Positions: Knitting of outerwear.
Requirements: Must be experienced and own knitting machine. Local residents only.
Provisions: Pays piece rates.

YARNWOOD, 871 Aztec, Muskegon, MI 49444.
Positions: Machine knitting of sweaters, hats, blankets, and ornaments.
Requirements: Prefers experienced knitters. Must be local.
Provisions: Training is provided.

YOUNG AMERICAN CLOTHING COMPANY, INC., 50 Columbia Street, P.O. Box 657, Newark, NJ 07101.
Positions: Sewing of linings for ladies' coats and jackets.
Requirements: Must be very experienced in this particular type of work. Must be local in order to pick up and deliver supplies and finished work.

Provisions: Sewing machine is provided. Pays piece rates. "People come to us looking for home work all the time. Unfortunately, most don't have the kind of experience that is necessary for this kind of work."

ZAUDER BROTHERS, INC., 10 Henry Street, Freeport, NY 11520.
Positions: Hand work involved in the manufacture of wigs and toupes.
Requirements: Must have specific experience with this kind of work. Must be local resident.

Chapter 4
Telecommuting and Other
Employee Options

Telecommuting is an often-misused term. It means transporting work to the worker rather than moving the worker to the workplace. This can be accomplished in a number of ways, but most often it involves the use of telephones, computers and modems, and facimile (FAX) machines.

In this book, telecommuting refers to an option open to employees who are currently working for a company and have an express need to take their work home. A temporary need might be illness, temporary disability, pregnancy, or the need to take care of family members. Some workers prefer to move home in order to work more productively on long projects, cut down on commuting, or spend more time with family.

Some telecommuting is done temporarily, some is part-time, and some is permanent. It is becoming a very common option in the corporate world wtih as many as 500 corporations reporting some kind of work-at-home option available to employees on an informal basis. A few of those have formal programs with the rules for working at home laid out in very specific detail.

If you are already working and you want to work at home, look in your own back yard first. Many employees have the opportunity to work at home and just don't know it. Before looking elsewhere for a new job that can be done at home, why not first talk to your manager about the possibility of moving your present job home? You may be surprised at the answer.

The listings in this section should be considered examples of successful telecommuting programs. None of them are open to inquiries from those not currently employed by the company.

AMF BOWLING PRODUCTS GROUP, INC., Jerico Turnpike, Westbury, NY 11590.
Office-based employees are provided with computer terminals and telecommunicatons equipment for after-hours telecommuting. Most telecommuting is done by company programmers.

AMTRAK, Union Station, Customer Relations, 50 Massachusetts Avenue, N.E., Washington, D.C. 20540.
Amtrak's Customer Relations Group has increased its productivity and employee morale by implementing telecommuting on a small scale. Nine writers in the group work at home on a rotating schedule, with one writer working one day at home, then the next taking one day, and so on.

ANASAZI, INC., 7500 North Dreamy Draw Drive, Suite 120, Phoenix, AZ 85020.
Programmers, engineers, and other high level technical personnel work at home. Company is very careful who is selected for telecommuting. Only persons who have proven to be self-managing, have some experience working at home, and have proper technical equipment can participate. Employee status remains intact.

ANDREWS GLASS COMPANY, INC., Northwest Boulevard, Vineland, NJ 08360.
Glass lampwork and tool work on laboratory glass products is offered as an option for extra income for after-hours work for established employees only.

A-TOP NOTCH SERVICE, INC., 1132 South Jefferson, Chicago, IL 60607.
This is a direct mail house. Employees type envelopes at home during peak periods.

AUTODESK, 2320 Marinship Way, Sausalito, CA 94965.
Autodesk is a software design firm. About one third of its programmers work at home as a matter of personal preference, returning to headquarters for meetings once a month. The company provides equipment and tools.

BANKERS TRUST COMPANY, 1 Bankers Trust Plaza, New York, NY 10006.
Bankers Trust recently conducted its initial telecommuting pilot program with the help of Electronic Services Unlimited. 20 employees worked at home for six months on a part-time basis only. The usual time spent at home working was two days a week unless the particular project allowed for longer periods of time. Employees were supplied with IBM PCs tied into the mainframe in Manhattan. The work was done in the local mode, using and transferring floppies. The pilot was successful so the program has been expanded to include 10 more people.

BATTERYMARCH FINANCIAL MANAGEMENT COMPANY, 600 Atlantic Avenue, Boston, MA 02210.
Batterymarch is an international investment counseling firm with $12 billion worth of funds, mostly corporate pensions, to manage. Operation requires a 24-hour vigilance in order to keep up with world markets. Most employees, 30 out of 35, have terminals at home connected to the company's mainframe. 20 professional brokers are also "on-line" with their own PCs. If a broker has a problem with the system, he/she can call one of the others at home for help. Throughout the night, the company's "Phantom Program" monitors the system automatically and transmits wake-up calls if something goes wrong.
"We've been using this system for over 10 years. Since starting the work-at-home routine, our productivity has increased tremendously. The owner had a vision that at

some time everyone would work at home unless they absoulutely could not."

BELL COMMUNICATIONS, Business Information Center, North Road, P.O. Box 688, Chester, NJ 07930.

Experienced employees in the Research Department can make arrangements with their managers to take their work home on a project-by-project basis. There have been some full-time telecommuters, but that situation is not the rule.

BELL SOUTH, Division of Mountain Bell, 3010 East Camelback Road, Phoenix, AZ 85038.

Bell South is conducting an experimental two-year telecommuting program. Telecommuters are all regular employees of Bell South and include both high-tech ad low-tech personnel, mostly middle managers and marketers.

BEST WESTERN HOTELS INTERNATIONAL, 2-6201 North 24 Parkway, Phoenix, AZ 85008.

This is an interesting project where the home workers telecommute from their home in prison. About 10 women prisoners in the Arizona State Prison handle telephone reservations for the hotel chain. They are provided with computer terminals, telecommunications hookups, extra phone lines, and complete training.

BLUE CROSS/BLUE SHIELD OF THE NATIONAL CAPITOL AREA, 550-12th Street, S.W., Washington, D.C. 20065.

This program was fashioned after the similar program at Blue Cross/Blue Shield of South Carolina's data entry program. Basically, cottage keyers key in data from insurance claims. The main difference is that here, all cottage keyers are former employees. Also, instead of keying onto tape, these workers key directly into the company's mainframe.

Each worker has a quota of at least 400 claims per day. IBM terminals with modems are leased to the home workers. Pays so much per claim on a biweekly basis.

BORG-WARNER CHEMICAL COMPANY, International Center, Parkersburg, WV 26101.

Sales personnel are equipped with PCs at home which are hooked up to company's mainframe. Telecomunications capabilities include E-mail. Sales people can now do analysis and forecasting without going into the office. Other professionals on staff are similarly equipped and can work at home as the need arises.

BRONNER MANUFACTURING AND TOOL COMPANY, 286 Ridgedale Avenue, Hanover, NJ 07936.

Work to take home is assigned only to regular in-house employees that wish to earn extra money at home. Work involves milling, turning, deburring, drilling, and lathe work. Pays piece rates.

BROWN WILLIAMSON TOBACCO COMPANY, P.O. Box 35090, Louisville, KY 40232.

Systems programmers work on a contract basis and divide their time between home and office. Only programmers that were previously employed in-house are chosen.

CALIFORNIA STATE DEPARTMENT OF GENERAL SERVICES, Telecommunications Division, 601 Sequoia Pacific Boulevard, Sacramento, CA 95814-0282.

After two years of planning, The California State Telecommuting Project is finally underway. State workers from 14 different state agencies can volunteer to participate. Anyone who thinks his/her job can be done at home can volunteer. A minimum of 200 will participate with job titles ranging from clerk typists to managers. Locations have been scaled back to include the greater Los Angeles area, San Francisco, and (primarily) Sacramento.

Those chosen will be outfitted with PCs and ergonomically correct furniture. An electronic bulletin board will replace the "water cooler" as the center of internal communications. All workers are required to return to the office of origin once a week.

Jack Nilles, sometimes known as the "father of telecommuting" wrote the 150-page "Plan For Success" and has been selected to direct the project. David Fleming, who initiated the idea, hopes the experiment will serve as an example of successful telecommuting and thereby open up telecommuting opportunities elsewhere in government and private industry. To that end, many aspects will be monitored and evaluated to conclude how much fuel was saved, effects on traffic flow, possible effects on air quality, etc.

CERTIFIED METALS COMPANY, 175 Entin Road, Clifton, NJ 07014.
Current employees can take advantage of the company's home work option and do polishing, finishing, assembly of rings, and some diamond setting at home.

CHATAS GLASS COMPANY, 570 Broadlawn Terrace, Vineland, NJ 08360.
Glassblowing and grinding of laboratory glassware can be done as a secondary income opportunity by established employees. Only part-time work is allowed at home. Pick up and delivery of supplies and finished work is provided. This is handwork, so no machinery is needed. Pays piece rates.

CHILTON CREDIT REPORTING, 6 St. James Avenue, Boston, MA 02116.
In-house employees must be thoroughly experienced before moving work home. About 14 workers have taken advantage of the option. They proof computer sheets and analyze the "decisions" made by the computers. Pays piece rates equalling approximately the same as in-house workers doing similar work.

CHRISTIAN WOLF, INC., P.O. Box 88 Troy, IL 62294.
This is a manufacturer of communion wafers. Employees earn extra income by cutting and packaging the products at home.

CITIBANK, 399 Park Avenue, New York, NY 10043.
Citibank offers telecommuting as an option to regular employees on an informal basis as the need arises. Employees most often work at home during temporary disability or pregnancy.

COLORADO NATIONAL BANK, 17th and Champa, Denver, CO 80202.
This major Colorado bank is currently conducting a pilot telecommuting program within the MIS department only. The purpose of the project is to determine whether telecommuting can help cut costs as it has in so many other organizations. The telecommuters write systems documentation four days a week. The PCs are provided by the workers. Colorado National expects to expand the program to perhaps two dozen telecommuters at the end of the pilot phase.

COMPONENT PLASTICS, INC., 700 Tollgate Road, Elgin, IL 60170.
Employees are provided the opportunity for additional income by performing secondary operations and light inspection of plastic molding products.

A Closer Look: Fort Collins, CO

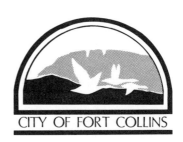

CITY OF FORT COLLINS

Ft. Collins, Colorado, a city of 85,000 located 60 miles north of Denver, is the first municipality to institute routine telecommuting.

The foundation for the project is a large electronic mail network set up by Peter Dallow, Information and Communications Systems Director. The system was originally designed as a good means of communications between city employees and city council members. Each user had to be supplied with a computer, of course, and once several hundred of them were linked together by the system, telecommuting was simply the next logical step.

Asked about surveys or other scientific bases for the project, Dallow shrugs off any such notion. "It was no big deal once the equipment was in place."

As a matter of fact, the program's policies and procedures are found on a one-page sheet outlining blanket acquisition procedures for necessary hardware and software. Any other issues that may arise will be handled on a case-by-case basis. Thus far, no problems have been reported.

"Normally, you don't tell an employee to be sure and take home some supplies—that would be called pilfering. But, now we encourage them to take home the whole office," says Dallow.

It would take a lot of software, disk drives and other equipment and supplies to equal the cost of building more office space. The personal computers had to be purchased regardless of where they would be used, and telecommuting has proven to be an excellent way to deal with Ft. Collins' office space crunch.

Several hundred city workers on many different levels are now participating in the project, which includes council members, accountants, data processors, rate analysts for the utility department and secretaries. Most work at home part of the time with a small percentage doing so full-time. Prime candidates for telecommuting, says Dallow, are top level professionals such as programmers and systems engineer. Just about everybody is eligible for part-time participation except the police and fire fighters.

Dallow cites benefits for both the workers and the city. For the workers, there is flexibility, job enrichment, a way to retain employee status during maternity leave, and new opportunities for Ft. Collins' handicapped citizens. For the city, there is increased productivity, a partial solution to the office space problem, lower costs, greater employee retention and the ability to attract employees in otherwise hard-to-fill jobs.

COMPUTERLAND, 30985 Santana Street, Hayward, CA 94544.
Computerland is conducting a two-year telecommuting experiment for current company marketing personnel and their managers. All necessary equipment is provided.

CONNECTICUT MUTUAL LIFE, 140 Garden Street, Hartford, CT 06154.
Data processing personnel are provided with PCs at home "for their convenience." Other employees are allowed to work at home on a "need to" basis. The use of networkers was pioneered by CMU.

CURTIS 1000, 150 Vanderbilt Avenue, West Hartford, CT 06119.
Company offers home work arrangement as option to in-house employees with proven need. For example, one disabled worker does hand inserting and other mail processing work at home.

CYMATICS, INC., 31 West 280 Diehl Road, Naperville, IL 60540.
Cymatics is an electronics manufacturer. Some employees assemble circuit boards at home after several years experience in the plant.

DATA GENERAL CORPORATION, 4400 Computer Drive, Wstboro, MA 01580.
Data General manufactures, designs, and sells business systems. One product is the "Comprehensive Electronic Office" system which includes E-mail, spreadsheet analysis and more. Working at home is an option for in-house employees on a departmental level. Those taking advantage of the option are most often programmers, engineers, and word processors involved in software development.
Employee's department is responsible for providing necessary equipment, generally a PC and modem which will be logged onto the company mainframe. This is usually older equipment that has already been costed out. "Working at home has proven to be a convenient and useful tool. The key benefits are convenience and being close to family."

DECORATED PRODUCTS COMPANY, 1 Arch Road, Westfield, MA 01086.
About 8 employees here make extra money by taking work home. They inspect nameplates manufactured at the plant. They are required to pick up and deliver the work themselves. Pays piece rates.

DETROIT FREE PRESS, 321 West Lafayette, Detroit, MI 48231.
Reporters, columnists, and editors telecommute. PCs (IBM, AT&T #6300, or Leading Edge) are supplied. Work is transmitted to mainframe via telecommunicatons network. Examples of telecommuters include one-person bureaus in Los Angeles and Toronto, and a columnist who lives 40 minutes away fom the office and has no reason to commute anyway for that type of work. Telecommuting was implemented as a company policy in 1984. Detroit Free Press also has several home-based freelance photographers who work on an assignment basis. Currently has about 20 home workers. All telecommuters are staff members and are paid the same salary and benefits they would receive if they were in-house. Freelancers are paid by the job.

ELECTRONIC SERVICES UNLIMITED, 142 West 24th Street, New York, NY 10011.
Electronic Services Unlimited (E.S.U.) is a New York based research and consulting firm that plans, advises, and implements telecommuting programs for major corporate

clients. They have also conducted two very extensive surveys of the"work-at-home universe". President and founder Marcia Kelley says, "We are a model of what we propose." Company has seven telecommuters from New Hampshire to California. Inquiries only accepted from employers needing consulting services.

EQUITABLE LIFE ASSURANCE, Pension System Department, 200 Plaza Drive, Secaucas, NJ 07094.

Several programmers and managers are participating in a pilot telecommuting program. Work involves database development, technical support, troubleshooting, budgeting, project monitoring and progress reporting. All equipment is supplied. Home terminals are connected to the large mainframe IMS. There is also a $400 allowance for furniture. Employees are salaried with employee status intact. After final review of pilot, Equitable will decide whether to expand telecommuting option to other departments. So far, it is reported to be successful.

Success is a word that is rapidly becoming synonymous with telecommuting pilot programs. Equitable Life Assurance is no exception.

Last year Equitable relocated some of its departments from corporate headquarters in midtown Manhattan to Secaucus, New Jersey. For most employees involved, this was merely a matter of traveling in a different direction; some even lived in New Jersey and the move meant less traveling. But, for those who lived on Long Island, travel time would double and it was feared that that would be too much of an increase for some.

It was clear that something had to be done to avoid the costs of replacing valuable personnel. Telecommuting was offered to key people as an incentive to stay with Equitable. Six people—programmers, analysts, and one administrative assistant—were encouraged to stay home two or three days a week. They were allowed to reatin their salary levels and employment status and were given all necessary equipment and a $400 furniture allowance.

Telecommuting project coordinator Jack Tyniec, credits Electronic Services Unlimited with providing the necessary training and guidance. ESU worked closely with Equitable's legal department, personnel manager, and prospective telecommuting managers to avoid problems in advance.

"We had no idea how many things could just creep out of the woodwork. ESU helped us spell out the issues and deal with them in advance — things like local zoning restrictions, labor laws, insurance liability both for company-provided medical coverage and Workmen's Compensation, and even seemingly innocent wordings in our company personnel policy."

Words like "...work to be performed in company office...," found in standard employment contracts, may not have been intended to restrict working at home, but that is the legal effect, Tyniec points out. To rectify that situation, a supplementary contract was drawn up to specifically allow work at home.

The first formal review of the Equitable telecommuting program indicates that all is going well. The telecommuters love it, Tyniec says, and their managers are equally enthusiastic. "Not only have we kept good people, but productivity has increased as well. We've measured productivity in terms of quality, not quantity, from a managerial point of view. The managers are unanimously in favor of continuing the program. The consensus is that these people (telecommuters) were good anyway, but now they're even better."

It is expected that telecommuting will be formally integrated into Equitable's overall personnel policy. In the meantime, though, "It will spread now of its own accord," says Tyniec. "Our personnel manager gave a presentation to other company PMs at their urging. It seems that somebody has to slay the dragons first, but once that's been done and it's been clearly demonstrated that it works, others will follow. At least for corporations, someone has to champion the effort to get telecommuting started."

FEDERAL RESERVE BANK, 104 Marietta NW, Atlanta, GA 30303-2713.

Federal Reserve Bank offers a work-at-home option to its regular professional staff. First started as an experiment in the early 80's with more than 65 employees in the research department participating, working at home is now an option incorporated into departmental policy for anyone who performs tasks such as writing or editing either full-time or part-tme. Computers, when used, are usually PCs owned by the employees. "Reports of our home work program have been greatly exaggerated by the media. When they (employees) can work better at home, they do. It's a simple as that.

FIRST NATIONAL BANK OF CHICAGO, 1 First National Plaza, Chicago, IL 60670.

Company has a formal home work program intended especially for data processing and other non-technical personnel. Program guidelines are designed to insure success. "It basically uses a foundation of trust and it's up to the managers to make it work. There is support from top management in the company." There are no number goals or monitoring of employees. Working at home is considered a careeer option which managers can use as a possible solution to employees' problems as they arise. "We've had some good experiences. In the case of some clericals, there has been a 30% increase in productivity." Any necessary equipment is paid for by the business unit budget. This is a program for experienced current employees only.

GENERAL TELEPHONE, Information Management Department, 1 GTE Place, Thousand Oaks, CA 91362-3811.

GTE first experimented with telecommuting during the '84 Summer Olympics as part of a citywide call for people to reduce commuting as much as possible. The pilot program involved technical and programming personnel and systems analysts. All were provided with PCs, modems,

printers, and pagers and all were kept on straight salary. The experiment was considered

Linda Anapol, Director of Teleservices Applications for Pacific Bell, at work in her home office.

a complete success and now GTE is broadening the scope of telecommuting across departmental lines. Planners of the program feel management skills should improve after telecommuting employees are trained in self-management skills and managers learn to gauge productivity rather than count heads. GTE is also participating in telecommuting as part of the Southern California Association of Governments' plan to reduce trafic congestion and pollution. "We think telecommuting over a period of time will have a substantial impact on traffic in Southern California. There is a lot of potential here."

GRAYLINE HOUSEWARES, 1616 Berkley Street, Elgin, IL 60170.

Some employees perform after- hours work for extra income by packaging screws for this manufacturer.

HARRIS TRUST AND SAVINGS BANK, 111 West Monroe, Chicago, IL 60603.

Harris Trust has an informal agreement that allows certain experienced employees to work at home on computer terminals to complete paperwork.

HARTFORD INSURANCE GROUP, The Hartford Plaza, Hartford, CT 06115.

Data processors and programmer analysts. Hartford has conducted a telecommuting pilot project with guidelines developed by a special committee. Employees, all volunteers, were required to have a good performance record with the company, be highly productive, not be working on "sensitive projects," and have a manager's approval. Each worked four days a week at home and one day a week at the office. Hartford supplied computer equipment hooked up to the company's mainframe plus extra phone lines. Employee status and salary remained unchanged. Although some problems were reported, telecommuting was integrated into Hartford's overall personnel policy, mostly as a reward for highly productive, experienced employees.

HEWLETT PACKARD LABORATORIES, Research and Development, 3000

Rick Higgins, Pacific Bell Marketing Manager

A Corporate Profile
Pacific Bell

Pacific Bell has a work-at-home program that, after only five months, was hailed as a complete success. While most telecommuting programs to date have been designed specifically for data processing personnel only, from the start Pac Bell wanted to prove that any job could be done at home. And, they have done just that.

75 employees went home in the program's first year, and 100 more are expected to make the move shortly. All are volunteers and no re-

strictions have been placed on job titles. The range of job classifications is broad—everything from marketing personnel to engineers.

Computers are used only by those who needed them before moving their work home. Second phone lines and pagers are the most often added equipment. The home workers are spread out geographically all over the state of California.

Being closer to clients was the first noticeable benefit. "This made us much more effective in servicing our clients," says Leslie Crawford, Marketing Manager for the Pacific Bell Telecommuting Department. "We soon realized how much 'windshield time' (time wasted behind the wheel commuting) was actually being spent on driving to the office first, then to the client."

The company was naturally pleased to improve service to clients, but there have been other benefits as well. For one thing, moving the work home has resulted in closing three offices with savings on space leases totaling $40,000 annually. There were no deliberate plans to close the first office; all the employees went home and there simply was no one left to mind the store. Two other offices then closed down and several more are expected to close soon.

But the biggest advantage to the program, according to Crawford, is flexibility for everyone concerned—for the company, for the employees, and for the clients. Increased flexibility has meant many jobs have been redefined with a new look at what they are, what they should accomplish, and how.

The program is working so well that Pac Bell's account executives have been looking at telecommuting as a possible solution to client's problems. Pointing to themselves as a prime example is often the best way to sell the idea. "To some, however, the very word 'telecommuting' sounds foreign. To them, we point out that their own salespeople have been doing it for years. Telecommuting is just a new word to describe it. When they realize that, it doesn't seem like such a weird idea after all."

This may all sound unrealistically positive, but when asked about disadvantages, Crawford said she couldn't think of any. "Maybe it's because everyone in the program volunteered," she said. "They knew their jobs, their managers knew them, and they knew from the advance planning what to expect. No one has voiced a problem and no one has left the program."

If there is a problem, she added, it would be not enough people. "More bodies in more homes around the state would be good for us," she laughs. "We are very, very pleased with the success of our telecommuting program and the enthusiasm with which it has been received. It has already been established that telecommuting works for data processing professionals. Now we have proved it is possible for all fields."

Hanover Street, Palo Alto, CA 94304.

Working at home as an option is offered department-wide. Home workers are usually programmers, hardware and software engineers, applications engineers, research scientists, speech writers, and managers. Most work at home part of the time during the week; some do so in addition to in-house work. Equipment is provided as necessary. Individuals are responsible for their own phone bills, but can avoid toll charges by calling the company mainframe and requesting a callback - made at company expense.

HIGHLAND SUPPLY CORPORATION, 1111 - 6th Street, Highland, IL 26249.

Highland Supply is in the business of converting aluminum foil and films. Employees perform packaging tasks for extra income.

HOLT, RINEHART, & WINSTON, Division of CBS Publishing, 111 5th Avenue,New york, NY 10003.

In-house copy editors and proofreaders can get permission to work at home if they have a need for any personal reason. Employees must have editor's approval.

HOMEQUITY, INC. a subsidiary of PHH Group, Inc., 249 Danbury Road, Wilton, CT 06897.

Telecommuters do programming, evaluating, systems analysis, and software development. Homequity is a leading relocation service company. Its primary business consists of finding new housing for transferred corporate employees. Phase One of the telecommuting pilot project lasted about four months and gave the comnpany a chance to evaluate cost savings and productivity. The initial findings were excellent and Phase Two, "continuation and expansion," is now in progress. Since most of the participants in Phase One were computer personnel, they were supplied with PCs and modems. "Telecommuting only makes sense because the future of this business is in computer."

HONEYWELL, INC., Honeywell Plaza, Minneapolis, MN 54087.

Working at home is an informal option for Honeywell employees on a departmental level. One example of its use involves handicapped phone operators. The operators have dedicated phone lines in their homes which route long distance calls on weekend and nights. Calls are relayed from Honeywell employees on the road who don't have access to touch-tone phones. Home operators patch through the calls, using a network. Pays salary plus benefits.

IBM, Old Orchard Road, Armonk, NY 10504.

Home work is a company option for IBM employees only. IBM has provided over 8,000 PCs for its employees to use at home, either part-time during regular business hours or after hours. Home work is allowed during regular hours on a project basis as a convenience to employees. Company recently participated in a formal two-year telecommuting experiment conducted by The Center for Futures Research at U.S.C.

INDUSTRIAL INDEMNITY INSURANCE, Division of Crum & Foster, P.O. Drawer E, Walnut Creek, CA 94596.

Approximately 125 insurance auditors in the company have been outfitted with Visual Commuter Portable Computers, Hayes modems, HP printers, and Super Audit software at the expense of the company. The purpose was to reduce commuting time to and from the ofice and to increase overall productivity. Both goals have been achieved.

INFORMATION ACCESS COMPANY, 11 Davis Drive, Belmont, CA 94002.

This company collects information from magazines and trade journals to maintain databases, including Magazine Index, Management Contents, and Trade and Industry Index; all of which are found in most libraries. At one time, Information Access had a fairly large home work operation with over 150 home-based indexers. Upon moving the operation to California, however, the home work program was scaled back severely. Now home-based indexers work only on weekly or monthly publications so deadlines can be met comfortably.

Workers come in once or twice a week to get supplies, materials, and any special instructions and to meet with their supervisor.

Company provides Apple PCs and special software. (Indexes are written on diskettes which are returned to the office.) Workers are full employees with benefits and promotional opportunities equal to those of their in-house counterparts. Home indexers are used because they are more productive and have fewer errors.

KEATING OF CHICAGO, INC., 715 South 25th Avenue, Bellwood, IL 60104.

Keating is in the business of commercial kitchen equipment. Typing for its sales department is performed at home by employees who are either previous in-house employees or referrals.

THE KEMPER GROUP, Corporate Headquarters, Overland Park, KS 64130.

Cost control analysts, inspectors, claims examiners, and processors are among the employees of Kemper who have chosen to move their work home.

LANIER BUSINESS PRODUCTS, INC, 1700 Chantily Drive N.E., Atlanta, GA 30324.

Lanier makes "Telestaf," a product used in telecommuting which was used in American Express' initial homebound training program. It includes features such as voice mail and is transcription- facilitated. Within Lanier, home work is allowed as a necessary option. Usually home workers are word processors and secretaries working at home part of the time as the need arises.

LENCO ELECTRONIC, INC., 1330 Belden Street, McHenry, IL 60050.

Lenco is an electronic manufacturing company. Experienced employees perform a small part of the job at home, connecting and soldering wires onto transformers.

ARTHUR D. LITTLE, INC.,25 Acorn Park, Cambridge, MA 02140.

Telecommuting is an informal option offered to staff members. Most telecommuting is done by information systems consultants. Equipment is provided as necessary.

MARINE MIDLAND BANK, 140 Broadway, New York, NY 10015.

Regular employees of Marine Midland have the option of working at home as the need arises. The option is most often taken by professionals on staff in cases of temporary disability or pregnancy. The company is planning to develop more definitive guidelines for telecommuting in the future after current reorganization is completed.

MCDONALD DOUGLAS, Information Systems Group, 2560 North First Street, P.O. Box 49019, San Jose, CA 95161.

At one time (before company went through reorganization) there were 200 full-time telecommuters, plus another 2,000 employees that worked at home part of the time. These were mostly consultants, project managers, sales and marketing personnel, programmers, and engineers. Home work is not nearly so prevalent now, but it is still

Homeworker Profile
Carol D'Agostino

In 1976, Carol D'Agostino's life was on a downhill track as she joined the ranks of divorced mothers. Reentering the workforce can be tough, and for Carol—who is physically disabled—it was near impossible.

Taking in borders in her Long Island home provided some income, but it was a difficult way to make a living. "It was eroding my health even further. I needed something else, something better."

She heard about the External Education Program for the Homebound at Queensborough Community College and enrolled with the hope of upgrading her rusty office skills.

The college provided an Apple computer on loan and lessons were sent to Carol's home via telephone hookups to the classroom. Before long, she had the word processing skills necessary to enter an intern program requiring 90 hours of work for an employer. Her internship was with Electronic Services Unlimited, a New York based research and consulting firm that plans, advises, and implements telecommuting programs for major corporate clients. The internship later became a permanent, full-time job.

Carol receives work assignments electronically. She handles database management, miscellaneous word processing, mailings and research, and is responsible for production of the company newsletter, *Telecommuting Report*. "The work changes every day. In a small company you have to be able to do a lot of different things."

While Carol originally intended only to upgrade her skills to improve her job prospects, she is now continuing in computer education with a good shot at an AS degree.

"Thanks to the Homebound program, I have new skills and new confidence. I went from no opportunities to unlimited opportunities. I'll never be unemployed again!"

---

possible on an informal basis. Any experienced worker whose job can be done at home can request permission from the manager in charge of their department.

MELLON BANK, 3 Mellon Bank Center, Mellon Square, Pittsburgh, PA 15259.

Mellon Bank has made personal computers available to its programmers and other personnel for several years. Mostly the PCs are used at home for after-hours work, but some employees, programmers in particular, can work at home full-time on a project-by-project basis. Working at home is also used as a perk to boost the morale of management-level employees.

METROPOLITAN LIFE INSURANCE COMPANY, 1 Madison Avenue, New York, NY 10010.

Metropolitan has several handicapped computer programmers trained by Lift, Inc. (see listing). Agents are also home-based. Necessary equipment and phone lines are provided. All home workers are paid full benefits.

MONTGOMERY WARD & COMPANY. INC., The Signature Group, 200 North Martingale, Schaumberg, IL 60194.

Montgomery Ward uses home-based workers to handle mail-opening and other jobs involved in the direct mail operation for insurance companies and other financial service clients. Only current employees or people referred by employees are considered. All are local residents.

MOUNTAIN BELL, Subsidiary of U.S. West, 7301 West Mansfield, Rom 101, Lakewood, CO 80235.

Over 100 engineers, writers, computer programmers and their supervisors work at home. Because Mountain Bell's telecommuting program is still in the experimental stage, only volunteer in-house workers can participate at this time. Equipment is supplied as necessary. Home workers are represented on the project-planning team by The Communications Workers of America. Employee status remains unchanged.

NORTHWESTERN BELL INFORMATION TECHNOLOGIES, 2120 South 72nd Street, Omaha, NE 68124.

Northwestern Bell is involved in a two-year telecommuting experiment involving middle managers, marketing personnel, and data processing personnel. The guidelines for the program were developed by the Center for Futures Research at USC. After conclusion of the experiment, telecommuting will be evaluated and considered as a permanent overall company policy.

PACIFIC BELL, 444 Market Street, Room 1105A, San Francisco, CA 94111.

Engineers, marketing planners, project managers, forecasters, programmers, analysts, and some technicians and service reps work for Pacific Bell at home. Currently has over 200 telecommuters in both Northern California and Southern California. Though not all positions require computers, PCs are supplied as necessary. Pagers and extra phone lines are also provided as necessary.

PEAT, MARWICK, MITCHELL & COMPANY, 345 Park Avenue, New York, NY 10154.

Throughout its 100 offices nationwide, this major accounting firm has provided its field auditors with MacIntosh computers in order to increase productivity. The auditors are now able to work for several days without actually returning to the office.

Like most major accounting firms, this one also has a "stable" of on-call accountants that handle assignments on a freelance basis during peak periods. These independent accountants are mostly former employees or are highly recommended by current employees.

J.C. PENNEY COMPANY, INC., 1301 Avenue of the Americas, New York, NY 10009.

Telemarketers take catalog orders in Milwaukee, Columbus and Atlanta, where the company catalog distribution centers are located. This program has increased from about

18 home workers in 1981 to 60 in 1987. Computer terminals (hooked up to the company mainframe) are supplied,
along with two phone lines - one for data and one for voice contact with the customer. Supervisors visit home workers to make sure the home work space is adequate. They expect a minimum of 35 square feet of work space that is isolated from family activities (noise).

Home workers are paid the same as in-house workers. In order to qualify to participate in the telecommuting program, a worker must have worked in a Penneys phone center for at least a year. The program is expected to grow even more, since it will save the company a lot of money by not having to build new facilities.

PUBLIC SERVICE COMPANY OF NEW MEXICO, Alverado Square, Albuquerque, NM 87158.

Working at home is an option offered to permanent employees who need
it. PCs are provided as necessary.

RISING STAR INDUSTRIES, 25500 Hawthorne Boulevard, Suite 2000, Torrance, CA 90505.

Entire company works from home. Workers are divided into core groups around the country for software development projects. Currently has 38 telecommuters nationwide. "There is no question that working at home is better for productivity, especially for creative work. The choice of people is important, though. They must be self-disciplined. Electronic cottagers and their managers have a different personality profile than 9 to 5 types. Management becomes very important - management of work, not people. We pretend it's a huge factory; if we need something, we don't walk over to talk about it, we pick up the phone instead. At the same time, working at home is not as special as people think. Professionals have always done it."

SOUTHERN CALIFORNIA ASSOCIATION OF GOVERNMENTS, 600 South Commonwealth Avenue, Suite 1000, Los Angeles, CA 90005.

SCAG started its telecommuting program two years ago with 20 staff members, including accountants, legal staff members, planners and writers. The purpose of the program is to find a way to reduce work-related driving in Southern California by 12% by the year 2000. This project is one of several being conducted under the umbrella of the Central City Association. During the initial project, the home workers kept a log of transportation charges, telecommunications usage and utilities usage. Each was periodically interviewed to determine the best methods for expanding the program. Workers have their choice of part-time or full-time telecommuting. There is no change in salary, benefits, or employee status for anyone who chooses to work at home.

SOUTHERN NEW ENGLAND TELEPHONE,227 Church Street, New Haven, CT 06510.

Working at home is an option open to all Southern New England Telephone employees. If the option is needed for any reason, working at home will be okayed as long as the job can be done at home.

STATE OF SOUTH DAKOTA, Pierre, SD 57501

Working at home is facilitated on a statewide level by several electronic networks and PCs that are provided to all professional personnel in all state agencies. Working at home is considered informal, but is clearly acceptable; especially since it is donated time.

TRAVELER'S LIFE INSURANCE, 1 Tower Square, Hartford, CT 06183.

Resident claims operations adjusters are provided with briefcase computers so they don't have to return to the office from the field to finish work. Data processors are also provided with home terminals, E-Mail, formal training in telecommuting procedures, and a telecommuting handbook. Telecommuting is a formal program for established DP employees only.

> "If you have the patience, you can make several thousand dollars a month."
>
> —Financial Acceptance

UNION MUTUAL LIFE INSURANCE COMPANY, Portland, ME 04122.

Union Mutual's "Flex-Program" is an option offered to employees as needed. Examples of need include, but are not limited to, pregnancy or temporary disability. "Currently, the program is driven solely by managers/employees' interests. After expressing a desire to work at home, employees must demonstrate a legitimate need for an alternative work arrangement to their managers."

UNITED SERVICES AUTOMOBILE ASSOCIATION, USAA Group, USAA Building, San Antonio, TX 75288.

Programmers for this insurance company are provided with PCs, both for after-hours work and also on a project-by-project basis.

UNIVERSITY OF WISCONSIN HOSPITAL AND CLINIC, 600 Highland Avenue, Madison, WI 53792.

Medical transcribers handle physicians' notes for 50 clinics. To qualify for working at home, employees must first gain experience by spending six months in the office doing the same work that will be done at home. Work is to completed on 24 to 48 hour turnaround schedule; same as for in-house workers.

Dictaphones and ;word processors are provided. Home workers are regular employees with salaries and benefits identical to that of in-house workers. Performance is measured by characters typed (home workers are found to be 40-50% more productive than in-house workers). Home workers are represented by Local 2412 of the Wisconsin State Employees' Union. "There is an interest here in expanding the program. We can add one home worker for every one-and-a-half in-house workers."

WEYERHAUSER COMPANY, Tacoma, WA 98477.

Marketing personnel can work out of their homes full-time. In-house employees in Washington have the option to work at home part-time on an informal basis. The option is usually used on a project-by-project basis. Weyerhauser has a very flexible time policy in general. The work-at-home option is most common among systems developers, technical professionals and sales personnel in the Research & Development and Data Processing departments.

Chapter 5
Computer-Based Opportunities

This section includes any situation that requires a computer to get the job done. This doesn't necessarily mean that you must own your own equipment. In the case of typesetting input, for example, many companies provide computer terminals to their home keyers. On the other hand, a contract programmer not only needs to own a computer, but often several different computers.

By its nature, computerized work generally pays more than office work that is done on conventional typewriters. Therefore, if you are a very good typist, you may find it to your advantage to transfer your typing skills to the computer keyboard. Word processors are in great demand to handle assignments from small businesses and huge corporations alike. It'll take a few months to get the hang of it all; the computer itself, the software, and the printer. There are classes available at most community colleges and vocational schools. If you're sharp, you can get paid while you learn by signing on with a temporary help agency. Kelly Services and Manpower, to name just two, have excellent training programs including cross-training on different systems available to anyone who is on the roster and available for work.

Experienced typists with exceptional accuracy can make money by becoming a typesetting input operator. Typesetting is a job that was done on very expensive equipment in composition shops before the personal computer came along. Now it is common for home-based operators to do the job at home by typing material into the computer and embedding code into the text that will instruct the shop's specialized printer to use certain fonts, type size or style, and special characters. Most shops have their own special code and train typists in how to use it. It is most common for typesetters that handle books (rather than advertising or brochures) to use home keyers. Typesetting input operators are paid for each character typed and average earnings run from $10 to $25 an hour.

Contract programmers will find the field a little crowded these days. There is still a lot of work in converting programs to run on different computers than they were written for, but that work will soon disappear. Computers are being programmed to do the conversions automatically. Writing programs to specifications pays better, but only very experienced programmers get this work. The key to getting work as a programmer is to continue learning about languages, compilers, and systems design. Employers like programmers who are enthusiastic about what the company is doing, pay attention to deadlines, document their work properly, and submit bug-free programs.

ABLE AMERICA NETWORK, 10010 Broadway, Suite 805, San Antonio, TX 78217.
Positions: This network is a new nonprofit organization providing contract work to home workers who are mentally or physically disabled, economically distressed, and "anyone in need of our help". Jobs include word processing, database management, and computer programming.
Provisions: Pay varies according to the contract. Inquiries are welcome from all 50 states as the network has national contracts.

ACADEMY SOFTWARE, Box 6277, San Rafael, CA 94903.
Positions: Contract programmers and technical writers. Contract programmers are used for conversions from Commodore software to Apple, Atari, and IBM. Also buys unique educational software from freelancers. Some original programming to company specifications available. Technical writers work on user manuals.
Requirements: Must be local resident. Extensive experience required.
Provisions: Payment for both positions can be by the job, by the hour, or on a royalty basis. Credit is given to both in most cases.

ADDISON-WESLEY PUBLISHING CO., Jacob Way, Reading, MA 01867.
Positions: Contract programmers. Company publishes over 100 programs for the Apple, IBM, and Macintosh. Freelance programmers can submit educational programs for consideration or seek assignments in conversions or original programming to company guidelines.
Requirements: Send resume indicating particular expertise and equipment availability and knowledge.
Provisions: Assignments pay by the project.

ALPHA MICROSYSTEMS, 3501 Sunflower, Box 25059, Santa Ana, CA 92799.
Positions: Contract programmers for Alpha Micro computers only. Contracts include vertical applications in specific business areas.
Requirements: Resume and references required.

ALTERNATE SOURCE, 704 North Pennsylvania, Lansing, MI 48906.
Positions: Contract programmers. Company seeks submissions of vertical applications software for any MS-DOS or CP/M computer. Submissions must include complete documentation and be bug-free.
Requirements: Send letter of interest that describes finished software. Guidelines are available for SASE.
Provisions: Pays 20% royalties.

AMERICAN EXPRESS BANK, LTD., American Express Plaza, New York, NY 10004.
Positions: Word processors.
Requirements: Must be local, physically handicapped and disabled. Job requires transcription skills.
Provisions: Complete training is provided. Equipment provided includes Wang word processing terminals, Lanier central dictation system, and Exxon telecopier. Telephone lines link the home work station to company headquarters on Wall Street. A company supervisor can dictate into the system from anywhere; likewise a home worker is able to access the system any time 24 hours a day to transcribe the dictation. The finished product in hard copy form is then sent back to headquarters via the telecopier. All activity is identified and monitored through the Control Center. "Project Homebound" currently

has 10 full-time regular employees of American Express.

AMERICAN STRATFORD, Putney, Box 810, Brattleboro, VT 05301.
Positions: Typesetting input operators. Currently has 14 home keyers.
Requirements: Must be local. Must own computer and be competent word processor.

> "It's really nice to be able to kick back when I want to. I can go out and mingle with my goats and geese and not worry about work for awhile. It'll get done."
> --Paul Farr, Remote Control

ANDENT, INC., 1000 North Avenue, Waukegan, IL 60085.
Positions: Contract programmers. Company publishes business software for the Apple II series. Submissions of original programs are accepted for consideration. Some contract programming, mostly conversions, is also available from time to time.
Requirements: Send proposal before submitting program. Work samples and references required for contract work.
Provisions: Contracts pay by the project. Original programs accepted for publication are either bought outright or royalties are paid.

APPALACHIAN COMPUTER SERVICES, Highway 25 South, P.O. Box 140, London, KY 40741.
Positions: Appalachian Computer Services is among a growing number of service bureaus that has solved the problem of stabilizing workflow with a home work program. The initial pool of cottage keyers was formed out of former in-house employees. Most of them had left their jobs because they needed to be at home with their families. The program accomplished what it was supposed to. The workflow went smoothly, the keyers were happy with the arrangement (no one dropped out), and the company overhead fell. Now that Appalachian Computer Services is sure the home work program is the solution they've been looking for, plans are underway to expand the program to an ultimate goal of 100 home keyers. These additional workers will be hired from outside the company.
Requirements: Since there are no telecommunications available, all recruiting will have to be done within the township of London. The only requirement will be a typing speed of 45 wpm. Experienced applicants will spend two days in-house learning to use the Multitech PC. Those with no experience in data entry will spend an additional 3 days in the company's standard training program. There is no pay for time spent in training. Each worker goes into the office to pick up the work and receive instructions. When the job is finished, he or she returns the work on disks (which are provided).
Provisions: The cottage keyers are all treated as part-time employees, not independent contractors. Each works a minimum of 20 hours a week. No one works over 30 hours a week at any time so the part-time status remains intact. There are no benefits due to this part-time status; however, the company is looking into ways of providing some benefits as the program progresses. In the meantime, there are production bonuses offered in addition to the guaranteed hourly wage. Multitech PCs are provided at no charge.

APPOLLO SOFTWARE, Box 6434, Kent, WA 98064.
Positions: Contract programmers and technical writers. Programmers are needed for conversion work both computer to computer and language to language. Some original programming assigned according to company specifications. Technical writers are used to produce users' manuals. Some copy writing is available.
Requirements: Resume and work samples required.
Provision: Pays by the job.

AQUARIUS PEOPLE MATERIALS, INC., Box 128, Indian Rocks Beach, FL 33535.
Positions: Contract programmers. Company publishes educational software for all grade levels. Original programs will be considered for publication. Contracts are available for conversions.
Requirements: Must be very experienced with IBM or Radio Shack equipment.

ARTSCI, INC., 5547 Satsuma Avenue, North Hollywood, CA 91601.
Positions: Contract programmers to translate programs between IBM and Macintosh.
Requirements: Resume and references required.
Provisions: Pays by the project.

ARTWORX SOFTWARE COMPANY, 1844 Penfield Road, Penfield, NY 14526.
Positions: Programmers are contracted to do conversions from other computers to major brand computers.
Requirements: Resume, work samples, and references required.
Provision: Pays by the job.

ATC SOFTWARE, 804 Jordon Lane, Huntsville, AL 35816.
Positions: Contract programmers. Original programs are considered for publication; any type of business application software for AT & T, IBM, or CP/M computers. Only programs written in C, BASIC, Cobol, dBase or Fortran will be considered. Also assigns contracts for programming in these languages. Programmers' guides for coding are available for each of the five languages ($20 each or $79 for all five).
Requirements: Extensive knowledge and experience required. Resume and references required.
Provisions: Pay methods vary.

AWARD SOFTWARE, 130 Knowles Drive, Los Gatos, CA 95030.
Positions: Contract programmers write data management programs to company specifications.
Requirements: Prefers local programmers. Must have extensive knowledge of BIOS and IBM, NEC, Sperry, or Heath/Zenith. Submit resume and references.
Provisions: Pay methods vary according to project.

BAXTER'S BUSINESS SERVICE, 3660 Wilshire Boulevard, Los Angeles, CA 90010.
Positions: Word processors for legal and insurance work.
Requirements: Must be local resident. Must own word processor and transcribing machine. References required.

BELJAN, LTD., 2870 Baker Road, Dexter, MI 48130.
Positions: Beljan has been using home workers in its book typography business for 30

Close Up: Appalachian Computer Services

London is a town of 7,000 cradled in the hills of Southern Kentucky. It is home to **Appalachian Computer Services,** a data processing service bureau.

A common problem among service bureaus is the ebb and flow of work as contracts come and go. Stabilizing the workflow is a constant source of frustration for managers in this situation. There is also the cost of keeping enough employees on the payroll to handle peak workloads even though they may not be needed some of the time.

Appalachian Computer Services is among a growing number of service bureaus that have solved these problems with a home work program. Last summer a pool of cottage keyers was formed out of former in-house employees. Most of them had left their jobs because they needed to be at home with their families. All were considered valuable employees and were highly recommended.

The cottage keyers are all treated as part-time employees rather than independent contractors. Each works a minimum of 20 hours a week. Peak periods push the hours up to 30 hours a week. No one works over 30 hours a week at any time so the part-time status remains intact. This suits the workers well since none are available for full-time work. The disadvantage, however, is the lack of benefits for part-time work. Marietta Bargo,

project supervisor, says the company is looking into ways of providing benefits as the program progresses.

In the meantime, there are production bonuses offered in addition to the guaranteed hourly wage. The equipment—Multitech PCs—are provided at no charge.

There is no on-line work involved. Each worker goes into the office to pick up the work and receive instructions. When the job is finished, he or she returns the work on disks (which are also provided).

So far, Ms. Bargo says, the program is successful. The workflow is being handled smoothly, the keyers are happy with the arrangement and company overhead is down.

Now that Appalachian Computer Services is sure the home work program is the solution they've been looking for, plans are underway to expand the program to 200 home keyers. These additional workers will be hired from **outside** the company. Since no telecommunications are available, all recruiting will have to be done within London.

The only requirement will be a typing speed of 45 wpm. Experienced applicants will spend two days in-house learning to use the Multitech PC. Those with no experience in data entry will spend an additional 3 days in the company's standard training program. There is no pay for time spent in training.

years. There are now 6 typesetting input operators and 2 proofreaders.
Requirements: Must be local resident in order to pick up and deliver work. Fast and accurate typing skills required.
Provisions: Computers and training provided. Work comes from overflow from the plant and is part-time only.

BIONIC FINGERS, 312 South Adams #3, Glendale, CA 91205.
Positions: Medical transcribers.
Requirements: Minimum of three years experience in general, acute care, and hospital medical transcription is required. Must own word processor and transcribing machine (standard or micro okay). Must live in the area.
Provisions: Pays by the line. Some benefits available. Courier service picks up and delivers work as far away as Orange County, "but only for top notch transcribers!".

BI-TECH ENTERPRISES, INC., 10 Carlough Road, Bohemia, NY 11716.
Positions: Contract programmers write communications and database software according to company specifications for Radio Shack, IBM, and Epson computers.
Requirements: Must be local resident. Extensive experience required. Submit resume and references.
Provisions: Pays by the project.

BLACK DOT, INC., 6115 Official Road, Crystal Lake IL 60014.
Positions: Typesetting input operators. Company has a very long waiting list.
Requirements: All operators are independent contractors and own their own equipment. Previous typesetting experience is required. Local residents only.

BLUE CROSS/BLUE SHIELD OF SOUTH CAROLINA, Columbia, SC 29219.
Positions: Local cottage keyers (data entry operators) for coding health claims. Full-time, 8-hour days. Openings are offered first to in-house employees, who are preferred for their company experience, but will also hire from outside applicants. Prefers to train in-house for 6 to 12 months if possible. Currently has over 100 workers.
Requirements: Must live in the area.
Provisions: Pays by the line on computer. Training and equipment (including computer and modem) is provided. Home workers are considered part-timers and receive virtually no benefits; employer/employee relations are excellent, however, and the program is considered by all parties concerned to be very successful. Inquiries are welcome, but you should expect to be put on a waiting list.

BRAUN-BRUMFIELD, INC., 100 North Staebler Road, Ann Arbor, MI 48106.
Positions: Typesetting input operators for book typography.
Requirements: Local residents only. Experience and equipment required.
Provisions: Pays by the keystroke.

BOYD PRINTING COMPANY, INC., 49 Sheridan Avenue, Albany, NY 12210.
Positions: Typesetting input operators.
Requirements: Local, experienced operators with own equipment only.
Provisions: Pays by the word.

B/T COMPUTING CORPORATION, Box 1465, Euless, TX 76039.
Positions: Contract programmers. Company publishes business software for Macintosh.

Requirements: Thorough knowledge of Macintosh and Assembly language programming. Submit resume, work samples, and references.
Provisions: Pays royalties.

BUSINESS GRAPHICS, 3314 Baser N.E., Albuquerque, NM 87107.
Positions: Typesetting input operators.
Requirements: Must be local resident. Experience and computer required.

CAC, 2348 Eden Lane A, Bethlehem, PA 18018.
Positions: Part-time data processing. Work involves processing information from fund raising projects and producing reports and invoices.
Requirements: Must own or have use of an IBM or compatible PC. Access to a printer is preferred, but not necessary. Must live within close proximity to a populated area. When inquiring, send letter of interest, including personal data, computer hardware configuration, printer model, and location relative to the nearest city.
Provisions: Training and all necessary software is provided. Work is seasonal. Pays piece rates set for each form. A good entry operator should make $10 an hour. This is a new home work company expected to expand. Inquiries from anywhere in the U.S. are welcome.

CAL-WESTERN LIFE, 2020 L Street, Sacramento, CA 95814.
Positions: Claims processors.
Requirements: Experience and proven track record for quality of work are required in-house for at least one year. Upon leaving the company environment, telecommuters become independent contractors. Written contract calls for a minimum quota of 350 claims per week. Local residents only.
Provisions: Pay is based on a per claim basis. No benefits. IBM terminals are supplied by the company on a lease plan that costs the workers $50 a month. Yearly income ranges from $15,000 to $20,000. Currently has 21 telecommuters in the program. Will not consider hiring home workers that have not worked inside the company first.

CARLISLE COMMUNICATIONS, 2530 Kerper Boulevard, Dubuque, IA 52001.
Positions: Typesetting input operators. Currently has 17 home keyers.
Requirements: Must live in Dubuque in order to pick up and deliver manuscripts and disks. Must be excellent typist with high rate of accuracy.
Provisions: Training and equipment provided. Pays by the character.

CATERED GRAPHICS, 9823 Mason Avenue, Chatsworth, CA 91311.
Positions: Typesetting input operators for book typography.
Requirements: Local residents only. Must be experienced in this business. Must own IBM equipemnt. Apply with resume.

CHECKMATE TECHNOLOGY, INC., 509 South Rockford, Tempe, AZ 85281.
Positions: Contract programmers and technical writers. Company manufactures peripherals such as RAM disks and memory cards for the Apple IIE series, Macintosh, and IBM. Software is needed by company to enhance marketability of programs written to company specifications and also for conversion from Apple programs to others. Technical writers may be needed for documentation.

CIRCLE GRAPHICS, INC., 7484-K Candlewood Road, Harmans, MD 21077.

Positions: Typesetting input operators. Company has 12 operators on call.
Requirements: Must be local resident in order to pick up and deliver work. Computer required; any brand okay.
Provisions: Pays by the character. Will train for company code.

CLEAR STAR INTERNATONAL, 3233A Golden Avenue, Cincinnati, OH 21214.
Positions: Contract programmers, computer consultants, software developers, and educators. Clear Star is an eight year old software development company operating worldwide. It operates seven days a week, 24 hours a day. Company works with 5th generation applications, PC and home computers, super-micros, and is extremely active in telecommunications packaging. Company "educators" (consultants) have a goal of dispelling the myths associated with high tech. Personnel pool also includes mining and business consultants, database developers, commercial artists, and musicians.
Requirements: Should own PC and modem. Type of equipment depends on particular contract. Equipment will be provided if necessary. C language most commonly used, but prefers to use 5th generation application environments due to leveraging capabilities. "It allows us to compete with high-end applications."
Provisions: Pay varies on an individual basis. "There is no norm here." Usually pays on an hourly or project basis. 80% of Clear Star workers are at home (50-60). "This is an unconventional setup. We use almost completely independent, very diversified types of people. The best programmers are a combination of hacker, professional, and creative person - someone who doesn't fit into the 9 to 5 mold. We prefer a couple of years of systems design. You should understand that the state of the industry is focused on applications for the foreseeable future. We're always open to inquiries. All applications are added to our database for possible use in the future.

COGHILL COMPOSITION COMPANY, 1627 Elmdale Avenue, Richmond, VA 23224.
Positions: Typesetting input operators. Company handles all types of commercial typesetting jobs.
Requirements: Must own IBM compatible and have telecommunications capabilities. Local residents only.
Provisions: Pays by the character.

COMBASE, INC., 333 Sibly Street, Suite 890, St. Paul, MN 55101.
Positions: Contract programmers and technical writers. Combase is a growing company in the courseware development field. It developed some of the biggest selling programs for Control Data. Freelancers are used for design and development of software according to specifications. In this case, programmer gets program-ready sheets and does the coding. There is also general development work available and some conversion work.
Requirements: Experience and appropriate equipment are necessary. Prefers people in the twin cities area.

COMMERCIAL PRINTERS, 3 Hilltop Road, Norwich, CT 06360.
Positions: Typesetting input operators. Company uses combination of courier and telecommunications to transfer work.
Requirements: Local residents only. Must be fast and accurate typist. Prefers people with computer experience.
Provisions: Equipment provided. Operation is small so opportunities are limited.

COMPUTER CENTRAL CORPORATION, 8 Westbury Drive, St. Charles, MO

Close Up: Clear Star International

"We're always open to inquiries," says Daniel Sternklar, president of Clear Star International.

Clear Star is a seven year old software development firm operating world-wide from headquarters in Cincinnati on a seven days a week, 24 hours a day schedule.

The company is "extremely active" in telecommunications packaging, developing voice mail systems and the like.

"Our software developers, and particularly our computer consultants, are more like educators half the time." Sternklar says. "We spend a lot of time trying to dispel the myths that still surround the world of computers. Even though we are on a high level of development, we know our clients probably are not. Even with big corporations, we often have to start at the very beginning and show them how to use computors the right way in their businesses and then we can go on to integrate our software into their systems."

Eighty per cent of Clear Star workers are at home (50-60). In addition to programmers, there are database developers and consultants with expertise in business, mining, art, and music.

Workers should own a PC and modem. The type of equipment depends upon each particular contract. If a contract calls for equipment other than the kind owned by the programmer, whatever is necessary will be provided for the duration of that particular project. The company works with PC and home computers, super-micros, and 5th generation applications.

"Knowledge of 'C' language is enough to get in our door, but we really prefer to use 5th generation application environments due to the leveraging capabilities. It allows us to compete with high-end applications."

Pay varies on an individual basis. "There is no norm here." Usually it's an hourly or project rate."

"This is an unconventional setup. We use almost completely independent, very diversified types of people. The best programmer is a combination of hacker, professional, and creative person — someone who doesn't fit into the 9 to 5 mold. Paperwork has almost been eliminated here to leave more room for pure creativity.

"We prefer a couple of years of experience in systems design. Actually, experience levels around here run the whole gamut, from "kids" with tremendous unused potential to highly trained "old pros."

"Anyone interested in computer programming as a career should understand that the state of the industry is focused on applications for the foreseeable future."

63301.

Positions: Computer Central has been using home-based data entry operators since 1969. While 20 people do work in the office, about 50 work at home.

Requirements: Must be local resident. Must pick up and deliver own work daily. Must be able to type 60 wpm accurately. Must be able to work five hours a day.

Provisions: A two-day training session is provided to learn the equipment and work procedures. PCs are provided. Social Security and unemployment insurance coverage is provided. Pays piece rates which equals about $4 an hour. There is an opportunity to earn more with production bonuses for fast and accurate keyboarders.

COMPUTER PRODUCTS, P. O. Box 4408, Parkersburg, WV 26101.

Positions: Contract programmers and possibly technical writers. Programs are written to company specificatons. Location is unimportant; telecommunications are used.

Requirements: Need PC of any kind commonly used by mid-sized businesses; IBM, Apple, Sperry, etc. No mainframe work. Experience in business applications using assembly. Most important is attitude and knowledge of the industry you're writing for.

Provisions: Pays by the project. Uses from 5 to 20 programmers at a time.

COMPUTER SUPPORT SERVICES UNLIMITED, 10573 West Pico Boulevard, Suite 215, Los Angeles, CA 90064.

Positions: This is a service bureau for customer support reps. Reps will work as on-call consultants either directly for this company or subcontracted to other companies. Expertise in any hardware or software (especially dBase and word processors) will be considered. Some freelance programming will be assigned as well.

Requirements: No experience as a customer support rep is necessary. For the time being, opportunities exist only in the state of California; can be anywhere in the state. To be considered, send your name, address, phone number, and request an application questionnaire.

Provisions: Pays a percentage of the contract. Company president, Judith Woods says, " I am building a network of people I can call upon (at home). Flexible scheduling will be offered so this work won't interfere with any other work the rep might be doing."

COMPUTERWARE, Box 668, Encinto, CA 92024.

Positions: Freelance and contract programmers. Computerware has been publishing software for Radio Shack and other 6809 computers since 1975.

Originally all programs were entertainment oriented, now they are mostly business. Software is now being written for IBM PCs as well. All programming is done in Assembly language. Freelancers are encouraged to submit programs with documentation for consideration. Also assigns programming contracts.

Requirements: Freelancers can request Computerware's "Authorship Guidelines" before submitting program. All others submit resume, samples, and references.

Provisions: Pay methods vary.

CONTROL DATA, 880 Queen Avenue South, Bloomington, MN 55431.

Positions: Control Data has two home work programs, both of which were started in the late 1970s. "Alternative Worksites" is a volunteer option open to Control Data programmers, word processors, analysts, and managers.

Requirements: The only requirement for participation is an okay from the individual's manager. Currently there are 24 programmers.

"HOMEWORK" is Control Data's program for the severely disabled. While the number of people participating in this program fluctuates, it is "going strong" and inquiries from homebound disabled persons are welcome. HOMEWORK is a combination training and placement program. Training in data processing is provided in the worker's home via computer. Previous experience is not necessary. Equipment, which is technically the financial responsibility of the individual, varies according to the needs of the company (or government agency) where the individual is eventually placed. Computer hardware and training software plus optional devices like modems are available.

In the case of a CD employee who has become disabled, either temporarily or permanently, free training is provided with salary and benefits retained intact. The training program is also marketed to companies and governments as a package by the Disabled Services Division of CD. In this case, the client employer would handle the bill for the training of its disabled employee.

It isn't necessary to be currently employed to take advantage of the program. If you're interested, you should first contact your vocational rehabilitation counselor and ask them to contact CD on your behalf. From there a program can be worked out whereby training costs are funded by disability insurance, the State Department of Rehabilitation, or the company that will hire you upon completion of the training.

CREATIVE GRAPHICS, INC., P.O. Box 6048, Allentown, PA 18103.
Positions: Typesetting input operators and proofreaders. Currently has 12 home keyers.
Requirements: Local residents only. Must be fast and accurate typist.
Provisions: Will train on terminal "only if we think they're worth it". Provides Radio Shack equipment.

CYGNUS, Box 57825, Webster, TX 77598.
Positions: Contract programmers for conversions and some original programs written to company specificatons.
Requirements: Should have 8-bit PC and thorough experience. Documentation should be complete. Resume and work samples required.

DATA COMMAND, Box 548, Kankakee, IL 60901.
Positions: Contract programming. Company publishes high quality educational programming for the top five computers.
Requirements: Innovative thinking is most important here. New ideas in educational programming are highly sought after. You can merely submit a great idea for a new program or submit a resume and references for possible contract assignments to company specs.

DATA DESIGNS, 1703 Fairfield Road, P.O. Box 6177, Lindenhurst, IL 60046.
Positions: Writers and editors for database design and administration, and upgrading of technical manuals. Also uses online search specialists, vocabulary developers and indexers for new database development and other information systems services.
Requirements: Need home computer system including PC, modem, and printer.
Provisions: Temporary or part-time freelancers must let their full-time employers know that they are working for Data Designs (if they have other jobs). Hours are totally flexible; company is accessible by computer 24 hours a day. "One worker starts at midnight...". Pays by the project. Currently has a pool of 40 freelancer workers to draw on, plus several permanent full-time workers. 100% of workers are home-based. Applications are kept on file.

DILITHIUM PRESS, Box 606, Beaverton, OR 97075

Positions: Company publishes educational and business programs for five top computers. All programs are written by freelancers.
Requirements: Send proposal with work samples and SASE.

DISCWASHER, 4309 Transworld Road, Schiller Park, IL 60176.
Positions: Contract programmers and technical writers. Programming is usually conversion work, but company also assigns programs written to client's specifications. Technical writers are occasionally used for documentation.
Requirements: Must own and have thorough knowledge of Apple, IBM, Atari, Commodore, or CPM computer. Resume should indicate knowledge and experience with languages and operating systems. Include previous work experience and references.
Provisions: Pays by the job or by the hour.

EDWARDS BROTHERS, INC., 2500 State Street, Ann Arbor, MI 48106.
Positions: Typesetting input operators, proofreaders, and layout for book typography business.
Requirements: Local residents only. Must have necessary skills.
Provisions: Equipment and specific training provided. Home workers are considered company employees.

ELECTRONIC ARTS, 2755 Campus Drive, San Mateo, CA 94403.
Positions: Contract programmers for conversion work. Also regularly backs talented software developers on original programs. Company mainly produces entertainment software for the home market. Some technical writing is assigned for documentation.
Requirements: Must have experience on equipment owned. Prefers Apple, Atari, IBM, or Commodore. Must have fervent interest in company's products. "We look for someone specifically suited to the project."

ELITE SOFTWARE DEVELOPMENT, INC., Drawer 1194, Bryan, TX 77806.
Positions: Contract programmers for program components such as algorythms. Currently has pool of six.
Requirements: Must own and have experience with IBM-AT or clone. Also has some CPM 8-bit work. Prefers programmers who properly test their work and are capable of writing their own documentation.
Provisions: Generally pays by the hour, total sum not to exceed predetermined amount.

ELIZABETH TYPESETTING COMPANY, 26 North 26th Street, Kenilworth, NJ 07033.
Positions: Typesetting input operators for book typography. Work is transferred via modem and FAX.
Requirements: Local residents only. Accurate keyboard skills required.
Provisions: Equipment is provided. Pays by the character.

EN FLEUR CORPORATION, 2494 Sun Valley Circle, Silver Spring, MD 20906.
Positions: Contract programmers for program sub-routines.
Requirements: Should own and be extremely familiar with MacIntosh, HP, or IBM. Assembly is the language most often used. Send work samples with resume. All work must be well documented.
Provisions: Pays by the job.

EPS GROUP, INC., 1501 Guilford Avenue, Baltimore, MO 21202.

Positions: Typesetting input operators for book typography. Currently has 8 home keyers.
Requirements: Local residents only. Skilled keyboarders only.
Provisions: Equipment and courier provided when necessary. Pays by the character.

EXSPEEDITE PRINTING SERVICE, 12201 Old Columbia Pike, Silver Spring, MD 20914.
Positions: Typesetting input operators for book typography.
Requirements: Must be local resident in order to pick up and deliver work. Experience and computer equipment required.
Provisions: Work is part-time from overflow. Pays by the character.

FEDERATION OF THE HANDICAPPED, Automated Office Services, 211 West 14th Street, 2nd Floor, New York, NY 10011.
Positions: Automated Office Systems is the newest of the Federation's programs for homebound disabled workers. It is similar to the typing/transcription department, except that all workers use computers and telecommunicaitons equipment to perform the work.
Requirements: All positions require evaluation through lengthy interviews and personal counseling. All workers must live in New York City.
Provisions: Automated Office Services provides training in word processing procedures. Computers, telecommunication equipment and a phone-in dictation system are provided. All positions pay piece rates.
Disability insurance counseling is provided.

THE FIELD COMPANIES, dba Field Premium, Pleasant Street, P.O. Box 78, Watertown, MA 02172.
Positions: Data entry operators. Work consists of computer data entry (mostly names and addresses for mail order fulfillment).
Requirements: Experience is required. Must be local resident.
Provisions: Equipment and pick up and delivery are provided. Pays piece rates.

FREELANCE NETWORK, 5550 Denny Avenue #203, North Hollywood, CA 91601.
Positions: Freelance word processors. The network publishes a directory of freelancers listing their equipment, specialty, experience level, and location. The directory is then distributed to companies throughout greater Los Angeles that regularly use the services of freelance word processors.
Requirements: There is no cost for the service. References are required.
Provisions: Each operator receives a copy of the directory. Pay is worked out between the responding companies and operators.

GENERIC SOFTWARE, Box 790, Marquette, MI 49855.
Positions: Contract programmers and technical writers. Programmers used for conversions, both computer to computer and language to language, and original programs written to company specifications. Technical writers used for writing manuals and some copy writing. Location is unimportant; "We are worldwide; our people are everywhere."
Requirements: Programmers must be familiar with CPM or MS-DOS microcomputers. Before sending resume, get a good understanding of the company's needs. Writers send resume with work samples.
Provisions: Both positions pay by the job.

GRAPHIC TYPESETTING, 3929 South Broadway Place, Los Angeles, CA 90037.

Phil Neal
Contract Programmer, Maine

"I live in such a remote area I do as much as possible over the phone. I start each job by traveling to the worksite to do a requirement analysis and determine what needs to be done. I then report on what the client will need, how long it will take, and when they can expect parts of the system to be tested. From there, all the work is done strictly from my house. Living in such a remote area, it would be difficult to envision working in any other way."

Positions: Typesetting input operators for work in working all over the U.S.
Requirements: Must be former employee or come with recommendation from another book typography firm.

GUILD PRINTING COMPANY, INC., 380 West 38th Street, Los Angeles, CA 90037.
Positions: Typesetting input operators for book typography.
Requirements: Must be former in-house employee.

HANDI COMPUTING, 3490 Taylor, East Lansing, MI 48823.
Positions: Contract programmers for database development. Owner Kirby Morgan is an extremely talented, well-educated handicapped individual who writes educational courseware in physics and calculus for Control Data. He moved to East Lansing where zoning ordinances allow him to use more home-based programmers and expand his business. East Lansing is also within a local calling area for hooking workers up to the major electronic networks.
Requirements: Must live in the area. Minimum five years experience in developing courseware is required.
Provisions: Workers are independent contractors and are paid by the job.

HRM SOFTWARE, 175 Tompkins Avenue, Pleasantville, NY 10570.
Positions: Computer programmers for freelance submissions, computer to computer conversions, and company-directed programming. HRM publishes only interactive home education programs
Requirements: Experience programming on Apple, Commodore, or IBM. Freelancers can submit finished programs for consideration. All others submit resume, samples, and references.

ICOM SIMULATIONS, 1110 Lake Cook Road, Buffalo Grove, IL 60090.
Positions: Contract programmers write original business application software accord-

ing to company specifications.

Requirements: Thorough knowledge and experience required. Submit resume, references, and work samples.

Provisions: Pay methods vary.

IMPRESSIONS, INC., P.O. Box 3304, Madison, WI 53704.

Positions: Typesetting input operators for book typography.

Requirements: Local residents only. Excellent keyboarding skills are required. Must own computer equipment.

Provisions: Hours are flexible. Pays by the character.

INTELLIGENT MACHINES, 1440 West Broadway, Missoula, MT 59802.

Positions: Contract programmers and technical writers. Programmers write software according to company specifications. The company primarily produces business software for most major computers. Technical writers write manuals.

Requirements: Resume and references required for both positions.

Provisions: Pays by the hour and by the job.

INTELLIGENT MICRO SYSTEMS, INC., 1249 Greentree Lane, Narberth, PA 19072.

Positions: Contract programming of utility programs for AT&T, IBM and Macintosh.

Requirements: Extensive knowledge and experience with operating systems and languages. Must live on East Coast.

ISLAND GRAPHICS, 1 Harbor Drive, Sausalito, CA 949675.

Positions: Computer programmers used to develop computer graphics.

Requirements: Must be local resident. Experience is required.

Provisions: All equipment is supplied by the company. Employees are salaried. 10% of company employees work at home. 'We are an opportunity based company."

J & L GRAPHICS, INC., 2200 Carlson Drive, Northbrook, IL 60062.

Positions: Typesetting input operators for book typography.

Requirements: Local residents only. Must be experienced, skilled operator with own computer equipment.

Provisions: Courier service provided. Pays $0.55/1,000 characters.

KJ SOFTWARE, INC., 3420 East Shea Boulevard, Suite 161, Phoenix, AZ 85028.

Positions: Freelance programmers and technical writers on contract. Company produces only management training programs with workbooks for IBM computers.

Requirements: Programmers can submit finished programs for consideration. Technical writers submit resume, samples, and references.

Provisions: Programmers are paid royalties. Writers are paid by the project.

LAKE AVENUE SOFTWARE, 77 North Oak Knoll, Suite 105-A, Pasadena, CA 91101.

Positions: Contract programmers and technical writers. Company develops accounting software for any size business using dBase III on IBM compatibles. Contract programmers are usually called upon to modify existing programs. Technical writers are used on occasion to write manuals. Most workers are local, but some are out of state. Work is handled through the transfer of disks; no telecommunications available at this time.

LASSEN SOFTWARE, INC., Box 1190 Chico, CA 95927.
Positions: Contract programmers and technical writers. Company produces business utility software, some of which is specifically useful for the home-based business person. Contract programmers are used mostly for conversions. Technical writers are used for documentation and copy writing.
Requirements: Programmers should first send for programming guidelines. Both positions require resumes and samples of previous work.
Provisions: Pays by the job.

THE LEARNING COMPANY, 545 Middlefield Road, Suite 170, Menlo Park, CA 94025.
Positions: Contract programmers and technical writers. Company produces educational software with an emphasis on graphics and sound. Contract programmers are used for conversions from computer to computer. Technical writers produce manuals.
Requirements: Exceptional ability in working with graphics and sound effects is especially sought in programmers. Must be very familiar with IBM, Commodore, and Apple computers. Must be local resident. Ability to meet deadlines is important Writers should be experienced and their experience should be documented in their resumes.
Provisions: Pays by the job.

LEARNING WELL, 200 South Service Road, Roslyn Heights, NY 11577.
Positions: Contract programmers for conversions and programs written to company specifications. Company publishes educational programs for Apple, Commodore, and IBM.
Requirements: Thorough knowledge and experience programming in Assembly language on one of the mentioned computers. Submit resume, samples, and references.

LIFT, INC., P.O. Box 1072, Mountainside, NJ 07092.
Positions: Lift, Inc., is a nonprofit organization that trains and places physically disabled people as home-based computer programmers for corporate employers. In the past 10 years, program participants have been placed with 52 major corporations.
Requirements: Applicants must have a severe but stable disability, such as MS or impaired limbs. Pilot programs for blind and deaf workers are underway, too. Standard aptitude tests are applied to find traits as motivation, drive, self-control, and an aptitude for computer programming. Occassionally the candidate already has some training, but prior training is not necessary for entry into the program. Each candidate is trained to specifically meet the needs of the corporate client using whatever language and equipment the employer chooses. Most candidates are trained in systems programming and business applications.
Provisions: Upon completion of training, the programmer will work under contract with Lift for one year. The salary is comparable to that of any other entry level programmer, with medical and life insurance provided. After the year is up, the corporate employer then has the option of employing the programmer directly. The placement record has been exceptional. Lift operates in 15 states now, but expansion is underway, with plans to include all 50. Qualified persons are encouraged to apply from any urban location. (All workers are required to go into the employer's office at least once a week and most corporations are located in densely populated areas.)

THE LINTON FACTOR, 1355 Creeeekside Drive, #407, Walnut Creek, CA 94596.
Positions: Data entry, order taking, bookkeeping, and customer service.
Requirements: At least four to five years of experience is required. Ability to produce

quality work and manage oneself is necessary. Must live in Northern California.
Provisions: Pays different piece rates for different types of work. For example, bookkeepers earn about $20 an hour about 20 hours a week. All resumes are kept on file.

E.T. LOWE PUBLISHING COMPANY, 2920 Sidco Drive, Nashville, TN 37204.
Positions: Typesetting input operators for book typography.
Requirements: Local residents only. Experience and equipment required.
Provisions: Pays by the character.

MANUFACTURERS HANOVER TRUST CORPORATION, 4 New York Plaza, 21st Floor, New York, NY 10015,
Positions: Data processing personnel. Purpose of telecommuting program is to establish a pool of data processing professionals who can work on a project-by-project basis on rush jobs, overflow, etc.
Requirements: Must live in the NY metropolitan area in order to attend occasional meetings, conferences, or problem-solving sessions. Must meet strict criteria set up by the bank's legal department in order to conform to state labor laws.
Provisions: Pays set rates per project that equal higher pay per hour than in-house employees receive. No benefits. Equipment is supplied on an interest-free lease/option basis. Manufacturers Hanover is the first corporation to hire home workers from the "outside"; it quickly formed a waiting list.

MARYLAND COMPOSITION CO., INC., 6711 Dover Road, Baymeadow Industrial Park Glen Burnie, MD 21061.
Positions: Typesetting books, catalogs, and directories is done here by a pool of independent home keyboarders and is proofread by another pool of homeworkers.
Requirements: Keyboarders need good typing skills only; must be fast, but it is even more important to be accurate. Must be available for a minimum of 20 hours a week and live nearby. Workers pick up their own work.
Provisions: Company provides 40 to 50 hours of initial training. PCs are loaned to workers. Pays an hourly rate for the first six months, then the rate changes to a formula based on quality, quantity, and difficulty. "We look for people who have kids and can't get out to go to a full-time job. Usually their motivation is not money so much as it is getting out into the mainstream. We try to satisfy their needs by offering a flexible situation that we can all live with." There is usually a backlog of applicants, but inquiries from reliable people are welcome.

MAVERICK PUBLICATIONS, P.O. Box 5007, Bend, OR 97701.
Positions: Keyboarding and proofreading. This is a small book producing company, established in 1968, that uses cottage labor where economics make it advantageous. An optical character reader is used to transfer manuscripts to magnetic disks. Computerized photo-typesetting allows corrections to be made on a video screen.
Requirements: Must be local resident.

MCFARLAND GRAPHICS & DESIGN, INC., Blair Mt. Road, Route 2, Dillsburg, PA 17019.
Positions: Typesetting input operators for mass market book typography. Currently has 8 operators working full-time and another 4 part-timers handle overflow.
Requirements: Uses former typesetters only. All are independent contractors. Local residents only. Must be disciplined. New applicants are tested.
Provisions: "We are different in that we pay an hourly rate. If an operator is getting paid

by the character, there is too much stress built into the situation. They're likely to skip over problems rather than stop and call for help. In order to make a program like this work, there has to be a trust factor and a lot of give and take."

MEGATREND SYSTEMS, 2506 Cole, Oakland, CA 94601.
Positions: Claims processors.
Requirements: Need PC (prefer IBM compatible) and modem. Experience is required. Must live in the Bay area.
Provisions: Write for details. Company is new, but will be focusing on telecommuting as a primary method of employment.

MOLECULAR, INC., 251 River Oaks Parkway, San Jose, CA 95134.
Positions: Contract programmers and technical writers. Company produces multi-user software packages for Concurrent CPM 86, 3.1 and Xenix 3.0 Programmers write according to company specifications. Technical writers handle documentation and copy writing.
Requirements: Send resume and references. Must be local resident.
Provisions: Pays by the job.

MONARCH/AVALON HILL GAME COMPANY, 4517 Hartford Road, Baltimore, MD 21214.
Positions: Monarch/Avalon has been making adult board games for 30 years. Company now produces adult computer strategy games. Contract programmers are used for conversions from one computer to another and also for original program writing to company specifications.
Requirements: Must own and have experience with IBM, Apple II, Commodore 64, or Atari. Some game experience is preferred, particularly with "our type of games." Send resume and include references. Programmers are encouraged to send for free "Programmer's Guidelines."
Provisions: Pays by the job or royalties or a combination of both. Can live anywhere. "We have programmers as far away as Hungary." Currently has up to 25 contract programmers working at a time.

MONOTYPE COMPOSITION COMPANY, 2050 Rockrose Avenue, Baltimore, MD 21211.
Positions: Typesetting input operators for book typography. This is a union shop, so in-

---

Close Up
F-International

F-International, Berkhamsted, England, is not only the single largest company in the world that employs primarily home-based workers, but it is also one of the oldest to do so.

It was founded in 1962 by Steve Shirley, who was at the time a Sr. Assistant Programmer at ICT. She was also expecting her first child.

Even back then, the world of computer programming moved so fast that a career could be ruined in the time it takes to have a baby. Since there were no opportunities for her to continue work, Mrs. Shirley started her own computer consultancy and software house, F-International. ("F" stands for freelance.)

Today, 24 years later, the company has over 1,200 workers, 90% of whom are home-based. Positions for programmers, spec writers, estimators, sales executives, telemarketers, and managers are included.

Employees are recruited through ads placed in the trade press and also through recommendations of friends and client's friends. Publicity brings in applicants, too. Sometimes, posters are used touting the flexibility of home work as an enticement to would-be employees.

Though the firm has an open-door policy regarding new applicants, the requirements are by no means lax.

Even with a tremendous shortage of qualified computer personnel, a minimum of four years of experience is required. Just as important is the requirement of credibility. F-International needs to know that its people can work with a minimum amount of supervision. 13.5 years of experience is average for their personnel.

In return, workers have as much flexibility as they need. They have the unique opportunity to progress in their careers in whatever way they see fit. For women this has proven to be particularly important, and women here move into management positions much faster than in conventional companies.

What holds the company together in a fast-paced industry when its employees are spread throughout several countries? In any one month there are 250 projects going on for about 150 clients at at time! A self-designed management auditing system keeps the company machine running smoothly. The gears which turn and mesh together are committees representing every aspect of the business. They meet regularly to discuss management, project, and operational problems. All the committees work with each other at some point and issue follow-up reports. Everybody knows what's going on all of the time, so there's no room for slippage. All of this internal communication is an absolute must for the success of the company.

And it works. Annual growth is a healthy 30% and F-International is looking to expand throughout the rest of Europe with new services, such as their newly designed telecommunications networks.

At the same time, the rest of the world is watching. Delegations from all over—Australia, Japan, the U.S.-have come to learn from these pioneers of telecommuting.

Spokeswoman Rosie Symons says, "The home work force will grow quite quickly in the next five to ten years, mostly due to the availability of cheaper equipment."

Having an established model of success like F-International can't help but speed the process.

house workers are guaranteed work first. Any overflow goes to independent contractors. There are about 6 full-time and another 12 on-call home keyers on the roster.
Requirements: Local residents only. Must own computer equipment and have experience.
Provisions: Pays by the character.

MOUNTAIN VIEW PRESS, Box 4656, Mountain View, CA 94040.
Positions: Freelance programmers. Publishes hundreds of programs of all types for all types of computers. All programs are FORTH language programs.
Requirements: High level experience writing in FORTH with resume, samples and references to prove it. Send along with proposal.

MUTUAL SERVICE LIFE INSURANCE COMPANY, 2 Pine Tree Drive, St. Paul, MN 55112.
Positions: Claims processors. Work comes from hospitals, doctors, dentists, and other medical clients. Currently has 15 home workers.
Requirements: Must have demonstrated good claim quality. "I'm not likely to let anyone work outside of the office setting if they won't be able to meet our quality standards." Must pay own phone charges incurred on the job. 10 hours is required in-office every quarter for staff meetings. There is no pay for this time, but any extra time beyond the required 10 hours will earn the specified hourly rate. Must be local resident.
Provisions: Equipment is provided (IBM 3161 computer terminals are hooked up to the company mainframe). Pays on a per claim basis. Minnesota Workman's Comp is provided.

NETWORK TYPESETTING, 5058 South 107th Street, Omaha, NE 68127.
Positions: Input operators that key in formats for typesetting. Workers are independent contractors. Currently has six input stations. "We would welcome inquires from high quality input people. They don't necessarily have to be here in Omaha."
Requirements: Although actual experience is not required, quality of work is important. Need IBM PC with Wordstar and a 50,000 word (minimum) spelling checker; sometimes a modem and/or printer is also necessary. "You should understand the business and the importance of doing quality work."
Provisions: Equipment is supplied if necesssary. Pays by the job. No benefits. "Our input people are highly paid—more than in-house workers."

NEW YORK LIFE INSURANCE COMPANY, 51 Madison Avenue, New York, NY 10010.
Positions: Insurance claims processors and contract programmers. Currently has 25 home workers.
Requirements: Must be current or recent employee of New York Life. Must live in the New York City area.
Provisions: Equipment is provided as necessary. Employees retain in-house status.

NPD, 900 West Shore Road, Port Washington, NY 11050.
Positions: NPD is one of the largest market research firms in the country. They have begun to employ home-based data entry operators to process batches of source documents. The operators are divided into groups of 20 each, with a supervisor for each group. Supervisors are also home-based and are treated the same as in-house data entry supervisors with salaries, benefits, etc. They are provided with PCs for their homes, but do not do data entry work.

Requirements: Good typing skills are necessary. Must be local resident. Must attend quarterly meetings. Must pick up and deliver work about every three days.
Provisions: PCs and all necessary supplies are provided. Training is provided in NPD office for one to two weeks. Work is part-time, therefore only sick leave and vacation benefits (prorated) are provided; no insurance benefits. Pays piece rates equal to that of in-house workers. Applications are accepted, but there is a waiting list.

ORANGE CHERRY MEDIA, P.O. Box 390 Pound Ridge, NY 10576.
Positions: Freelance and contract programmers. Company publishes highly graphic educational programs for Apple, Atari, IBM, and Commodore computers.
Requirements: Freelancers can submit either finished program with documentation or proposal with samples and resume. Contract programmers are sometimes assigned to write to spec. Submit resume, samples, and references.

OREGON SOFTWARE, INC., 6915 S.W. Macadam Avenue, Portland, OR 97219.
Positions: Technical writers for user manuals.
Requirements: Must be local writer with minimum five years experience in computer documentation. Submit resume, work samples, and references.
Provisions: Pays hourly rate.

PARKWOOD COMPOSITION SERVICE, 1345 South Knowles Avenue, New Richmond, WI 54017.
Positions: Typesetting input operators, proofreaders, and layout for book typography.
Requirements: Local residents only. Experience and equipment required.
Provisions: All workers are independent contractors with no guarantees of continuous work. Work flow is very seasonal.

POLARWARE, P.O. Box 31, Geneva, IL 60134.
Positions: Freelance programmers write all types of programs for the home computer user. Contract programmers for conversions.
Requirements: Experience programming for Apple, IBM, Macintosh, Commodore, or Atari. Freelancers can submit finished program with documentation for consideration. Contract programmers submit resume and references.

PONY-X-PRESS, 909 West Fifth Avenue, Columbus, OH 42312.
Positions: Typesetting input operators, proofreaders, and layout for book typography. Currently has 15 regulars on the roster.
Requirements: Local residents only. Must possess necessary skills. Operators must own computer equipment.
Provisions: "Although most of our home workers are former employees, we will try new people. They must have a word processor and be very familiar with their own equipment and software. If someone comes to us claiming to be an input operator, we'll assign one trial project. We will teach them our code. It's been customized for our type of work here so that it's very streamlined." All work is overflow.

POPULAR PROGRAMS, 135 Lake Street, Suite 180, Kirkland, WA 98033.
Positions: Contract programmers and technical writers. Company produces business software for IBM PCs only. Programming is written to specification; both original and modifications of existing programs.
Requirements: Must know Microsoft C and Assembly 8080. Send resume with references.

Provisions: Pay methods vary; by the job, by the hour, or royalty.

PORT CITY PRESS, INC., 1323 Greenwood Road, Baltimore, MD 21208.
Positions: Typesetting input operators for book typography.
Requirements: Local residents only. Experience and equipment required.
Provisions: Pays by the character.

QUEUE, INC., Intellectual Software, 562 Boston Avenue, Bridgeport, CT 06610.
Positions: Contract programmers for writing educational software for Apple and/or IBM computers. Freelance programmers also do conversions and programming to company specifications.
Requirements: Local people are definitely preferred. Apply with resume and references or work samples. Quality of work is very important.
Provisions: Pays by the job or royalty. Inquiries are welcome.

QUORUM INTERNATIONAL, UNLIMITED, Industrial Park Station, Box 2134, Oakland, CA 94614.
Positions: Contract programmers and technical writers. Company produces industrial software, usually graphic simulations used for training purposes. Programmers must own and be thoroughly familiar with either the Apple II or Amiga. Technical writers have not been used in the past, but the company plans to use freelancers in the future.
Requirements: Send letter of interest with work samples. "Prior talent and interest in the project is most important. Enthusiasm counts for a lot."
Provisions: Pay methods vary.

REMOTE CONTROL, P.O. Box 2861, Del Mar, CA 92014.
Positions: Company is a software development firm. Uses customer support representatives in all areas of the country. Product being marketed now is "Telemagic", a telemarketing software package.
Requirements: Must have IBM PC or compatible.
Provisions: Can work full-time or part-time. Training is provided. Pays by the call. Write for details.

REPRODUCTION TYPOGRAPHERS, 244 West First Avenue, Roselle, NJ 07203.
Positions: Typesetting input operators for book typography. All operators are independent contractors and can work for other companies simultaneously.
Requirements: Must be experienced operators with own equipment. Local residents only. Must pick up and deliver own work.
Provisions: All work is overflow from the plant. Pays by the keystroke.

RESOURCE SOFTWARE INTERNATIONAL, 330 New Brunswick Avenue, Ford, NJ 08863.
Positions: Contract programmers work on various assignments writing new programs to company specs or modifying existing ones.
Requirements: Must have experience programming in Assembly language on Apple, IBM, HP, or Radio Shack. Submit resume, samples, and references. Prefers programmers on East Coast.
Provisions: Pays by the project.

RIGHT BROTHERS SOFTWARE, 1173 Niagara, Denver, CO 80220.
Positions: Right Brothers is a new software publishing company looking for good

Carolyn Hyde
Data Entry Operator
Blue Cross/Blue Shield of SC

"The best thing about working at home is being able to work my own hours, not being confined to a 9 to 5 job. The pay is better too. Since I get paid by the line, all I have to do is work more to get paid more. It's nice to get paid for what I do."

educational programs for the Color Computer I, II, and III. Especially wants thought provoking, problem solving courseware for higher education levels. Programs are highly interactive and are games only if there is also a strong educational value.
Requirements: Thorough knowledge of BASIC and Assembly languages (only). Submit disk, printed listing, and any other support materials available.
Provisions: Programs will be analyzed for commercial value and if accepted will offer standard royalty of 12-15%.

RIGHT ON PROGRAMS, Box 977, Huntington, NY 11743.
Positions: Contract programmers for computer to computer conversions. Company produces educational programs for Apple, IBM, and Commodore. Also accepts freelance submissions.
Requirements: Must be highly qualified. Submit resume and references.

ROXBURY PUBLISHING COMPANY, P.O. Box 491044, Los Angeles, CA 90049.
Positions: Freelance home-based typesetters are used by this textbook publisher.
Requirements: Must have typesetting equipment (not PC; this is not embedding but typesetting). Los Angeles residents only. Minimum of five years experience. Send resume and indicate equipment type.
Provisions: Pay method varies. Inquiries welcome from qualified people, but there is a waiting list.

THE SAYBROOK PRESS, INC., P.O. Box 629, Old Saybrook, CT 06475.
Positions: Typesetting input operators for book typography. Currently has 8 home keyers.
Requirements: Local residents only. Must be accurate typist. Must pick up and deliver own work.
Provisions: Training and equipment provided. Pays by the character.

SELEX, 10 Carlisle Drive, Livingston, NJ 07039.

Positions: Software developers. Company develops highly interactive text on any subject. Some technical writers.
Requirements: Must own and have thorough knowledge of major brand PC and printer. Send list of equipment availability with letter of interest.
Provisions: Pays royalty plus other benefits.

SET TYPE, 1717 West Beltine, Madison, WI 53713.
Positions: Typesetting input operators.
Requirements: Local residents only. Experience and own equipment required.
Provisions: Pays by the character.

TOM SNYDER PRODUCTIONS, INC., 123 Auburn Street, Cambridge, MA 02138. Contract programmers and software engeneers. Company produces educational games for Apple, Atari, Commodore and IBM. Most of the available work is conversion from machine to machine.
Requirements: Send resume and work samples.
Provisions: Pays by the job or hourly rate of $10 to $40 and hour.

SPSS, INC., 444 North Michigan Avenue, Suite 3000, Chicago, IL 60611.
Positions: Contract programmers and technical writers. Programmers do conversions of business graphics software. Technical writers are used for documentation and promotional materials.
Requirements: Programmers must have experience with mainframe or super-minis. Applicants for both positions must send resume and previous work samples.

STRATEGIC SIMULATIONS, INC., 883 Stierlin Road, Building A-200, Mt. View, CA 94043.
Positions: Contact programmers for computer to computer conversions. Company publishes over 100 games for Apple, Atari, and Macintosh computers.
Requirements: There is a lot of conversion work available. However, only programmers with a high level of proficiency and ownership of both computers will be considered. Submit resume and references. Include request for current conversion needs.

STYLISTS SOFTWARE, Box 916, Idaho Falls, ID 83402.
Positions: Contract programmers and technical writers. Programmers do some conversions and some original programs written to company specificatons. Company produces business and typesetting packages for 68,000 UNIX clones and Macintosh.
Requirements: Must be extremely familiar with Macintosh, Assembly and C languages. Technical writers must be local residents.
Provisions: Pays by the job.

TAX ONE, 4553 - 34TH Avenue South, Minneapolis, MN 55405.
Positions: Tax One designs and sells software to CPAs via a network of home-based telemarketers. In addition, a nationwide bookkeeping service bureau now has home-based bookkepers working on monthly service projects from small business accounts to construction union payrolls.
Requirements: Competence is the essential requirement for bookkeepers, who are considered independent contractors and must supply their own computer systems. The type of equipment doesn't matter since
Tax One can provide any software conversions necessary.

Provisions: Training and manuals are provided as well as ongoing company support. Work can be part-time or full-time. For bookkeepers, Tax One obtains all accounts and handles all billing. "A competent bookkeeper working with our system should easily gross $30 an hour." Telemarketers are paid $6 an hour plus lead bonus.

TECHNICAL BOOKS, 4300 West 62nd Street, Indianapolis, IN 46268.
Positions: Technical writers. Company publishes computer related books that are sometimes supported by computer programs.
Requirements: Writers should first send for free catalog. Then submit resume.
Provisions: Pays by the project.

TEKTRONIX, INC., Box 4600 MS 92-680, Beaverton, OR 97075.
Positions: Company publishes thousands of programs that are programming tools for software engineers. All programs are written in C language for AT&T, Compaq, DEC, and IBM. Contract programmers write programs according to company specifications.
Requirements: Must be highly experienced., Submit resumes and references.

TYPETRONICS, 341 State Street, Madison, WI 53703.
Positions: Typesetting input operators.
Requirements: Local residents only. Experience and equipment required.
Provisions: Pays by the keystroke.

THE ULTIMATE SECRETARY, 18231 Los Alimos Street, Northridge, CA 91326.
Positions: Medical and x-ray transcribers.
Requirements: Must live in the Valley. Ability to learn and a "way with words" is the primary prerequisite here. (It is very unusual for transcription companies to offer training to inexperienced medical transcribers, but this one does.) Must own word processor (and have experience using it) and transcribing machine with either standard or micro cassettes.
Provisions: Training provided. For now workers will have to pick up and deliver their own work, especially during the training period, but a courier service is planned for the near future. Turnaround time on x-ray material is 24 hours and 48 hours on all others. Work can be part-time or full-time. Pays by the line.

UNITRON GRAPHICS, INC., 47-10 32nd Place, Long Island, NY 11101.
Positions: Typesetting input operators for book typography.
Requirements: Experience and equipment required. Local residents only.
Provisions: Pays by the keystroke.

UNIVERSITY GRAPHICS, INC., 11 West Lincoln Avenue, Atlantic Highlands, NJ 07716.
Positions: University Graphics provides services to the book publishing industry and has three pools of home workers: keyboarders for typesetting with embedded code, proofreaders, and page makeup people who key in data to the mainframe. Currently has over 70 home workers.
Requirements: Keyboarders must type 50 to 60 wpm with a low error rate. Proofreaders must have good English skills, "maybe an English major." Local residents only.
Provisions: Training is provided. Keyboarders are provided with IBM PCs; others receive terminals which are hooked up to company's mainframe. Pays piece rates. "We were one of the first in the composition industry to use cottage labor. Now it's becoming the norm because it helps stabilize costing in an industry which is cyclical in nature. By

**Wanda Welliver
Typesetting Input Operator
Network Typesetting
Omaha, NE**

"I worked at home for eight years as a typist and never even saw a computer. When I met my boss, he explained typography to me and said if I could type 100 words a minute, the job was mine. A couple of months later, I was completely comfortable working with Wordstar on my new IBM PC. Now I make a lot more money than I would just typing. But, even more important than that is the freedom. I really don't want to go back out there."

using home workers, we can keep tight controls on our costs and overhead. Inquiries are always welcome."

WAVERLY PRESS, INC., Guilford & Mt. Royal Avenues, Baltimore, MD 21601.
Positions: Waverly Press has been using home keyers for over 10 years to embed code for typesetting medical and scientific publications. This is a high volume operation typesetting over 250,000 pages a year.
Requirements: Applicants must type fast and very accurately. "Some are surprised at the level of skill required for this work. This is not just a typing job." Must live in the area. Also has a pool of proofreaders; must be able to read at a certain rate (about 27,000 characters per hour while simultaneously checking for errors in the copy. A test is given upon applcation).
Provisions: Initial training is conducted in the plant for six weeks. Workers are then supplied with 640 K IBM PC compatible, dual disk drives, modified text editor, furniture, miscellaneous office supplies, and "an endless supply of manuscripts." Pay is dependent upon accuracy with 3 different rates: low, medium, and high. "Two thirds of our keyers are in the high range." Pays by the keystroke with the complexity taken into consideration; the computer is programmed to measure the work. Piece work with no benefits except a pension plan is available to those with over 1,000 hours a year. Daily van service is available to those who need it.

J. WESTON WALCH, Box 658, Portland, ME 04104.
Positions: Company publishes educational courseware. Freelance programmers can submit finished program with documentation for consideration. Contract programmers are also used for conversions and modificatons.
Requirements: Freelancers should send only proposal. Contract programmers should submit resume, work samples, and complete information describing particular expertise.

WENGER CORPORATION, 555 Park Drive, Owatonna, MN 55060.
Positions: Contract programmers for conversion, modifications, and original program-

ming to company specifications. Company publishes educational programs on the subject of music only. All programs are written by freelancers.
Requirements: Submit resume, samples, and references.

WESTCHESTER BOOK COMPOSITIONS, 40 Triangle Center, Yorktown Heights, NY 10598.
Positions: Typesetting input operators.
Requirements: Local residents only. Experience and equipment required.
Provisions: Pays by the character.

JOHN WILEY & SONS, INC., 605 - 3rd Avenue, New York, NY 10158.
Positions: Contract programmers and technical writers. Company produces technical applications software for the engineering and scientific fields. Various types of work are contracted out to programmers, including conversions, testing, debugging, and some original development. Technical writers do documentation work.
Requirements: Must own and have thorough knowledge of Apple or IBM PC. Send resume, work samples, and references.
Provisions: Payment methods vary according to the situation.

WILLIAM BYRD PRESS, 2905 Byrdhill Road, Richmond, VA 23261.
Positions: Typesetting input operators, proofreaders, and pasteup people. Company produces scientific, medical and other very technical journals. Currently has about 104 cottage workers.
Requirements: Experience is required. Must live in Richmond. Send resume with proof of experience.
Provisions: Workers are considered part-time employees. Pays piece rates depending on the difficulty of the project. No benefits. There is a waiting list.

THE WISCONSIN PHYSICIANS SERVICE, 1717 West Broadway, P.O. Box 8190, Madison, WI 53708.
Positions: Claims processors.
Requirements: Apply with resume. Must be local resident.
Provisions: Pays piece rates.

WOOLF SOFTWARE SYSTEMS, INC., 22048 Sherman Way #106, Canoga Park, CA 91303.
Positions: Contract programmers and technical writers. Company develops business and communications software for most computer systems. Programmers do conversions and some original programming to company specifications.
Requirements: Both positions require resumes, references, and work samples.
Provisions: Pays by the hour.

YORK GRAPHICS SERVICES, INC., 3600 West Market Street, York, PA 17404.
Positions: Typesetting input operators and proofreaders for book typography.
Requirements: Local residents only. Operators must have good typing skills. Proofreaders must be detail oriented and have excellent English skills.
Provisions: All home workers are independent contractors and should understand that there are no guarantees of work assignments. All available work is overflow.

Chapter 6
Opportunities in Office Support Positions

"Desk jobs" are among the fastest-growing categories of home work opportunities. Just about any kind of job that is performed in an office setting can just as easily be done at home. The availability of inexpensive office equipment combined with new telephone service options makes it easier now than ever before.

Some companies hire home office workers directly. More often than not, however, they are hired through service bureaus. For instance, insurance policies have been typed by home workers for many years. But the insurance companies have nothing to do with the hiring of home typists. Instead, the insurance companies contract with policy typing service bureaus. The service bureaus are responsible for all phasaes of the policy-typing process and do all the hiring and training of the home typists.

Service bureaus are popping up everywhere in the medical transcribing field. Medical transcribing is the top of the line for home typists. Not only is it the most financially rewarding of all home typing jobs—it is also an industry that is growing at a breakneck speed and there are more openings for jobs than most employers can fill.

The job involves typing doctors' reports and correspondence from cassette tapes. Employers often require several years of experience and test applicants to ensure they have a thorough knowledge of medical terminology. To get the necessary background, there are "Medical Secretary" courses available through community colleges and private vocational schools. A complete course takes from three to six months. But even then, you will need some practice in order to keep up with the 24-hour turnaround time required by most companies. One good way to gain some experience is to sign up with one or more temporary employment agencies. Explain what you're trying to do and ask to be assigned to any medical office jobs that come up.

Foreign language translation is included in this section because so much of the work requires office skills such as typing, proofreading, typesetting, and transcribing. Again, this is a field handled almost entirely by service bureaus. Most translators work at home and many work for service bureaus located in another state or even another country.

Translation is not a job for amateurs. It requires a high level of proficiency in a foreign language and some bureaus will only hire native language translators. It is also necessary to have special expertise in a given field in order to be able to work with the terminology peculiar to that field. For instance, if you are a translator specializing in the legal field, you would need an understanding of legal terminology not only in English, but in the foreign language as well.

AA INTERNATIONAL TRANSLATIONS & LINGUISTICS, 2312 Artesia, Redondo Beach, CA 90278.
Positions: Foreign language translators; all languages and all subjects.
Requirements: Experienced native translators only. Send resume.

ABLE AMERICA NETWORK, 10010 Broadway, Suite 805, San Antonio, TX 78217.
Positions: This network is a new nonprofit organization providing contract work to home workers that are mentally or physically disabled, economically distressed, and "anyone in need of our help". Jobs include word processing, telemarketing/research, and bulk mail services. Inquires are welcome from all 50 states as the network has national contracts.

ACADEMIE LANGUAGE CENTER, 8032 West Third, Los Angeles, CA 90048.
Positions: Foreign language translations of documents.
Requirements: Certification required. Local residents only. Apply with resume.

ACCURAPID TRANSLATION SERVICES, INC., 806 Main Street, Poughkeepsie, NY 12603.
Positions: Technical translators in all languages. Company specializes in business, engineering and scientific documents.
Requirements: Thorough knowledge of foreign language and English is required. Must also have experience in one of the three specialties. For translators outside the area, a computer and modem is preferred. Submit resume noting areas of technical expertise and type of computer and telecommunicatons equipment.
Provisions: Pays by the word on most contracts.

ACTION TRANSLATION & INTERPRETATION BUREAU, 7825 West 101st, Palos Hills, IL 60465.
Positions: Foreign language translators work in all languages and subjects.
Requirements: Thorough knowledge of both foreign language and English is required. Some particular of expertise is also necessary. Residents on Northern Illinois only. Submit resume and references.

ACTIVE TRANSLATION BUREAU, 1472 Broadway, Suite 306, New York, NY 10036.
Positions: This is a very old translation bureau that handles all languages and all subjects. Native language translators handle literary, chemical, electronics, commercial, medical, legal, technical and industrial documents.
Requirements: Must be native language translator. Minimum five years professional translating experience required. Submit resume with references.
Provisions: Pay rates vary with different projects.

AD-EX TRANSLATIONS INTERNATIONAL/USA, 525 Middlefield Road, Suite 150, Menlo Park, CA 94025.
Positions: Translators and some technical writers for translation of technical, sales, and legal documents, as well as literature, into any major language, or from other language into English. Word processors and typesetters also used, but only those with foreign language expertise. Work is sent via the U.S. mail, Federal Express, or telecopiers.
Requirements: Expertise in any technical field is #1 priority. Knowledge of foreign language is secondary, but must be thorough. Need typewriter or word processor.

Provisions: Payment methods varies. 90% of staff works at home. Average 10 to 40 workers a day.

ADVANCE LANGUAGE SERVICE, 333 North Michigan Avenue, Suite 3200, Chicago, IL 60601.
Positions: Translators and typesetters with foreign language expertise work in all languages and subjects.
Requirements: Experienced local translators only. Submit resume and references.

ADVANCED INTERNATIONAL TRANSLATION, 150 Broadway, New York, NY 10038.
Positions: Translation from and into all languages. This bureau handles a wide array of subjects: financial, legal, engineering, electronics, medical, literary, technical, advertising, and others. Translators that are also technical writers are especially desirable.
Requirements: Thorough knowledge of foreign language and English is required. Experience working in one of the areas mentioned above should also be noted on resume. Prefers New York residents.
Provisions: Pays by the word on most projects.

AF TRANSLATIONS, 324 North Francisca, Redondo Beach, CA 90278.
Positions: Foreign language translation of general and technical documents. All major languages.
Requirements: Prefers to work with Southern California translators. Experience required. Apply with resume and references.

A I C I, 9911 Inglewood Avenue, Ingleweed, CA 90301.
Positions: Freelance technical translators work at home for this translation service bureau.
Requirements: Must be able to work from and into English with French, German, Italian, Spanish, or Japanese. Will consider experienced translators only. Prefers computer users; any type. Apply with resume and references. Can live anywhere.
Provisions: Pays by the word.

ALLIED INTERPRETING & TRANSLATING SERVICE, 7471 Melrose Avenue, Los Angeles, CA 90046.
Positions: Foreign language translation of legal and medical documents. All languages.
Requirements: Certification required. Los Angeles residents only. Apply with resume.

ALL-LANGUAGE SERVICES, INC., 545 Fifth Avenue, New York, NY 10017.
Positions: Translators handle legal, technical, financial, medical and engineering documents.
Requirements: Prefers native language translators. Prefers New York residents because some projects require coming into headquarters. Resume and references required.
Provisions: Pay methods vary according to assignment.

ALL-WORLD LANGUAGE TRANSLATIONS, 8665 Wilshire Boulevard, Suite 309, Beverly Hill, CA 90211.
Positions: Translators handle legal, technical, scientific, and sales documents from and into most foreign languages.
Requirements: Must live in California. Thorough knowledge of foreign language and

English is required. Experience is necessary. Submit resume.
Provisions: Usually pays by the word.

ALPHA GAMA, 1 Scripp Drive, Suite 303, Sacramento, CA 95825.
Positions: Medical Transcribers.
Requirements: CMT or qualified acute care experience is necessary. Must reside within the delivery area.
Provisions: Full-time or part-time work available. Pick up and delivery of supplies and finished work is available from Roseville to West Sacramento. Pays for production.

ALTRUSA LANGUAGE BANK OF CHICAGO, 25 East Washington Street, Chicago, IL 60602.
Positions: Foreign language translators. All languages; all subjects.
Requirements: Prefers native language Translators will accept certificaton instead. Submit resume and references.

AM-PM TRANSCRIPTIONS, 1030 North State Street, Chicago, IL 60611.
Positions: Transcribing of tapes from focus groups, round table discussion, etc.
Requirements: Minimum two years experience transcribing. Good keyboard skills required. Must live nearby.
Provisions: Provides word processors. Pays $1 to $2 per page depending on the project. (Workers average 15 to 18 pages per hour.) Currently has 10 transcribers.

ASSOCIATED TRANSCRIPTS, 5251 Index Street, Granada Hills, CA 91344.
Positions: Independent medical transcribing/typing.
Requirements: Experience in medical transcribing is required. Must be able to prove a working knowledge of general medical terminology. Must type at least 65 wpm accurately. Also need transcribing equipment that uses either standard or micro-cassettes. Pick up and delivery required.
Provisions: Pays piece rates.

ASSOCIATED TRANSLATORS INTERNATIONAL, Box 3689, Stanford, CA 94305.
Positions: Translators and interpreters for conferences and court reporting. Also uses proofers. Company deals with all fields of business; high-tech, scientific, industrial, agricultural, manufacturing, legal, finance, and others. Work might include letters of incorporation, computer manuals, literature, or transcripts.
Requirements: "We look for various skills and abilities. Some have no experience, but have good verbal skills. Must be fluent in a foreign language." Most workers own PCs with modems, which are necessary for typesetting jobs. So far, typesetting is done only in Roman alphabet, though some Vietnamese will be added soon. Most workers are hooked up to the major electronic networks.
Provisions: Pay for translators is on a per-word rate, which fluctuates depending on the technicality, quality, length of time needed, and whether there is typesetting involved. Inexperienced workers are usually paid on a per-hour basis, part-time only. Interpreters are paid by the hour. Currently there are 2,000 employees in a nationwide network. Company reports more are "urgently needed."

BBT&T, 8920 Wilshire Boulevard, Suite 404, Los Angeles, CA 90211.
Positions: Medical transcribers.
Requirements: Acute care experience necessary.

A Closer Look: Transcriptions Limited

With over 1,000 home-based medical transcribers associated with 27 offices around the country, Transcriptions Limited may be the largest home work organization in the U.S.

Founder and president Mark Forstein started the company in 1970, he says, "By happy accident." It is by no accident, however, that Transcriptions Limited reached its present level of success.

Forstein says home workers are a tremendous resource in the work force. Aside from the cost savings to employers like himself, he claims home workers are fiercely loyal and supportive of the work-at-home movement and each other.

Some transcribers have been with the company for many years. "These are mostly women who start out with us when they have young children. After the family is older, some of them want to get out of the house and back into the office routine for social contact. These women have been loyal to us and we return the trust by offering them the opportunity to come to work in our offices."

The offices, which are actually a separate business entity, handle any overload that comes up. Since the transcribers are independent contractors, they can refuse work at any time, for any reason. This gives them some latitude (and greatly reduced stress) within the structure which requires a 24-hour turnaround time as a rule.

The company operates on a seven-day week, 24 hours a day. It is managed by key people on a management pyramid.

Inquiries from experienced transcribers are always welcome, but you should be prepared to prove your worth. Experience in acute care would be best and you will be given an extensive test in medical terminology.

The training session lasts only for a few hours—just long enough to get an overview of how things work and what is expected. "We do not offer the luxury of on-the-job training."

If you know your stuff, though, you can make good money. Pay is based on production and varies depending upon the part of the country you are in. In California, average pay is more than $13 an hour and in Chicago, one woman made $60,000 last year.

You will need a typewriter and transcriber, but if you don't own one, Transcriptions Limited will rent it to you at a nominal fee. The same principle applies to pick-up and delivery; it is an option that is available for a small price if you choose. You can also choose the option of working part-time or full-time hours.

These options are the result of Forstein's efforts over the years to comply with any and all aspects of using independent contractors. "Nothing," he says, "has been left to chance."

Provisions: Pick up and delivery available over large area of Los Angeles. Pays piece rates equal to about $12 an hour

BERLITZ TRANSLATION SERVICE, 660 Market Street, San Francisco, CA 94104.
Positions: Berlitz is a huge translation bureau with offices all over the country and in 23 foreign countries as well. Freelance translators in all languages work in all subject areas.
Requirements: Thorough knowledge of foreign language and English required. Only experienced translators are considered. Can live anywhere, but for those not near a Berlitz office, a computer and modem is preferred. Make note of equipment type on resume.
Provisions: Pays by the word.

BERTRAND LANGUAGES, INC., 633 Third Avenue, New York, NY 10017.
Positions: Freelance translators handle engineering, scientific, medical, legal, commercial, financial, and some advertising documents.
Requirements: Prefers native language translators. Must have expertise in one of the areas mentioned above. Translators outside the New York area should have telecommunications capabilities. Submit resume and references.

BUREAU OF OFFICE SERVICES, 3815 North Cicero Avenue, Chicago, IL 60604.
Positions: Typing, transcription and word processing. Currently has 57 home workers.
Requirements: Must own good equipment and have at least three years experience. Must be local resident. Must obtain home worker certificate from the State Department of Labor.

BUFFINGTON'S BUSINESS SERVICES, 2905 West 116th, Inglewood, CA 90303.
Positions: Medical transcribers.
Requirements: Must live in Inglewood area. At least five years medical transcribing experience is required.
Provisions: Pays piece rates.

CALIFORNIA REPORTING, 1049 Dolores Street, #3, San Francisco, CA 94110.
Positions: Transcribers for court reporting firm. Work is part-time only.
Requirements: Experience is required. Must live in San Francisco. Word processor is required. Apply with resume.

CALIFORNIA TYPING EXCHANGE, P.O. Box 3547, Hayward, CA 94540.
Positions: Typists and transcribers for major metropolitan areas of California.
Requirements: Good typing/transcribing skills needed. Must own good typewriter.
Provisions: Pick up and delivery available within certain boundaries. Pays production rates.

CALLAGHAN & COMPANY, 3201 Old Glenview Road, Wilmette, IL 60091.
Positions: Manuscript typing for law book publisher.
Requirements: Must own good typewriter. Good typing skills required. Must be local resident. Must obtain home worker certificate from State Department of Labor.

CCA, INC., International Marketing Communications, 7120 Havenhurst Avenue, #205/208, Van Nuys, CA 91406.
Positions: Technical translators and multilingual editors for computer manuals and data

Steven Green
Owner, Green's Machine

Word processing businesses are popping up everywhere, but the field has a long way to go before reaching the saturation point. So says Steven Green, who operates Green'es Machine with his wife, Joy , from their Milwaukee home.

Steven and Joy have taken their word processing business to an exceptionally high level. Their clients are major corporations which they cultivated over a long period of time. They now have so much business, the work is formed out to 30 independent contractors in the Milwaukee area.

Steven thinks working at home is great, especially if you need a flexible schedule. But he warns about expecting to make a good living if you have inferior skills. "If you're not good enough, you'll fail. In the 'real world' of jobs, you can hide in the bureaucracy. As an independent contractor, you can't hide. You may think because on a typing test you type 90 words a minute, that means you're good. It doesn't. Typing different material from day to day is not the same as practicing a few paragraphs over and over. To make it as an independent word processor, you have to be better than good."

On the other hand, Steven says that at home, without the office rituals and distractions, you'll find you can accomplish in three hours the same work that used to take you eight hours. The other three hours (not to mention commuting time) can be spent any way you wish.

---

sheets.

Requirements: Must be highly experienced. Must own computer and modem. IBM compatible preferred; Macintosh okay. In general, Americans are used only for proofing and quality control work. Translators are usually native. Must be professionals, usually degreed. Being able to speak/write in a foreign language is not enough; technical expertise in a particular industry is an absolute must. Time deadlines are critical.

Provisions: Work is transfered nationwide via telecommunications or, in some cases, using Federal Express. Freelance and retainer positions are available. Freelancers are paid on a per-word basis. "A good freelancer can make $50,000 a year.." Translators in all languages are invited to send resume with references.

CERTIFIED TRANSLATION BUREAU, INC., 6218 Pacific Boulevard, Huntington Park, CA 90255.

Positions: Foreign language translators for all subjects.

Requirements: Experienced translators only; any language. Apply with resume and references.

CHILTON CORPPORATION, Mortgage Credit Reporting, 6 St. James Avenue,

Boston, MA 02116.
Positions: Auditing of mortgage credit applications.
Requirements: Must be experienced and local.
Provisions: Pick up and delivery provided daily. Pays $5 an hour.

COMMUNICATION ARTS INTERNATIONAL, 55 East 43rd Street, New York, NY 10017.
Positions: Freelance translators work in all languages and handle technical translations; commercial documentation; medical, legal, engineering and literary translating and editing; advertising and public relations projects; and international financial documemntation.
Requirements: Must be very experienced; a proven professional. Resume and references are required.
Provisions: Pay methods vary.

CONTINENTAL TRANSLATION SERVICE, INC., 6 East 43rd Street, Suite 2100, New York, NY 10017.
Positions: Freelance translators handle technical manuals, legal documentation, marketing projects, and medical transcription in most foreign languages.
Requirements: Thorough knowledge of foreign language and English required. Must have expertise in one of the areas mentioned above. Submit resume. Prefers New York residents.
Provisions: Pay methods vary.

DAVID C. COOK PUBLISHING COMPANY, 850 North Grove Avenue, Elgin, IL 60120.
Positions: Manuscript typing.
Requirements: Must own good typewriter and have good skills. Must be local resident. Must obtain home worker certificate from State Department of Labor.

COSMOPOLITAN TRANSLATION BUREAU, INC., 116 South Michigan Avenue, Chicago, IL 60603.
Positions: Cosmopolitan is a very old translation bureau that handles all languages and subjects.
Requirements: Native translators are preferred, but will consider translators with absolute knowledge of a foreign language and good English skills. Must have a particular area of expertise for the terminology of that field (such as legal or medical). Chicago translators only. Submit resume and references.

DICKINSON PRODATA INC., 67 Federal Avenue, Boston, MA 02169.
Positions: Typing names and addresses on letters designed and printed by Dickinson.
Requirements: Must come from referral and be local resident.
Provisions: Typewriter is provided. Pays hourly rate of $4.

DIRECT MERCHANDISING SERVICES, INC., 1865 Miner Street, Des Plaines, IL 60016.
Positions: Collating and envelope stuffing of printed materials involved in the business of direct mail. The home worker pool is decreasing here: currently has 10.
Requirements: Must be local resident. Must obtain home worker certificate from the State Department of Labor.

DUN & BRADSTREET, 99 Church Street, New York, NY 10007.
Positions: Commercial reporters.
Requirements: Work is available only to home-based freelancers in towns with less than 75,000 population. Strong verbal and written communication skills are required.
Provisions: Pays by the report.

EURAMERICA TRANSLATIONS, INC., 516 Fifth Avenue, 9th Floor, New York, NY 10036.
Positions: Freelance translators work in all languages on straight documentation, typesetting and audio-visual services. Especially needs translators with knowledge of automotive, high-tech, medical, financial, legal, or promotional material. Assignments are given on-line only.
Requirements: Thorough knowledge of foreign language "equal to a native" is required. A computer, modem and FAX is required for transmitting work. Submit resume and references. Note any special areas of expertise.
Provisons: Pays by the word.

EXCELLENCE TRANSLATION SERVICE, P.O. Box 5863, Presidio of Monterey, Monterey, CA 93940.
Positions: Foreign language translators for general and technical documentation. All languages.
Requirements: Thorough knowledge of foreign language and English required. Can live anywhere in California. Submit resume and references.

FEDERATION OF THE HANDICAPPED, 211 West 14th Street, 2nd Floor, New York, NY 10011.
Positions: The Federation operates the Home Employment Program (HEP) for home-bound disabled workers only. Within HEP there is a typing/transcription department.
Requirements: All positions here require evaluation through lengthy interviews and personal counseling. All workers must live in New York City.
Provisions: The workshop provides training plus any extra help necessary to overcome any unusual problems an individual might have. Pick up and delivery of supplies and finished work is provided regularly. Necessary equipment is provided. Pays piece rates. Disability insurance counseling is provided.

GLOBAL LANGUAGE SERVICES, 2027 Las Lunas, Pasadena, Ca 91108.
Positions: Foreign language translators of general and technical documents. All languages.
Requirements: Prefers native language translators, but will consider certified translators. Some special area of expertise is required. Submit resume.

GLOBALINK, 2911 Hunter Mill Road, Suite 201, Oakton, VA 22124.
Positions: Foreign language translators for general and technical documents. All languages.
Requirements: Thorough knowledge of foreign language and good English skills are required. Computer and modem is also required. All work is transferred via electronic mail and FAX. Submit resume along with equipment details. Can live anywhere.

GREEN'S MACHINE, 2031 North HiMount, Milwaukee, WI 53208.
Positions: Medical transcription, word processing, legal transcription, database development, and other typing." We put forward a professional image on behalf of the

independent contractors who would otherwise not be able to attract the top corporate clients we have." Currently has 30 home workers.
Requirements: Must live in Milwaukee. Typing skills are needed; accuracy is most important. Must have good typewriter. Workers must own good typewriters. Workers must pick up and deliver their own work.
Provisions: Pays production rate equal to a minimum of $10 an hour.

ARLEAN GUERRERO'S MEDICAL TRANSCRIPTION, 4606 Meridian Avenue, San Jose, CA 95118.
Positions: Medical transcribers.
Requirements: Must live in San Jose. Hospital medical records experience is required.

HELEN'S LEGAL SUPPORT, 601 West Fifth, Los Angeles, CA 90071.
Positions: Legal transcribers handle overflow work only.

Requirements: Must own good equipment, have several years of legal transcribing experience, and references. Los Angeles residents only.
Provisions: Pay methods vary, but usually pays by the page.

HOGARD BUSINESS SERVICES, INC., 462 South Schuyler Avenue, Bradley, IL 60915.
Positions: Typing and other clerical work involving direct mail services. Currently has 26 home workers.
Requirements: Must be local resident. Good typewriter and typing skills are important. Must obtain a home worker certificate from the State Department of Labor.
Provisions: Pays piece rates.

HOMEWORK COMPANY, 10210 NE 8th, Bellevue, WA 98004.
Positions: Policy typing, transcription, insurance rating and collating. Homework Company is a 35 year old company with 37 ofices west of the Mississippi. Currently has about 800 home workers.
Requirements: Workers are independent contractors and must supply own equipment for particular jobs; typewriter, transcription equipment, or calculator. Insurance raters need three years experience. Typists must be accurate.
Provisions: Training is provided. Choice of part-time or full-time. Pays piece rates for typing and transcribing. Pays hourly rate for insurance rating and collating.

HOOPER-HOLMES BUREAX, Box 428, Basking Ridge, NJ 07920.
Positions: Commercial reporters. Work consists of gathering information over the phone from businesses, usually for insurance company clients, then writing up the information in a narrative-style report. Company has 100 offices nationwide. Some use homeworkers, some do not. "In rural areas, it's common to have public servants like firemen and policemen do this to supplement their incomes. In this case, there may not even be an office."
Requirements: Excellent verbal and written communication skills required. Typewriter is needed.
Provisions: Training is provided. Workers are independent contractors and are paid per report.

INDEX RESEARCH SERVICES, P.O. Box 3201, San Mateo, CA 94403.
Positions: Typing of reports from insurance adjusters after they have performed property inspections. Currently has over 15 home workers working from the company's three offices in San Mateo and Sacramento.
Requirements: Must have good typewriter and type at least 65 wpm. Must live near one of the three offices.
Provisions: Any extras such as transcription machines or supplies are provided. Work is part-time only. Workers are independent contractors and are paid on a per report basis with a guarantee of $5 to $6 an hour.

INLINGUA TRANSLATION SERVICE, 690 Market Street, Suite 700, San Francisco, CA 94104.
Positions: Inlingua is a major translation bureau with more than 200 offices all over the world. Freelance translators handle legal, business, and medical documentation in all languages.
Requirements: A thorough knowledge of foreign language and English is required. Submit resume and note special areas of expertise.
Provisions: Pays by the word.

INTER TRANSLATION & INTERPRETING, 1840 North Winona, Los Angeles, CA 90027.
Positions: Foreign language translators for legal and insurance documents. Arabic, Armenian, Italian, Japanese, Russian, and Persian and Turkish languages.
Requirements: Native or certified translators only. Must be Los Angeles resident. Experience in legal and/or insurance field required. Submit resume and references.

INTERNATIONAL DOCUMENTATION, Box 67628, Los Angeles, CA 90067.
Positions: Freelance translators are used by this service bureau.
Requirements: Thorough knowledge of any language for all types of translating; technical writing, medical transcribing, booklets, brochures, etc. Experience is necessary.
Provision: Pays by the word. Work is transferred via modem or conventional methods.

INTERNATIONAL LANGUAGE & COMMUNICATIONS CENTERS, INC., 33 North Dearborn, Chicago, IL 60602.
Positions: Freelance translators handle business documents.
Requirements: Must be expert in a foreign language and English. Experience working with business documents is required. Prefers translators with own computers. Must live in the Chicago area. Submit resume and references.

LEO KANNER ASOCIATES, P.O. Box 5187, Redwood City, CA 94063.
Positions: Freelance translators in all languages work in all subject areas.
Requirements: Must be a West Coast resident. Only professional-level translators will be considered. Apply with resume and references.
Provisions: Pays by the word.

MORTAN KRITZER, M.D., INC., 6221 Wilshire Boulevard, Los Angeles, CA 90048.
Positions: Medical transcribers.
Requirements: Must be very experienced in internal medicine terminology. Must be local. Good typewriter and transcribing machine is necessary.
Provisions: Pick up and delivery of supplies and finished work is provided daily since a 24-hour turn-around is required. Hours are part-time.

LAD TRANSCRIPTIONS, 17772 Irvine Boulevard, Suite 205, Tustin, CA 92680.
Positions: Medical transcribing.
Requirements: Minimum three years experience in basic four reports. Local residents only. Must own good typewriter and transcribing machine.
Provisions: Pays by the line.

THE LANGUAGE LAB, 211 East 43rd Street, New York, NY 10017.
Positions: Freelance translators work in all languages for clients in industry, law firms and government agencies.
Requirements: Only highly experienced professionals are considered. Submit resume and references.

LANGUAGE SERVICE BUREAU, Dupont Circle Building, Washington, D.C. 20036.
Positions: Freelance foreign language translators.
Requirements: Experienced professionals only. Must be nearby resident. Submit resume and references.

LANGUAGES UNLIMITED, 4900 Leesburg Pike, Suite 402, Alexandria, VA 22302.
Positions: Freelance translators work in all languages on documentation for international businesses.
Requirements: Must be very experienced in foreign language translation and in working with business documents such as patents, taxes, or finance.
Submit resume and references.

LIBRARY OF CONGRESS, National Library Service for the Blind and Physically Handicapped, Washington, D.C. 20542.
Positions: Homebound disabled proofreaders in the Braille Development Section.
Provisions: A training program is available to teach blind people to proofread Braille materials. A certificate is awarded upon completion of the program. Work is farmed out to homebound workers from the Library's production department on a piece rate basis. Number of participants varies.

LINDNER TRANSLATIONS, INC., 29 Broadway, Suite 1707, New York, NY 10006.
Positions: Lindner is a 30-year-old translation bureau with freelance translators working in all languages. Areas include legal, medical, technical, chemical, financial, commer-

cial and advertising.

Requirements: Must be proven professional with references. Prefers New York residents.

Provisions: Pays by the word on most assignments.

LINGUAMUNDI INTERNATIONAL, INC., 1483 Chain Bridge Road, McLean, VA 22101.

Positions: Freelance translators; all languages. Company specializes in foreign language typesetting.

Requirements: Must be experienced professional translator with some area of technical expertise. Especially prefers translators with own computer equipment. Submit resume and references.

LINGUAASSIST, 4 DeHart Street, Morristown, NJ 07960.

Positions: LinguaAssist is a translation bureau that offers translation in 60 different languages. Freelancer translators handle technical and legal documentation, typesetting and printing services, and word processing services.

Requirements: Thorough knowledge of foreign language and English is required. Prefers local residents, but does have FAX capabilities for qualified translators outside the area. Submit resume.

Provisions: Pay varies according to project.

LOS ANGELES PROFESSIONAL TYPISTS NETWORK, 6532 Lindenhurst Avenue. Los Angeles, CA 90048.

This network consists of about 70 members, all of whom are home-based typists. Purpose of the Network is to share information on clients and equipment as well as providing a social outlet. Overflow work is often available and almost all members have at least one home worker. "We are all specialists, so when something comes up that doesn't fit within our area of expertise, we pass it on to another member. We have turned competition into cooperation and we all have more work because of it.": Bi-monthly meetings are held in public locations around the greater L.A. area, with different outside speakers each time. Anyone interested is invited to attend. "We go out of our way to get work for those members who need it."

MARKET FACTS, INC., 676 North St. Clair Street, Chicago, IL 60611.

Positions: Coding, keypunch, clerical, and statistical tabulation relating to market research work. Currently has 94 home workers.

Requirements: Must be local resident. Must obtain home worker certificate from State Department of Labor.

Provisions: Pay varies according to job functions.

MASS INSURANCE CONSULTANTS & ADMINISTRATORS, INC., 55 East Jackson, 8th Floor, Chicago, IL 60604.

Positions: Clerical work concerned with the handling of insurance claims.

Requirements: Must be local resident. Experience working in claims administration preferred. Must obtain a home worker certificate from State Department of Labor.

MCGINLEY PROCESS SERVICE, 5922 SW 29th Street, Miami, FL 33155.

Positions: Certified process servers. Company is setting up a nationwide network of process servers and related services.

Requirements: Certification is necessary where required by law. PC and modem are necessary. Send letter of interest.
Provisions: Can be located anywhere in U.S.

MECHANICAL SECRETARY, 1220 Broadway, New York, NY 10001.
Positions: Typists and transcribers. Work covers several areas: medical, legal, insurance, advertising and general business. Currently has 15 home workers.
Requirements: Must have good typing skills and own approved equipment. Experience is required. Send letter of interest. Must be resident of Manhattan, Brooklyn, or Queens.
Provisions: Pick up and delivery of supplies and finished work is provided. Pays production rates.

MEDICALLY SPEAKING, 6363 Wilshire Boulevard, Suite 412, Los Angeles, CA 90048.
Positions: Medical transcribers.
Requirements: Hospital transcribing experience is required. Must have good type-writer and transcribing machine. Must be local resident.
Provisions: Offers choice of part-time or full-time hours. Pays piece rates.

MEDI-TRANS, 236 West Portal, Suite 328, San Francisco, CA 94127.
Positions: Medical transcribers handle all types of work: medical and legal reports regarding personal injury, compensation, EMT, psychiatry, orthopedics, neurosurgery, etc.
Requirements: Must live in San Francisco. Must pick up work, preferably daily. Experience is required along with strong medical terminology. "You must know your anatomy and physiology. Fast typing is required along with your own equipment. Prefers computers to typewriters. Most tapes are micro cassettes; need a cassette system.
Provisions: Pays $2.50 per single space page. "Good transcribers type about seven pages per hour."

MODERN SECRETARIAL SERVICE, 2813 South La Cienega Avenue, Los Angeles, CA 90034.
Positions: Typists and word processors. Company specializes in insurance policy typing, but does all types of legal and general work. "We're always looking for good people."
Requirements: Must have good equipment and skills. Test will be given. Los Angeles residents only.

NATIONAL PROTECTION SYSTEMS, Division of National List, 16 Buyson Place, Irvington, NJ 07039.
Positions: Monitor agents are set up as "decoys" to detect unauthorized use of rented mailing lists. Currently has 44 agents around the country. "Some of our people have been with us for 15 years. If you apply, be prepared to be put on a waiting list."
Provisions: Pays flat fee of $50 a month to return all mail pieces to the company. (There are 100s, up to 1,000 pieces of mail in any given month.)

THE OFFICE CONNECTION, INC./NORTHWEST POLICY TYPING, 209 Dayton Avenue, Suite 103, Edmonds, WA 98020.
Positions: Insurance policy typists and legal transcribers. Workers are independent contractors. Currently has about 100 home workers.
Requirements: Good typing skills are required. Accuracy is much more important than

speed. 24-hour turn-around time is required with a five-day work week. Must own good typewriter. Apply with a typed letter of interest.

Provisions: Training is provided. The initial training sesssion lasts about a week in the company facilities; minimum wage is paid for training time. Pick up and delivery is provided daily. Semi-regular meeting are required to discuss changes in methods, new contracts, etc. Meeting time pays minimum wage plus car allowance. Pay for work is both by the hour for handling and by the piece for typing. Different rates are set for each type of form. "Our top typists average $15 an hour." Pays once a month. Work is available only in the Seattle area.

> "We have lots of work coming up. In addition to our established line, we are open to any new ideas."
> —Rocking Horse

OMNILINGUA, INC., Account Services Department, 150 First Avenue, N.E., Cedar Rapids, IA 52401.

Positions: Native-speaking translators for work in many different fields. All languages are eligible.

Requirements: Expertise in any area of business is necessary.

Provisions: Can live anywhere. Pay methods vary. Inquiries are welcome from qualified translators.

PAPERWORKS, 816 South Illinois, Carbondale, IL 62901.

Positions: Typing of general business forms and correspondence.

Requirements: Must be local resident. Experience is required. Must own approved typewriter. All typists are given a two-hour typing test.

Provisions: Pays piece rates.

PARADISE MAILING, INC., 607 Harbor View Boulevard, Somerset, MA 02725.

Positions: Typing addresses on envelopes and flyers for direct mail processing.

Requirements: Good typing skills and typewriter are required. Must be local resident.

Provisions: Pays minimum wage.

THE PAUL REVERE LIFE INSURANCE COMPANY, 18 Chestnut Street, Worcester, MA 01608.

Positions: Address typing, labeling, and envelope stuffing for direct mail projects.

Requirements: Work is available only from this office, not from other Paul Revere offices around the country. Must be local resident.

Provisions: Pays piece rates equal to about $5 an hour.

PETERS SHORTHAND REPORTING CORPORATION, 3433 American River Drive, Suite A, Sacramento, CA 95825.

Positions: Court reporting and transcribing.

Requirements: Must be local resident. Some travel is required. Experience is necessary.

Provisions: Pays hourly, plus piece rates, plus expenses.

PHYSICIANS MEDICAL TRANSCRIBING, Chatsworth, CA (818) 938-1553.
Positions: Medical transcribers.
Requirements: Must live in or near the San Fernando Valley. Experience is required in acute care.
Provisions: Part-time hours only. Pays piece rates.

> "The whole idea of not wanting to lock a bunch of people up in a factory anymore . . . that's what we're all about"
> --Martin Paul, Cofounder, DEVA

PORTER & ASSOCIATES, 3120 Preston Highway, Louisville, KY 40213.
Positions: Translators; Japanese and Korean natives only.
Provisions: Offers freelance assignments only; pays by the assignment.

PRN TRANSCRIPTIONS, 6177 North Sauganash Avenue, Chicago, IL 60646.
Positions: Medical transcribers. (Pays per line rate.)
Requirements: Two years experience is required. Strong knowledge of general medical terminology is important. 20% of client doctors are Chinese, Korean, or Philippino; therefore, any experience with those languages is a plus. Must live on northwest side of Chicago. Good typewriter and transcribing machine with standard cassettes is required.

REESE PRECISION TRANSCRIBING, 9061 Keith Avenue, Suite 306, Los Angeles, CA 90069.
Positions: Medical transcribers; part-time only.
Requirements: Experience and an understanding of general medical terminology is required. Must own good typewriter and transcribing machine that takes regular size cassette tapes. Should live near West Hollywood in order to pick up and deliver work.
Provisions: Independent contractor status; pays by the line.

REMOTE CONTROL, P.O. Box 2861, Del Mar, CA 92014.
Positions: User support reps for computer software firm. Software package, "Telemagic" is a telemarketing package.
Requirements: Must own IBM PC or compatible.
Provisions: Training is provided. Company is expanding into all areas of the country so your name will be kept on file until your area opens up. Choice of part-time or full-time hours. Home workers are consultants and are paid hourly rates.

RSI, P.O. Box 5510, San Mateo, CA 94402.
Positions: Insurance inspectors/investigators. Independent contractors only.
Requirements: Extensive experience is required. Send resume. Must live in one of the Bay area counties.

SACRAMENTO PROFESSIONAL TYPISTS NETWORK, 9113 Sherrilee Way, Orangevale, CA 95662.
The Network got its start as the original chapter of Peggy Glenn's national home typing group. After the national group disbanded, the Sacramento Network continued as a

support group, then eventually formed an organization with bylaws and regular meetings which are held on the second Thursday of each month. Members are professional home-based typists and word processors. Members refer clients and work to other members when there is overflow, rush jobs, jobs that are too big to handle, and in cases of illness or vacations. Often, one member will bid on a large job and then enlist the help of other members to do the job. "This is our lifestyle; it's called freedom," says chairwoman Janice Katz. Currently has 50 members. Inquiries and new members are welcome.
Requirements: Only residents of Sacramento can participate. Annual dues are $25.

SKRUDLAND PHOTO SERVICE, INC., 1720 Rand Road, Palatine, IL 60074.
Positions: Typing, stuffing envelopes, and other clerical operations.
Requirements: Must be local resident. Must obtain home worker certificate from the State Department of Labor.

SECRETEAM, 455 Sherman, Denver, CO 80203.
Positions: Secretarial work mostly consisting of general transcription.
Requirements: Must be local resident. Must own good typewriter and transcribing equipment.
Provisions: Pick up and delivery of work is provided. Since this is a service bureau, all home workers are independent contractors. Pays by the line or by the page depending on the job, but either way it is a 50/50 split of whatever is charged to the client. This is a new company and there is a waiting list already.

SH3, INC., 408 West 83rd Terrace, Kansas City, MO 64114.
Positions: Freelance translators for this service bureau.
Requirements: Thorough knowledge of French, German, Italian, or Spanish. You must be experienced and able to provide telecommunications, IBM PC (or compatible) disks, or CPM disks. Send resume.

SPAULDING COMPANY, 660 Summer Street, Boston, MA 92210
Positions: Typing of reports, listings, and directories.
Requirements: Good typing skills are necessary. Must be local resident.
Provisions: Typewriter is provided. Pays $5.50 an hour.

TIM SWEENEY & ASSOCIATES, 101 California Street, Suite 300, San Francisco, CA 94111.
Positions: Tim Sweeney is a stock broker who conducts financial seminars around the Bay area. He uses home workers for bulk mail processing projects.
Requirements: Must live in San Francisco. Must be dependable for steady, part-time work. Work involves picking up supplies such as mailing labels, brochures, and envelopes, taking them home and stuffing them, then returning them for postage metering (they will be mailed from the office).
Provisions: Pays cash daily, $.03 or $.05 per envelope depending on the particular job.

TECHNICAL WRITING AND TRANSLATING ASSOCIATES, 5356 North Bernard, Chicago, IL 60625.
Positions: Foreign language translators work as technical writers and editors in all languages.
Requirements: Thorough knowledge of foreign language and excellent English skills are essential. Technical writing experience is required. Prefers to work with Northern Illinois residents. Submit resume and references.

THUDIUM MAIL ADVERTISING COMPANY, 3553 North Milwaukee, Chicago, IL 60641.
Positions: Typing, labeling, inserting and other clerical operations involved in letter shop work. Currently has 38 home workers.
Requirements: Must be local resident. Must obtain home worker certificate from State Department of Labor.

TRANSET GRAPHICS, 520 North Michigan, Chicago, IL 60611.
Positions: Foreign langauge translators. Company specializes in graphic arts and typesetting services.
Requirements: Absolute knowledge of foreign language and English is required. Experience in typesetting industry also preferred. Will only consider translators with own computers and modems. Submit resume and references.

TRANSCRIPTIONS LIMITED, 15 Henry Avenue, Feasterville, PA 19047.
Positions: Medical transcribers for hospital overflow work; discharge summaries and operative reports. Currently has over 1,000 home workers and 30 offices nationwide, including Los Angeles, San Francisco, Sacramento, Denver, and Chicago.
Requirements: Acute care experience is required. A test in medical terminology is given to all applicants.
Provisions: Choice of part-time or full-time hours is available. Equipment is provided on a rental basis if necessary. Daily pick up and delivery of supplies and finished work is provided. Pays production rates that vary depending on the part of the country where you're located. Average hourly pay is about $13 and hour. Inquiries are always welcome from qualified transcribers.

TRANSLATING ASSOCIATES, 104 East 40th , New York, NY 10016.
Positions: Freelance translators work on assignments in all subject areas.
Requirements: Must be New York resident. Only highly professional translators with verifiable references will be considered. Prefers translators with writing and editing experience.
Provisions: Pays by the word.

TRANSLATION COMPANY OF AMERICA, INC., 10 West 37th, New York, NY 10018.
Positions: Translators, interpreters, and typesetters.
Requirements: Prefers native language translators. Must own typewriter or word processor. Expertise in a particular area of business is required. Send resume and references.
Provisions: Pays by the word.

TRANS-LINGUAL COMMUNICATIONS, INC., 8 South Michigan Avenue, Suite 1200, Chicago, IL 60603.
Positions: Foreign language translators work in all subject areas. Company specializes in software and technical manual translation.
Requirements: Minimum five years verifiable experience as a professional translator is required. Must have own technical background. Prefers translators with own computer equipment. Can live anywhere.
Provisions: Pays by the word.

TRANS-LINK, 1850 Gaugh, Suite 701, San Francisco, CA 94109.

Positions: Translators in 55 different foreign languages handle freelance assignments in technical translation, international advertising and audio-visual dubbing.
Requirements: Absolute knowledge of foreign language and English is required. Must be West Coast resident, preferably California. Resume and references required. Note area of technical expertise.
Provisions: Pay methods very according to type of work.

TYPE-A-LINE, INC., 311 Woods Avenue, Oceanside, NY 11572.
Positions: Typing of labels, cards, envelopes, and some inserting for direct mail fulfillment company. Some OCR typing on computers also. Currently has 17 home workers.
Requirements: Typewriter and good typing skills are required. Must be local to either Oceanside or Brentwood in order to pick up and deliver supplies and finished work.
Provisions: Training is provided. If necessary and nearby, company will provide pick up and delivery services. Pays piece rates equal to about $5 an hour. "New York State is tough on home workers. The State demands 'good' reasons for being allowed to work at home. I'd like to hire more home workers, but unless you meet the requirements, I can't."

TYPE-A-SCAN, INC., 1358 Rockaway Parkway, Brooklyn, NY 11236.
Positions: Various kinds of typing in the mailing list industry, mostly involving address labels. Typing is converted to disk by use of an optical scanner in-house.
Requirements: Reliability is very important here. Typing speed of 60 wpm with a low error rate is required. Workers must pick up and deliver their own supplies and finished work. Currently has "many" home workers throughout Long Island, New York City and part of New Jersey.
Provisions: Pays piece rates. Company provides IBM Selectric typewriters. Training is provided. "We are unique in our methods. We are always looking for new people."

THE TYPING COMPANY, 129 E Street, Suite C-2, Davis, CA 95616.
Positions: Typists and transcribers. Most work is academic; term papers, theses, dissertatons, application forms, tables, and grants. Now expanding into medical transcribing.
Requirements: Must have good typewriter and excellent skills. Davis residents only. Home workers pick up and deliver own supplies and finished work whenever they want during the day.
Provisions: Some training is provided. Pays 60% of the fee paid to the company. The best typist earns up to $12 an hour.

BETTY VAN KEULEN, 1817 Kirklyn Drive, San Jose, CA 95124.
Positions: Medical transcribers.
Requirements: Hospital transcribing experience is required. Must be local resident in order to pick up and deliver supplies and finished work. A good typewriter is necessary.
Provisions: If a transcriber isn't available, company will lease a transcriber at half price. Pays by the line.

VERNA MEDICAL TRANSCRIPTIONS, 156 Smithwood Avenue, Milpitas, CA 95035.
Positions: Medical transcribers for all types of medical records.

Requirements: Experience is necessary. Must own good typewriter and transcribing machine with either standard or microcassettes. Must be local resident in order to pick up and deliver supplies and finished work.
Provisions: Pays piece rates. Part-time or full-time work is available.

WCC, 40 Skokie Boulevard, Northbrook, IL 60062.
Positions: Translators for computer-aided technical translation into all major languages.
Requirements: Thorough knowledge of both English and foreign language. Some word processing experience. Apply with resume and references. Prefers local people.

THE WORD SHOP, Equitable Building, 3435 Wilshire Boulevard, Lower Plaza #111, Los Angeles, CA
Positions: The Work Shop is a word processing service bureau that handles legal, insurance, advertising, transcribing, and mailing list work. Overflow work is available not just to word processors, but to skilled typists.
Requirements: Must have own equipment; IBM only. Experience and references are required.

WORKERS UNLIMITED, 59 Barefoot Hill Road, Sharon, MA 02067.
Positions: Typing for direct mail fulfillment center. Company is home-based.
Requirements: Must be experienced and own typewriter. Must be local resident in order to pick up and deliver supplies and finished work.
Provisions: Pays piece rates equal to $5 an hour.

WORLD WIDE, 9510 West Jefferson Boulevard, West Culver City, CA 90230.
Positions: Medical transcribers for home work out of three Los Angeles offices. Currently has over 100 home workers.
Requirements: Must have experience and knowledge of medical terminology. Work will be for hospitals, clinics, doctors, and government. Must have good typewriter and transcribing machine. Los Angeles residents only.
Provisions: Specific training is provided. Pick up and delivery of supplies and finished work will be provided if necessary. Pays piece rates equal to about $12 an hour. Part-time or full-time hours available. Inquiries are welcome.

WORLDWIDE TRANSLATION AGENCY, 1680 North Vine, Suite 610, Hollywood, CA 90028.
Positions: Foreign language translators work on a wide variety of documents.
Requirements: Los Angeles residents only. Must be experienced professional translator with resume and references.
Provisions: Pays by the word.

A Closer Look
The Linton Factor

The Linton Factor, Inc. considers itself the "leader in telecommuting employment contracts," and it is the first telecommuting company to go commercial in this way.

Founder and president Robert Linton left his career as a stock broker in late summer 1985 to start a company comprised solely of highly qualified, home-based telecommuters. So far, over 100 home workers are providing customer service, telemarketing, data entry, and bookkeeping services to client companies and government entities under contract.

Linton says he wants his firm to achieve a national reputation for excellence and spearhead a trend toward respectability for home workers.

The original company structure was developed by Electronic Services Unlimited, the New York based telecommuting consulting firm that has set up corporate work programs all over the country. A board of advisors was organized to provide ongoing expertise where needed. Among the members are Lynda Anapol, director of the telecommuting department at Pac Bell and Pat Green, who planned the successful J.C. Penney home telemarketing program.

Perhaps the most interesting staff member, however, is Glenn Gloss, a clinical psychologist. Goss has developed a pre-employment screening process to determine who is psychologically capable of working in an isolated, self-managed situation. After joining the company, all workers are monitored at least once a month by taking the "Happy Telecommuter Checkup."

We are very concerned about our workers," says Linton. "For instance, we don't allow our data entry operators to work more than four hours a day. That's the limit before mental and physical stress begins to take its toll on quality and productivity.

All others are on an eight-hour work schedule which can be maneuvered at the worker's discretion between 6 am and 6 pm.

Though training is provided on a job-by-job basis, at least four years of work experience is required. "I want people who are committed to a career in telecommuting, who can produce quality work, and are self-disciplined."

12,000 keystrokes an hour is the required level for data entry. Telemarketers and customer service reps must be able and willing to obtain strong product knowledge.

In return, workers receive competitive pay rates, company stock, and a group insurance plan. A lease program makes equipment available.

Chapter 7
Opportunities Working With People

In this section you will find jobs that have but one basic requirement—the ability to work with people. Both at-home and from-home jobs are included.

Telephone surveying involves calling consumers to ask specific questions about their buying habits, or more weighty questions of social significance. The names and numbers are supplied and the surveyor is paid for each call. The average pay works out to about $6 an hour. The work is not usually steady; it tends to come and go. This can be good for someone who cannot make a permanent commitment. If you want steady surveying work you should sign up with several companies in order to insure back-to-back assignments.

Customer service is a profession that is just beginning to come into its own. American companies are starting to realize the importance of listening to their customers and trying to satisfy their needs. A customer service representative is basically a problem-solver. The job requires an ability to listen and record customers' comments accurately.

Fund raising can also be an easy job. It doesn't pay as well as surveying, usually only minimum wage plus a small bonus for bringing in so-much in donations. It is, however, very easy work to get and it can be good experience leading to more sophisticated and higher-paying phone work.

Like customer service, staffing coordination is a fairly new opportunity for home workers. This work is found most often in the burgeoning health-care field. Agencies are used to fill the staffing needs of hospitals, nursing homes, and outpatients. Calls come in day and night, but most agencies don't keep their doors open 24 hours a day. After 5:00 on weekdays and on weekends, calls are forwarded to a staffing coordinator's home. It is the coordinator's job to dispatch nurses and home health care workers as they are needed during those hours. Most coordinators have electronic pagers, so they need not be completely homebound.

Field surveying is a job that is custom-made for someone with an outgoing personality. The word "field" indicates that most of the work is done outside-- which may mean in a mall, at a movie theatre, or door-to-door. The surveyor collects answers to survey questions in the field and then returns home to fill out the paperwork. It is perfect for the person that needs the flexibility that working from home offers, but who doesn't want to be stuck inside all the time.

Field surveyors work for market research firms and opinion pollers. They generally work as independent contractors, often working for more than one company at a time because each survey may last from only two days to two weeks on average and being on the roster at a number of companies makes steady work more likely.

ADULT INDEPENDENT DEVELOPMENT CENTER OF SANTA CLARA COUNTY, INC. 1190 Benton, Santa Clara, CA 95050.
Positions: Fund raisers request donations over the phone.
Requirements: Must be reliable and self-managing. Must live within Santa Clara County.
Provisions: Training is provided. Pays salary plus bonuses and fringe benefits.

AIS MARKET RESEARCH, 4955 East Anderson, Suite 134, Fresno, CA 93727.
Positions: Field surveyors in the San Joaquin Valley.
Requirements: Must be resident of either Fresno or Modesto. Market research or similar experience required. Send for application.
Provisions: Work is part-time and sporadic. Pays by the survey.

ALL CITY LOCKSMITHS, 160 Del Vale, San Francisco, CA 94127.
Positions: Customer service/dispatchers for locksmiths. Job consists of answering incoming calls at home and determining whether dispatch is necessary.
Requirements: Need to be friendly, alert, and articulate. Locksmith knowledge is preferred. Company works on a 24-hour a day, seven day a week schedule, with home workers working on shift rotations. Calls are forwarded to workers' homes for duration of each shift period only. Must live in San Francisco.
Provisions: Complete training is provided. Commission paid on successfully concluded calls. Company is expanding.

AMERICAN RED CROSS, 2700 Wilshire Boulevard, Los Angeles, CA 90057.
Positions: Telephone recruiters locate potential blood donors.
Requirements: Two years telemarketing experience required. Must be available Sunday through Thursday. Excellent comunications skills necessary. Los Angeles residents only. Send resume.
Provisions: Pays $4.63 an hour.

AMERICAN TELEMARKETING, INC., 3349 Cahuenga Boulevard West, Suite 5a, Los Angeles, CA 90068.
Positions: Market research is conducted solely over the phone. Part-time hours only. Work is available in most major metropolitan areas.
Requirements: Market research experience is preferred, but not required.
Provisions: Pays about $8 an hour.

AMVETS, 1111 Prospect, Indianapolis, IN 46203.
Positions: Fund raisers call for donations of clothing and household articles.
Requirements: Must live in Indianapolis.
Provisions: Pays hourly wage plus bonus plan.

A-ONE RESEARCH, INC., 2800 Coyle Street, Brooklyn, NY 11235.
Positions: Field surveyers for market research studies.
Requirements: Must be resident of New York City or one of the immediate suburbs. Good communication skills and interviewing experience required.
Provisions: Work is part-time only. Pays by the survey.

ARBITRON RATINGS, INC., 312 Marshall Avenue, Laurel, MD 20707.
Positions: Telephone interviewers and their area coordinators for market research surveys. Surveys are conducted regularly throughout the year in hundreds of cities.

Requirements: Both positions require exceptional communications abilities and private phone lines. Coordinators must have organizational and motivational skills and self-discipline. Send letter of interest.

AREA MARKETING RESEARCH ASSOCIATES, 303 West Capitol Avenue, Little Rock, AR 72201.
Positions: Field surveyors are subcontracted to out-of-state market research firms.
Requirements: Market research experience required. Must be local resident.
Provisions: Work is part-time, on-call. Pays by the survey.

ARTHRITIS FOUNDATION, 203 Willow Street, Suite 201, San Francisco, CA 94109.
Positions: Telephone recruiters find volunteers to go door-to-door for donations. This program repeats every fall and spring for about two months each time.
Requirements: Must live in the Bay area. Experience is not required, but the director says this work is very difficult and may not be suitable for newcomers. Must be available to be on call during the evening hours of 6 to 9:30 pm.
Provisions: Pays $1.50 per recruitment.

LESLIE R. ASHER, 400 Second Avenue, Suite 16b, New York, NY 10010
Positions: Field surveyers and some telephone interviewers for focus group recruiting.
Requirements: Work is only assigned to residents of metropolitan New York, Long Island, New Jersey, and Westchester County. Experience in market research required.

ATLANTA MARKETING RESEARCH CENTER, 3355 Lenox Road, Suite 660, Atlanta, GA 30326.
Positions: Field surveyers and occasionally, telephone interviewers.
Requirements: Atlanta residents only. Experience preferred.
Provisions: Pays by the survey.

AUDITS AND SURVEYS, INC., 1 Park Avenue, New York, NY 10016.
Positions: Field researchers for market research projects. All surveys are conducted in the field.
Requirements: Experience is preferred.
Provisions: Pays by the survey. Company has offices all over the country. Write and ask for the field supervisor nearest you.

FRANCES BAUMAN ASSOCIATES, 23 Girard Street, Marlboro, NJ 07746.
Positions: Field surveyers and telephone interviewers for market research assignments.
Requirements: Must live in tri-state area of New York, New Jersey, or Pennsylvania. Experience required.
Provisions: Work is part-time on-call only. Pays by the survey.

BLIND & HANDICAPPED, P.O. Box 23771, Oakland, CA 94623.
Positions: Telemarketing of household products for fund raising.
Requirements: Must live in Northern California.
Provisions: Training is provided. Pays salary or commission.

BURKE INTERNATIONAL RESEARCH CORPPORATION, 420 Lexington Avenue, New York 10001.
Positions: Market researchers for field surveys only.

Requirements: Some experience in market research is required. Will consider workers who have worked with the public in some capacity. The primary requirement is the ability to communicate effectively.
Provisions: Training and supplies are provided. Pays per survey. Write for field supervisor in your area; major urban centers only.

> "We make much more money than other employment counselors . . . up to $1,000 a week."
>
> --Escrow Overload

CALIFORNIA AMVETS, 747 Twelth Avenue, San Diego, CA 92101.
Positions: Fund raisers telephone for donations of household discards to be sold through thrift shops. Also has locations in El Cajon, Fresno, and Oceanside.
Requirements: Must be dependable and have good speaking skills. Must live in local area.
Provisions: Choice of part-time or full-time; hours flexible. Pays guarantee of minimum wage plus bonus plan. Training provided.

CALIFORNIA COUNCIL FOR THE BLIND, 8915 Reseda Boulevard, Northridge, CA 91324.
Positions: Fund raisers telephone for donations of household discards.
Requirements: Must be resident of greater Los Angeles area. Good phone manner necessary.
Provisions: Pays commission plus bonus plan averaging about $4 an hour.

CAMERON MILLS RESEARCH SERVICE, 2414 Cameron Mills Road, Alexandria, VA 22302.
Positions: Field surveyers and telephone interviewers for market research projects.
Requirements: Must live in Washington, D.C., Northern Virginia, or nearby Maryland. Some experience working with the public necessary.
Provisions: Pays by the survey.

CANCER FEDERATION, San Jose, CA. (209)287-3088.
Positions: Telemarketers call for household discards in fundraising effort. Work 5 hours each evening, 5 days a week.
Requirements: Some telemarketing experience is required. Must live in Northern California.
Provisions: Training is provided. Pays guaranteed salary plus bonuses.

CAR-LENE RESEARCH, Deerbrook Mall, Deerfield, IL 60015.
Positions: Field surveyers and telephone interviewers for market research assignments.
Requirements: Must live in Deerfield, IL; Pomona, CA; Santa Fe Springs, CA; Northbrook, IL; Hanover, MA; Dallas, TX; or Richardson, TX. Market research experience is required.
Provisions: Pays by the survey.

CERTIFIED MARKETING SERVICES, INC., Route 9, P.O. Box 447, Kinderhook, NY 12106.
Positions: Field and telephone interviewers for public opinion polls.
Requirements: Good communication skills required. Work outside Albany area is contracted through other market research companies. Write for information.

CHAMBERLAIN MARKET RESEARCH, 3865 Viscount Avenue #11, Memphis, TN 38118.
Positions: Field surveyers.
Requirements: Memphis residents only. Experience required.
Provisions: Pays by the survey.

CHECK II MARKET RESEARCH, 900 Osceola Drive, Suite 207, West Palm Beach, FL 33409.
Positions: Field surveyers.
Requirements: Local residents only. Experience is preferred.
Provisions: Work is part-time only. Pays by the survey.

CHILTON RESEARCH SERVICES, 201 King of Prussia Road, Radnor, PA 19089.
Positions: Market researchers for surveys conducted primarily in the field.
Requirements: Experience is preferred. Must live in one of Chilton's sampling areas. Send letter of interest requesting name and address of field supervisor nearest you.
Provisions: Pays by the job.

CONSUMER OPINION SEARCH, INC., 10795 Watson Road, St. Louis, MO 63127.
Positions: Field surveyers.
Requirements: St. Louis residents only. Good communication skills required
Provisions: Pays by the survey.

CONSUMERS SURVEYS, INC., 3505 North Hart Avenue, Suite 3210, Rosemead, CA 91770.
Positions: Market research by phone.
Requirements: Must be in Los Angeles area.
Provisions: Training is provided. Pays for completed surveys.

CSI TELEMARKETING, 1200 Denton Avenue, New Hyde Park, NY 11040.
Positions: Market research operators using the phone to gather data for surveys. Currently has over 1,000 home workers and expects to expand.
Requirements: Experience is not necessary, but any previous work experience using the phone helps. Must live in one of the survey cities: Los Angeles, San Diego, Dallas, Detroit, Chicago, Boston, Philadelphia, Miami, Albany, New York, and Newark.
Provisions: Training is provided during a one-week session at one of the office locations. Phone costs are reimbursed. Pays by the survey; approximately $1 per completed call. Full-time workers complete several hundred surveys a week, but part-time work is available, too. Incentive bonuses are also given.

DAKOTA INTERVIEWING SERVICE AND MARKET RESEARCH, 16 Vista Drive, Minot, ND 58701.
Positions: Opinion polls are conducted in the field and on the telephone.
Requirements: Local residents only. Good communication skills required. Must be able to follow directions exactly.

Provisions: Work is part-time, on-call only.

DALE SYSTEM, INC., 250 West 57th Street, New York, NY 10019.
Positions: Market research surveys are conducted in the field.
Requirements: Experience in market research is preferred, but other experience dealing with the public could suffice. Need to live in one of the company's sampling areas. Send letter of interest requesting name and address of field supervisor nearest you.
Provisions: Pays per survey.

DAVIS AND DAVIS RESEARCH, INC., 4840 North Armenia Avenue, Suite 2, Tampa, FL 33603.
Positions: Market research surveys are conducted in the field.
Requirements: Must be local resident. Experience required.
Provisions: Must be available for assignments as they come in. Pays by the project.

DAVIS MARKET RESEARCH SERVICES, INC., 23801 Calabasas Road, Calabasas, CA 91302.
Positions: Field surveyers.
Requirements: Local residents only. Previous experience working with the public required.

DC MARKET RESEARCH, INC., 9957 South Roberts Road, Palos Hills, IL 60465.
Positions: Field surveyers and telephone interviewers.
Requirements: Chicago area residents only. Market research experience required.
Provisions: Pays by the survey.

DELAWARE INTERVIEWING SERVICE, 811 Sunset Terrace, Dover, DE 19901.
Positions: Field interviewers for market research surveys. Surveys are conducted in Delaware and nearby parts of Maryland only.
Requirements: Interviewing experience required. Must live in one of the sampling points.

DENNIS RESEARCH SERVICE, INC., 3620 East Paulding Road, Fort Wayne, IN 46816.
Positions: Market research surveys are conducted in Northern Indiana by independent, part-time field surveyors.
Requirements: Must be resident of Fort Wayne or South Bend. No experience is required, but good communication skills are a must.
Provisions: Pays by the survey.

DEPTH RESEARCH LABORATORIES, INC., 1103 Albemarle Road, Brooklyn, NY 11218.
Positions: Field interviewers for various market research and opinion poll surveys. Some are conducted in local area; occasionally some are conducted at designated polling points in other parts of the country.
Requirements: Interviewing experience is required. Send for application.
Provisions: Pays by the survey.

EVELYN DREXLER INTERVIEWING SERVICE, 8807 Bridlewood Drive, Huntsville, AL 35802.
Positions: Market research surveys are conducted by field surveyers and telephone

Close Up: NORC

Founded in 1941, NORC is the oldest survey research organization established for non-commercial purposes. NORC is a not-for-profit organization affiliated with the University of Chicago.

Survey research is the collection of accurate, unbiased information from a carefully chosen sample of individuals.

Some organizations do opinion polls, asking people to rate the performance of public officials, for example. Others do market research, asking about such things as the products people use. NORC does social science research, asking about people's attitudes and behavior in areas of social concern, such as education, housing, employment (and unemployment), and health care.

NORC's clients include the American Cancer Society, Harvard University, the Rockefeller Foundation, the U.S. Dept. of Labor, and the Social Security Administration to name just a few. Nowhere will you find higher standards of quality in research of this kind.

To date, NORC has conducted more than 1,000 surveys. This may not sound like a lot considering the thousands that are conducted for companies like Gallup. Unlike Gallup, though, NORC's surveys are "longitudinal," meaning the same people are surveyed over long periods of time. Over 900 part-time NORC interviewers are located in cities, towns, and rural areas throughout the United States. Many, but not all, are home-based. Each assignment is on a temporary, per-project basis. The average project lasts about 6 months. All interviewers must be available to work at least 20 hours a week. 40 hour weeks are common.

About half of the people working for NORC have been with the company at least 5 years. That's an outstanding record in an industry where rapid employee turnover is the norm. Nevertheless, NORC is constantly seeking more qualified interviewers—especially in hard-to-staff metropolitan areas such as New York, Chicago, Los Angeles and Miami.

Field Director Miriam Clarke says "We look for someone who is people-oriented, outgoing, and somewhat aggressive. Someone who does not like to be tied to a desk is a good candidate actually. Being able to follow instructions precisely is important, too."

An hour and a half of general training is provided at a central location. After that, project briefings are handled by mail and phone.

The pay range depends upon where you live, but the entry level base rate is $4.50 an hour and up, depending upon experience. Any particular qualifications, such as foreign languages, pay extra. Pay raises come once a year and are based on performance.

interviewers in Northern Alabama and Southern Tennessee.
Requirements: Must live in one of the sampling areas. Previous experience is preferred.

DISABLED AMERICAN VETERANS,3355 South Main, Salt Lake City, UT 84115.
Positions: Telemarketers use the phone to ask for donations of household articles.
Requirements: No experience required. Must live in Salt Lake City.
Provisions: Pays minimum hourly wage plus bonus plan.

DISABLED AMERICAN VETERANS OF COLORADO, 8799 North Washington, Denver, CO 80229.
Positions: Fund raisers call for donations of household discards to be sold through thrift stores.
Requirements: Denver residents only. Must have good phone voice and self-discipline.
Provisions: Training provided. Pays small hourly wage plus bonus plan.

C.B. DUPREE ASSOCIATES, 1552 Salt Springs Road, Syracuse, NY 13214.
Positions: Field surveyers and telephone interviewers conduct market research surveys.
Requirements: Must be local resident. Market research experience required.

EL CAMINO MEMORIAL PARK, 5600 Carol Canyon Road, San Diego, CA 92121.
Positions: Telemarketers conduct surveys over the phone.
Requirements: Experience dealing with the public. Must live in San Diego.
Provisions: Training is provided. Pays salary plus bonus.

ELECTROTEL, 3810 Pierce, Wheat Ridge, CO 80033.
Positions: Phone surveyers work on a variety of projects.
Requirements: Experience is required. Must be self-motivated. Local residents only.
Provisions: Training is provided in office for one week. Pay based on performance.

ESCROW OVERLOAD, 4417 Sarah Street, Burbank, CA 91505.
Positions: Middle managers —i.e., recruiters—are completely home-based. Escrow Overload is a temporary help service operating from San Diego to Ventura, California. All home workers are considered independent managers. All have professional offices set up in their homes complete with waiting rooms for new applicants, WATS lines and file cabinets. On-line computer systems are being added. Work consists of interviewing new job applicants, phoning new accounts, and placing employees.
Provisions: Pays commission. "The down side to working at home is the long hours, since we're responsible for virtually all aspects of the business in our respective areas. The up side is we make much more money than other employment counselors because the company's overhead is so low. We make $2 per hour booked, up to $1000 a week." (The $2 per hour is earned for each temporary placed, so the recruiter earns $80 for a 40 hour placement.)

E-Z INTERVIEWING, P.O. Box 951, Farmington, CT 06032.
Positions: Field surveyers.
Requirements: Local residents only. Must have interviewing experience.

FACTS 'N FIGURES, Panorama Mall, Suite 78B, Panorama City, CA 91402.
Positions: Market research and public opinion surveys are conducted by field surveyers and telephone interviewers.
Requirements: Must be resident of greater Los Angeles. Interviewing experience is

required.
Provisions: Pays by the survey.

FAR WEST RESEARCH, INC., 1315 Twentythird Avenue, San Francisco, CA 94122.
Positions: Market researchers conduct surveys on the telephone at home. Surveys are conducted in major metropolitan areas on the West Coast only.
Requirements: Must have market research experience. Must live in one of the company's sampling areas.
Provisions: Pays by the survey.

FIBRE CLEANING CORPORATON, 999 Central Street, Boston, MA 01760.
Positions: Telemarketers do market research over the phone.
Requirements: Must live in the greater Boston area.
Provisions: Training is provided. Offers choice of part-time or full-time hours. Pays hourly wage of $4.80. Benefits include paid vacations and holidays.

FIELD RESEARCH, INC., 234 Front Street, San Francisco, CA 94111.
Positions: Market research surveys are conducted in the field; mainly in California.
Requirements: Experience is preferred. Must live in one of the sampling areas.
Provisions: Pays by the survey.

GEORGE FINE RESEARCH, INC., 220 North Central Park Avenue, Hartsdale, NY 10530.
Positions: Market research surveys are conducted both in the field and over the phone.
Requirements: Experience is preferred. Must live in one of the company's sampling areas.
Provisions: Pays by the survey.

FOGARTY MARKET RESEARCH, 4828 Ronson Court, Suite C, San Diego, CA 92111.
Positions: Market research by phone only. Work consists of phone interviewing part-time; some is temporary, some is ongoing.
Requirements: Must live in San Diego.

Provisions: Training is provided. Pays by the survey.

GALLUP POLL, Princeton Survey Research Center, P.O. Box 628, Princeton, NJ 08542.
Positions: Market researchers. Gallup has two separate programs. First, within the local area of Princeton, telephone interviewers have the option to come into the Gallup facilities to use the WATS lines or work at home. There are 40 home workers like this in Princeton.

Second, is Gallup's field research. Across the country, there are 360 sampling areas. In this case, market researchers conduct surveys in the field (usually door-to-door), returning home only to do the "paperwork." There are almost 2,000 of these home-based researchers around the U.S. This work is permanent part-time. It is conducted during weekends and/or evenings, approximately 16 hours per month.
Requirements: No experience required and no age restriction for persons over 18. You need only to be able to read well, talk with people and have a dependable car. Send work experience, address and phone number with letter of interest.
Provisions: Training is provided, after which interviewer is tested and graded on sample work before job begins. All workers are independent contractors and are expected to meet minimum quotas. Pays an hourly wage plus expenses. "We're always looking for responsible people, especially full-timers."

GARGAN & ASSOCIATES, P.O. Box 12249, Portland, OR 97212.
Positions: Market research and public opinion surveys are conducted by field surveyors and telephone interviewers.
Requirements: Experience is preferred. Must live in Astoria, Portland, Salem, Albany, Eugene, Bend, Coos Bay, Roseburg, or Medford.
Provisions: Pays by the survey.

L. TUCKER GIBSON AND ASSOCIATES, INC., 6655 First Park Ten, Suite 231, San Antonio, TX 78213.
Positions: Field surveyors and telephone interviewers for market research studies.
Requirements: Must be experienced local resident. Bilingual applicants only.

GIRARD & GIRARD CREATIVE CONCEPTS, 22260 Parthenia Street, Canoga Park, CA 91304.
Positions: Field surveyors and telephone interviewers for market research.
Requirements: Interviewing experience is required. Residents of Los Angeles only.

LUANNE GLAZER ASSOCIATES, INC., 98 Ocean Drive East, Stamford, CT 06902.
Positions: Field surveyors and telephone interviewers for market research.
Requirements: Must be local resident. Excellent communication skills and ability to follow directions explicitly required.
Provisions: Training is provided. Pays by the survey.

RUTH GOLDER INTERVIEWING SERVICE, 1804 Jaybee Road, Wilmington, DE 19803.
Positions: Field interviewers for market research.
Requirements: Interviewing experience required. Must live in Delaware, Chester or Delaware County, Pennsylvania, or Salem County, New Jersey.

AURELIA K. GOLDSMITH MARKETING RESEARCH SERVICES, INC.,
1279 Guelbreath Lane, #204, St. Louis, MO 63146.
Positions: Field surveyors and telephone interviewers.
Requirements: Local residents only. Interviewing experience preferred.

GOOD SHEPHERD HOME FOR MENTALLY RETARDED, Denver, CO
(303)232-7697.
Positions: Telephone fund raisers call for donations of household goods and donations.
Requirements: Denver residents only. Must be dependable and sincere. To apply, you must call; do not write. Must be available to work early mornings and evenings.
Provisions: Training is provided in a 2 hour interview/orientation. Names to call are provided. Pays commission per pick up scheduled, averages $3.50 to $6.50 and hour.

"We go out of our way to get work for those
who need it."
—Los Angeles Professional Typists Network

LOUIS HARRIS AND ASSOCIATES, 630 Fifth Avenue, New York, NY 10020.
Positions: Market researchers and opinion surveyors.
Requirements: No experience is necessary. Louis Harris has "several hundred" sampling areas and it is necessary to live in one of them. Write and ask for an application which will be kept on file. When something comes up, you will be called. If you are ready for work, you will receive your instructions over the phone. How you go about completing the assignment from there is up to you.
Provisions: Pays by the survey, about $10 to $44 per survey.

HARVEY RESEARCH ORGANIZATION, INC., 1400 Temple Building, Rochester, NY 14604.
Positions: Interviewers to work as independent contractors on continuing assignments. Work is available in all major cities. There are 50 to 100 interviewers in each sampling area. Most interviews are conducted in the field.
Requirements: Experience is necessary. Write a letter of interest. You will be sent an application, then a sample survey to complete before being hired permanently .
Provisions: Pays by the survey.

HAYES MARKETING RESEARCH, 7840 El Cajon Boulevard, Suite 400, La Mesa, CA 92041.
Positions: FIeld surveyors and telephone interviewers for market research.
Requirements: Local area residents only. Experience required.
Provisions: Pays by the survey.

HEAKIN RESEARCH, INC., 1853 Ridge Road, Homewood, IL 60430.
Positions: Field surveyors conduct market research survey in 15 areas.
Requirements: Experience is preferred. Must be resident of Los Angeles, Sacramento,

San Francisco area, Chicago, Kansas City, Baltimore, Independence, Pittsburgh, Memphis, or Houston.

PAT HENRY ENTERPRISES, 8505 Tanglewood Square, #101, Chagrin Falls, OH 44022.
Positions: Market research surveys are conducted in the field and over the phone.
Requirements: Market research experience required. Must be resident of Northeastern Ohio.

HIGHSMITH INTERVIEWING SERVICE, 3218 York Drive, Augusta, GA 30909.
Positions: Market research surveys are conducted in the field and over the phone.
Requirements: Market research experience is preferred. Surveys are conducted only in Eastern Georgia or Western South Carolina.

HOSPICE OF SAN FRANCISCO, 225 - 30th, San Francisco, CA 94121.
Positions: Staffing coordinator for non-office hours.
Requirements: Experience in medical staffing required. Must live in San Francisco. Good phone manner important. Knowledge of medical terminology preferred.
Provisions: Pays hourly rates.

IDEAS IN MARKETING, P.O. Box 621598, Orlando, FL 32862.
Positions: Market research surveys are conducted in the field and over the phone.
Requirements: Market research experience is required. Must be resident of Tampa, St. Petersburg, Sarasota, Orlando, or Lakeland.

ILLINOIS AMVETS, 4711 West 137th Street, Crestwood, IL 60445.
Positions: Fund raisers phone for donations of household articles.
Requirements: There are 10 locations in Illinois; you must reside in one of them. No experience necessary outside of good speaking ability.
Provisions: Part-time hours are flexible. Pays commission for every pick-up; averages about $4.50 an hour.

IMPERIAL ENTERPRISES, P.O. Box 20684, San Diego, CA 92120.
Positions: Telemarketing in the Southeast Los Angeles area. Project involves fund raising, such as for the Special Olympics.
Requirements: Experience is preferred, but not necessary. "We're looking for stick-to-itness. You cannot be put off by isolation in this business."Must live within the survey area.
Provisions: Training is provided with take home material included. Leads are provided within local calling area. Work averages 3 hours a day. Pays commission equal to $150 to $200 a week. "We're always looking for good phoners."

INFORMATION RESOURCES, INC., 150 North Clinton, Chicago, IL 60606.
Positions: Market research interviewers and supervisors. Interviewers conduct surveys by phone. Supervisors are home-based. Company is growing rapidly and is assigning many new areas in addition to the major cities covered now.
Requirements: Must have good communication skills and work well independently. Interviewers should write letters of interest. Supervisors need to send resume.
Provisions: Interviewers are paid by the project. Supervisors are paid a salary and benefits.

Close Up: CSI Telemarketing

Consumer Surveys, Inc., more commonly known as C.S.I. Telemarketing, is growing steadily and now has over 1,200 home workers according to president Sam Gower.

C.S.I. developed a unique program for its clients several years ago called Precision Target Marketing. It combines market research with telemarketing in a two-step technique that is designed to increase a manufacturer's market share of a given product.

Here's how it works. A C.S.I. interviewer calls a consumer living within the immediate area of a particiapating store and asks questions like "What kind of toothpaste do you use?" to discover what brands of various groceries they use and, more importantly, in which supermarket they shop. If the consumer responds that they use Ivory Soap, drink Pepsi-Cola and have never tried a steak sandwich, C.S.I. will then mail the customer a packet of money-saving coupons for Dove, Coke and Steck-Umm Sandwich Steaks—all C.S.I. clients.

If the customer says they shop at the participating market, only those coupons are sent. But, if they shop elsewhere, an additional coupon good for a discount at the participating market will be included as well.

The result is that the client company is able to identify its competitor's customers for the first time. By targeting those customers with high value coupons, there is a much greater return. And for the supermarkets, there is an immediate increase in customer traffic, too.

C.S.I. interviewer Jean A. has worked from her New York home for five years now. Her perspective on how people feel about being called is interesting because she herself was called at home and surveyed. As a matter of fact, that's how she found out about C.S.I. in the first place. She found the whole thing so interesting, she sent the company a letter asking for information. She then applied for work and was taken on as an independent contractor.

"One of the best things about this," says Jean, "is we are not selling anything. We are offering something of value to the customers, so they are very receptive. It doesn't take much of their time, maybe 3 minutes. It's extremely rare that anyone hangs up."

Jean says she works for a few hours in the morning and a few hours in the afternoon and sometimes for a couple of hours in the evening. She is paid for each survey completed. Since she is an independent contractor, she can work as little or as much as she likes, but there are bonuses available for high levels of production and she likes to reach a certain plateau each week. The result for Jean is about $1,000 a month.

C.S.I. operates in Los Angeles, San Diego, Dallas, Detroit, Chicago, Boston, Philadelphia, Miami, Albany, New York, and Newark.

INTEGRITY RESEARCH, 20201 Sherman Way, #109, Canoga Park, CA 91306.
Positions: Market research surveys are conducted in the field and over the phone.
Requirements: Some kind of interviewing experience is required. Local area interviewers only.

ISAAC RESEARCH, INC., P.O. Box 989, Columbus, IN 47202.
Positions: Market research surveys are conducted in the field and over the phone.
Requirements: Interviewing experience is required. Local residents only.

J & R FIELD SERVICES, INC., 747 Caldwell Avenue, North Woodmere, NY 11581.
Positions: Field surveyors.
Requirements: Market research experience is required. Must be local resident.

JACKSON ASSOCIATES, 3070 Presidential Drive, #123, Atlanta, GA 30340.
Positions: Field and telephone interviewers for market research surveys.
Requirements: Experience required. Must be local resident.
Provisions: Pays by the survey.

JAPAN EXCHANGE SERVICES, 1015 West 159th Street, #18, Gardena, CA 90247.
Positions: Home-based coordinators are needed by this nonprofit educational organization. Responsibilities include finding host families for Japanese students, coordinating activities and tours. Work is part-time, starting in March and ending in August each year.
Requirements: Must be responsible and have time and energy. Current community involvement is preferred.
Provisions: Pays $100 per student placement plus bonuses for initial paperwork. Also pays for parties, etc.

KELLY SERVICES, INC., Box 32668, Detroit, MI 48232.
Positions: Staffing coordinators. Kelly relies on home-based staffing coordinators to take calls and dispatch temporary personnel during the night as a service to clients who operate on 24-hour shift rotations.
Requirements: Some experience in personnel placement is required. Write to locate office nearest you or find it in your local phone book. Then apply directly to that office.
Provisions: Positions are considered part-time only. Pays flat salary.

THE KIDNEY FOUNDATION, National Headquarters, 2 Park Avenue, New York, NY 10016.
Positions: Fund raising on a local level. Work involves calling for donations of household items.
Provisions: Training provided. Pays hourly wage plus bonuses. The Kidney Foundation has branch offices in every city. Call the one nearest you for more information.

LOS ANGELES MARKETING RESEARCH ASSOCIATES, 5712 Lankershim Boulevard, North Hollywood, CA 91601.
Positions: Field interviewers.
Requirements: Interviewing experience.
Provisions: Pays by the survey.

MARC, 4230 LBJ Freeway, Dallas, TX 75234.
Positions: Opinion surveyers. MARC is reportedly the #3 company in U.S. in custom research. Most research is conducted in the field.

Requirements: Some market research experience is preferred.
Provisions: Some training is provided. Workers are independent contractors and receive no benefits. Usually pays $1 per name. There are 16 office around the country with "thousands" of surveyors working on assignment throughout the year.

MARKET INTERVIEWS, 33029 Schoolcraft, Livonia, MI 48150.
Positions: Field surveyors conduct market research in studies in dozens of sampling areas around the country.
Requirements: Must be experienced surveyor. Must live in one of the sampling areas. Send for application.

MARKET METRICS, INC., 6535 East Osborn, Suite 402, Scottsdale, AZ 85251.
Positions: Field surveyors.
Requirements: Experience required. Must be resident of Phoenix.

MARKET RESEARCH SERVICES OF DALLAS, 3201 East Highway 67, Suite B1, Mesquite, TX 75150.
Positions: Local field surveyors and telephone interviewers are contracted by out-of-town market research firms to conduct surveys in the Dallas area.
Requirements: Good communication skills are necessary. Prefers some kind of experience dealing with the public.
Provisions: Work is part-time on-call only. Pays by the job.

MARKETING FORCE, 805 Oakwood, Rochester, MI 48063.
Positions: Marketing Force conducts market research surveys in the field in sampling points around the country. Currently has over 18,000 surveyors and 1,500 supervisors on roster.
Requirements: Good communication skills and the ability to follow directions to the letter are most important. Send for application and ask for name and address of nearest field manager.

MARKETING INVESTIGATIONS, INC., Osborne Plaza, 1106 Ohio River Boulevard, Box 343, Sewickley, PA 15143.
Positions: Field surveyors for market research studies.
Requirements: Interviewing experience required. Must live in Pittsburgh area.

J.B. MARTIN INTERVIEWING SERVICES, INC., 4695 Main Street, Bridgeport, CT 06606.
Positions: Field surveyors.
Requirements: Market research experience required. Local surveyors only.

MARY LUCAS MARKET RESEARCH, Marietta Plaza, 13250 New Halls Ferry Road, Florissant, MO 63033.
Positions: Field surveyors and telephone interviewers.
Requirements: Market research experience is required. Must be resident of greater St. Louis area.

BJ MAYERSON INTERVIEWING SERVICE, 928 East Hampton Road, Milwaukee, WI 53217.
Positions: Field surveyors and telephone interviewers.
Requirements: Market research experience required.

Provisions: Pays by the survey.

MAZUR/ZACHOW INTERVIEWING, 4319 North 76 Street, Milwaukee, WI.
Positions: FIeld surveyors and telephone interviewers.
Requirements: Market research experience required. Must be Milwaukee resident.

T. MCCARTHY ASSOCIATES, INC., Penn-Can Mall, 5775 South Bay Road, Syracuse-Clay, NY 13041.
Positions: Market research surveys are conducted in the field and over the phone.
Requirements: Must be local resident. Interviewing experience required.
Provisions: Pays by the survey.

MEDICAL PERSONNEL POOL, 303 S.E. 17th Street, Ft. Lauderdale, FL 33316.
Positions: This franchised agency is a nursing staff placement agency with offices coast to coast. In some areas where "satellite offices" operate in outlying areas, home-based staffing coordinators are used to take incoming calls and dispatch nurses to work assignments. In some offices, this is done only at night and on weekends.
Requirements: Some phone experience is preferred. Staffing experience is also preferred, but not necessary. Must be self-directed. Write to find the office nearest to you or look it up in your local phone book.

METROPOLITAN FINANCE CORPORATION, 1127-1131 West 41st Street, Kansas City, MO 64111.
Positions: Credit collections brokers for business-to-business accounts only.
Requirements: Some experience in the collections field is necessary.
Provisions: Good company support and training is provided. Pays commission. Can be located anywhere. All brokers are independent contractors.

MEYER CARE, 760 Market Street, Suite 612, San Francisco, CA 94102. Offices also in Kansas City, Denver, and St. Louis.
Positions: Meyer Care is a home health care provider as well as a placement agency that dispatches medical personnel to nursing homes as needed. Home-based medical coordinators receive calls and assign staff to home care cases and facilities from home at night and especially on weekends.
Requirements: Home workers are also required to come into the office on Fridays for

a few hours to help with clerical support since this is a peak day. California Regional Director, Harris Perles, says this is not a job for moonlighters, but rather someone who is home because of a need to care for family for instance. Calls may come in at any time during the night and the coordinator has to be able to handle it properly with efficiency and genuine concern. "This takes a certain personality. It's hard for us to find the right kind of people."

Provisions: Some offices pay salary only; some pay an additional bonus. Electronic pagers are also provided, so the workers are not quite so homebound.

NATIONAL ANALYSTS, 400 Market Street, Philadelphia, PA 19106.
Positions: Opinion surveys are conducted in the field.
Requirements: Must live in one of the sampling areas. Experience is preferred.
Provisions: Training is provided. Pays by the survey.

NATIONAL FAMILY OPINION, Box 315, Toledo, OH 43654.
Positions: Opinion surveys are conducted primarily in the field.
Requirements: Experience preferred. Must have strong communications skills.
Provisions: Pays by the survey.

NATIONAL OPINION RESEARCH CENTER, Social Science Research Center of the University of Chicago, 6030 South Ellis Avenue, Chicago, IL 60637.
Positions: Interviewers for long-term social science projects. This nonprofit organization is the oldest research center in the country, founded in 1941. Research contracts come from government agencies and other institutional clients generally to study behavioral changes in specified areas of the population. There are 100 "area probability centers," specifically requested by the clients. All workers are considered part-time, temporary independent contractors though projects often last up to 14 months. Most work is done face-to-face, some is done over the phone. Currently has over 700 interviewers and is actively seeking more, particularly in metropolitan areas.
Requirements: Must be available a minimum of 20 hours a week; some work 40 hours a week. Need to be people-oriented, independent, outgoing, somewhat aggressive, able to follow instructions precisely and pay attention to details. Send letter of interest.
Provisions: Training is provided; general training takes about a day and a half in the office. Project briefings are a combination of written materials and oral instructions over the phone. Pays starting salary of $4.75 plus expenses. Pay goes up with experience or with particular qualifications that may be hard to find. Annual increases are based on performance.

NORTHWEST CENTER FOR THE RETARDED, 1600 West Armory Way, Seattle, WA 98119.
Positions: Telemarketers to call for donations of household goods.
Requirements: Must be local resident.
Provisions: Training is provided. Pays hourly wage of $3.55 plus bonus plan.

OLSTEN HEALTH CARE SERVICES, 1 Merrick Avenue, Westbury, NY 11590.
Positions: Staffing coordinators. Olsten now has over 300 offices nationwide in its health care services division. Each office has a minimum of two home-based staffing coordinators job sharing on a seven-days-on, seven-days-off routine. The job consists of taking calls during the day, at night, and on weekends to dispatch appropriate personnel for hospital and home health care positions.
Requirements: Some staffing experience or medical background is required. Write to

locate the office nearest you, then apply directly to that office.
Provisions: Pays weekly salary plus placement bonuses.

OPINION RESEARCH CORPORATION, Opinion Park, Princeton, NJ 08540.
Positions: Opinion surveyors conduct interviews in the field in several hundred sampling areas around the country.
Requirements: Ability to communicate effectively with people is a must. Send letter of interest.
Provisions: Pays by the survey.

PROFESSIONAL RESEARCH ORGANIZATON, INC., 10 Corporate Hill Drive, Suite 100, Little Rock, AR 72205.
Positions: Market research surveys are conducted in the field and over the phone.
Requirements: Must be experienced. Local residents only.

PROFILE MARKETING RESEARCH, INC., 321 Northlake Boulevard, North Palm Beach, FL 33408.
Positions: Field surveyors.
Requirements: Experience required. Southern Florida residents only.

PUBLIC REACTION RESEARCH, One Dillion Road, Kendall Park, NJ 08824.
Positions: Public opinion surveys are conducted in the field and over the phone.
Requirements: Some kind of interviewing experience is required. Must be resident of greater Princeton area.
Provisions: Pays by the job.

Q & A RESEARCH, INC., 519 Mid-Island Plaza, Hicksville, NY 11801.
Positions: Field surveyors.
Requirements: Market research experience required. Must be local resident.
Provisions: Pays by the survey.

QUALITY CONTROL SERVICES, 11042 Manchester Road, St. Louis, MO 63122.
Positions: Opinion surveyors and telemarketers go into the field to invite people to test products. "We use thousands of surveyors each year."
Requirements: Must be able to follow directions, read and write, and be "brave."
Provisions: Training is provided. Pays hourly wage that varies depending on which city the home worker lives in. Benefits include a retirement plan. Quality Control has offices in Atlanta, Nashville, Boston, Chicago, Dallas, Houston, Kansas City, Overland Park, Indianapolis, Philadelphia, Phoenix, San Francisco, and Whittier.

RESEARCH TRIANGLE INSTITUTE, Hanes Building, Research Triangle Park, Raleigh, NC 27601.
Positions: Interviewers for opinion research surveys conducted primarily in the field. Research Triangle is a nonprofit social research organization operating nationwide.
Requirements: Good communication skills needed. Send letter of interest.
Provisions: Pays hourly rate in some areas, pays by the survey in others. Training is provided.

THE ROPER ORGANIZATION, 566 Boston Post Road, Mamaroneck, NY 10543.
Positions: Opinion surveyers conduct research within sampling areas around the country. All research is conducted in the field.

Requirements: No opinion surveying experience is necessary, but experience involving some kind of public contact is preferred. Write and ask for name and address of nearest field supervisor.

SAGE SURVEYS, INC., Soundview Lane, Port Washington, NY 11050.
Positions: Field surveyors and telephone interviewers.
Requirements: Interviewing experience is required. Must be resident of New York CIty or one of the nearby suburbs.

SALEM SERVICES, 21 Poe Road, Thornwood, NY 10594.
Positions: Field surveyors and telephone interviewers.
Requirements: Experienced surveyors only. Must be resident of Westchester or Rockland County.
Provisions: Pays by the job.

"A competent bookkeeper working with our system should easily gross $30 an hour."
—Tax One

SALT LAKE ANIMAL SOCIETY, 1151 South Redwood Road, Suite 108, Salt Lake City, UT 84104.
Positions: Telemarketers call for donations.
Requirements: Must live in Salt Lake City.
Provisions: Training is provided. Pays commission and bonus plan.

SANDIA MARKETING SERVICES, 923 Coronado Mall, N.E., Albuquerque, NM 87110.
Positions: Field surveyors.
Requirements: Market research experience preferred. Must be local resident.
Provisions: Pays by the survey.

SANTELL MARKET RESEARCH, INC., 300 Mt. Lebanon Boulevard, Suite 2204, Pittsburgh, PA 15234.
Positions: Field surveyors.
Requirements: Market research experience preferred. Must be local resident.
Provisions: Pays by the survey.

SIMMONS MARKET RESEARCH BUREAU, 219 East 42nd Street, New York, NY 10017.
Positions: Opinion surveyors conduct research in the field. Both surveyors and their supervisors are home-based.
Requirements: Must live within one of the Simmons' survey areas. Send letter of interest and ask for the name and address of the field supervisor closest to you.

Provisions: No experience is necessary. Must attend short training sessions which are conducted regularly within survey areas all over the U.S. Pays by the survey.

SUCCESS SEEKERS MECCA, 717 Main Street, Suite 9, Fitchburg, MA 91420
Positions: Personnel field representatives (recruiters). This 20-year old personnel agency has a nationwide network of reps.
Requirements: Send resume and cassette recording of yourself reviewing experience, training, and goals.
Provisions: Training is provided. Constant and ongoing contact with company after initial training. Commission paid for both job orders generated and/or your referrals that are successfully placed by the company. Full-time or part-time. Can be located anywhere in U.S.

SURVEY CENTER, INC., 505 North Lake Shore Drive, Chicago, IL 60611.
Positions: Market research surveys are conducted in sampling points around the country. Field interviewers and their supervisors work part-time on-call.
Requirements: Write and request name and address of nearest field supervisor.
Provisions: Pays by the survey.

TAYLOR INTERVIEWING SERVICE, 1026 Horseshoe Road, Augusta, GA 30906.
Positions: Field surveyors and telephone interviewers.
Requirements: Market research experience preferred. Must be Augusta resident.

TAYLOR MANAGEMENT SYSTEMS, 9242 Markville, Dallas, TX 75243.
Positions: Telephone recruiters locate fund raiser volunteers.
Requirements: Telemarketing experience required. Must be Dallas resident.
Provisions: Pays piece rates based on number of volunteers recruited.

TAYLOR RESEARCH, 3202 Third Avenue, San Diego, CA 92103.
Positions: Field surveyors.
Requirements: Market research experience required. Must be San Diego resident.
Provisions: Pays by the survey.

TEMPOSITIONS, Home Health Care Division, 150 Post Street, San Francisco, CA 94104.
Positions: Staffing coordinator for evenings and weekends.
Requirements: Experience in medical staffing required. Must live in San Francisco.
Provisions: This is part-time work only.

TEXAS GULF MINERALS AND METALS, INC., 1610 Frank Akers Road, Anniston, AL 36201.
Positions: Buyers. Company recycles catalytic converters. Home-based buyers locate and purchase used catalytic converters which will in turn be sold to the company.
Requirements: Write for complete details.
Provisions: Pick up is provided weekly. Pays weekly. Training is provided. Can be anywhere in U.S.

TEXAS RESEARCH, 2200 Guadalupe, Suite 218, Austin, TX 87805.
Positions: This market research firm is now growing outside of its Texas based operations into New Mexico, Georgia, and California. Work consists of conducting short, two-minute, eight question surveys.

Requirements: Must live in one of the survey areas.
Provisions: Training is provided. Pays by the completed survey; from $.25 to $.40 each depending on overall volume. Can be part-time or full-time.

TRENDFACTS RESEARCH/FIELD SERVICES, 31800 Northwestern Highway, Suite 380, Farmington Hills, MI 48018.
Positions: Field surveyors work part-time on-call in Michigan only.
Requirements: Market research experience required.
Provisions: Pays by the survey.

TRI-COUNTY RESEARCH, 3 Rexal Court, New City, NY 10956.
Positions: Field surveyors and telephone interviewers.
Requirements: Market research experience required. Must live in Westchester, Rockland, Bergen, Passaic, or Upstate New York.

UCPA, 11401 Rainier Avenue South, Seattle, WA 98178.
Positions: Fund raising involves calling for donations of reusable household items.
Requirements: Must live in greater Seattle area.
Provisions: Pays base salary plus bonus plan. Benefits include paid vacation. Hours can be part-time or full-time. Training is provided.

UNITED CEREBRAL PALSY, 1217 Alhambra Boulevard, Sacramento, CA 95618.
Positions: Fund raising by phone. Job consists of calling for donations of household discards for about four hours a day.
Requirements: Must live in Sacramento.
Provisions: Pays hourly wage plus bonus plan.

THE UNITED STATES CENSUS BUREAU, U.S. Department of Commerce, Social and Economic Statistics Administration, Washington, D.C. 20233.
Positions: Surveyors and opinion researchers conduct regular monthly surveys and periodic special assignments throughout the country. All surveys are conducted in the field.
Requirements: Attendance at a paid training session is required.
Provisions: Pay is $6.28 per hour (plus $1.50 an hour more in inner cities) plus 20.5 cents a mile. Benefits include paid sick days, paid vacation time and pension. The Census Bureau is a huge bureaucracy and it is extremely difficult to reach the right people, such as the field supervisor in your area. The Personnel Department suggests watching the "Help Wanted" section of your local newspaper for notice of upcoming work. You can also write and request the name and address of your local field supervisor.

UNITED STATES TESTING, 1415 Park Avenue, Hoboken, NJ 07030.
Positions: Market research interviewers conduct surveys at various sampling points throughout the country.
Requirements: Must live within one of the sampling areas. Must enjoy talking to new people.
Provisions: Training is provided. Work is part-time with flexible hours available. Pays by the survey.

VALLEY RESEARCH & SURVEY, 2875 South Main, #102, Salt Lake City, UT 84115.
Positions: Field surveyors and telephone interviewers.

HOMER   BY RICH TENNANT

Requirements: Market research experience required. Salt Lake City residents only.

VALLEYWIDE RESEARCH, 94 North Park Plaza Mall, Chandler, AZ 85224.
Positions: Field surveyors.
Requirements: Market research experience required. Must be local resident.

VETERANS' REHABILITATION CENTER, 9201 Pacific Avenue, Tacoma, WA 98444.
Positions: Fund raisers phone for donations of household items, clothing, etc.
Requirements: Must come to Tacoma for short training session. (Can live in Seattle.)
Provisions: Paid training is provided. Pays guaranteed hourly wage. Inquiries are welcome.

VIETNAM VETERANS OF AMERICA FOUNDATION, Ventura, CA (805) 487-3977.
Positions: Fund raisers phone for donations of household items to be sold in thrift stores.
Requirements: No experience required. Must have good speaking voice. Local residents only. Apply by calling.
Provisions: Pays guaranteed minimum wage plus bonus plan. Training is provided.

VFW, SPECIAL EVENTS, San Francisco, CA (415)563-0406.
Positions: Fund raisers sell tickets to special charity events over the telephone.
Requirements: Good communication skills, reliability, and good phone voice are basic essentials. Do not write; applicants are chosen over the phone for voice quality.
Provisions: Pays commission and bonus.

VISION SERVICES, 1401 Madison, Suite 284, Seattle, WA 98104.
Positions: Phone work for nonprofit agency that offers programs to the blind and visually impaired. No sales is involved.
Requirements: Must live in Seattle. Touchtone phone required.
Provisions: One week of training is provided at headquarters. Pays $3.75 per hour. After four months a bonus plan is added.

WALKER RESEARCH COMPANY, 8000 Knue Road, Indianapolis, IN 46250.
Positions: Opinion surveyers conduct field interviews within sampling areas around the country.
Requirements: Send letter of interest asking for name and address of nearest field supervisor.
Provisions: Training is provided. Pays by the survey.

WE TIP, Los Angeles, CA (818) 506-5456.
Positions: Fund raisers sell tickets to charity events over the phone. This is a citizen's anti-crime organization.
Requirements: Must live in greater Los Angeles area and be available to work 25 to 40 hours a week. Accepts call-in applications only in order to judge phone voice and communication skills.
Provisions: Pays commission averaging $300 a week.

WEST STAT, 1650 Research Boulevard, Rockville, MD 20850.
Positions: Interviewers conduct social research surveys in the field.
Requirements: Must be able to attend training session.
Provisions: Training is provided. Write for the location of the nearest office.

WESTERN MEDICAL SERVICES, 572 Market Street, San Francisco, CA 94104-5494.
Positions: Answering service staff.
Requirements: Excellent communication skills are necessary. Some medical knowledge is required. Must live in the local calling area of San Francisco. Work is part-time, evenings only.
Provisions: Pays hourly wage.

WHITE VACCUM COMPANY, 215 Brownsville Road, Pittsburgh, PA 15210.
Positions: Telemarketers do customer service work.
Requirements: Must apply in person and live in Pittsburgh; after initial application all contact is done via the mail.
Provisions: Training is provided. Customer list is supplied. Work is part-time; three hours a day, five days a week. Pays salary plus commission.

WORLD EXCHANGE, White Birch Road, Putnam Valley, NY 10579.
Positions: World Exchange needs Program Directors for its exchange student program. This year 1,000 students will be arriving from France, Japan, Spain, and Holland and U.S. students will be sent to England, France, Spain and Holland for one month cultural exchange. Program Directors find and interview host families on a part-time, seasonal basis.
Requirements: Experience helps, but is not necessary. World Exchange is looking for people who are "internationally minded." Ability to work well with people and various civic organizations is important. Can live within 300 miles of Los Angeles or San Francisco on the West Coast, and anywhere from Southern Florida to the Canadian Border on the East Coast.
Provisions: Compensates for each placement.

ZYBEX, 5680 La Jolla Boulevard, La Jolla, CA 92037.
Positions: Zybex offers medical computer systems to doctors and clinics including hardware, software, and data processing services. Telemarketers are needed in Califor-

nia, particularly in the Bay area and Orange County, to survey potential prospects and set up appointments for demonstrations. There is no selling involved.

Requirements: Must live in the areas mentioned. Some kind of phone experience is preferred. Must be pleasant but assertive and able to fill out survey forms properly.

Provisions: Pays hourly rate of $5 plus bonus for each appointment set and additional bonus if a subsequent sale is made by the demonstrator. Part-time only.

Chapter 8
Industrial Home Work

Industrial home work is the kind of work that most people think of when you mention home work. It is work that is usually performed in a factory setting or sometimes in an office. It generally requires no special skills and therefore it doesn't generally pay very well.

It is simply a myth that this is the most common type of home work. Actually, it is the least common type of home work, because industrial home work is illegal in many states and some types of industrial home work are prohibited by federal labor laws as well. The states that do allow it have very strict standards and certification procedures. In Illinois, for example, any employer who wishes to hire home workers must obtain certification not only for the company, but for each and every employee as well.

All industrial home work is done locally. It is impossible for this type of work to be transported from one location to another, partly because of the labor laws. Also, it is not economically feasible to pay to transport materials to and from a worker's home, pay the worker, and expect to make a profit. Most of the time, an industrial home worker must pick up and deliver the materials and finished work himself. In rare instances, a courier service is set up within a short radius of the employer's factory or office.

As the manufacturing sector of our economic base continues to shrink, so will industrial home work. There is not very much of it available now, and there will be even less available in the future.

ALLEN SHOE COMPANY, INC., 266 River Street, Haverhill, MA 01830.
Positions: Work is very specialized; French cord turning for shoe manufacturer.
Requirements: Some experience specific to this work is necessary. Must be local resident.
Provisions: Machinery is provided by the company. Piece rates equal approximately $4 an hour.

ALLISON ELECTRONICS, INC., 406 West Fairway, P.O. Box "B," Big Bear City, CA 92314.
Positions: Electronic assemblers. Loading only, no soldering, of PC boards and ICs.
Requirements: Experience preferred, but not required. Must be local resident.
Provisions: Pays piece rates based on production. Will accept applications, but has a waiting line.

ATL CORPORATION, Brownville Avenue, P.O. Box 512, Piswich, MA 01938.
Positions: Hand weaving of parts used in manufacturing heating elements. No experience is necessary, but workers must be local residents.
Provisions: Pays hourly rate of $3.60.

AURA BADGE COMPANY, Clayton Avenue, Clayton, NJ 08312
Positions: Hand assembly includes inserting pins into cello buttons and acetate badgeholders.
Requirements: Must be local resident in order to pick up and deliver supplies and finished work. No experience or equipment is required.
Provisions: Pays salary and basic benefits provided by law. Currently has 15 home workers.

BALDY'S TACKLE, 100 McFadden Place, Newport Beach, CA 92633.
Positions: Wrapping threads onto the guides of fishing rods. "This is an old art; our best wrapper has over 20 years of experience."
Requirements: Experience is necessary. Must be local resident.
Provisions: Pays piece rates.

BROOKLYN BUREAU OF COMMUNITY SERVICE, Program for the Handicapped, 285 Schemerhorn Street, Brooklyn, NY 11217.
Positions: This is a non-profit organization offering many services to the elderly and handicapped citizens of Brooklyn. Home work involves manual assembly of products such as novelties and pharmaceuticals. Products are chosen for suitability - i.e., must be small enough to store in an apartment for a week at a time, light enough to carry up stairs, and suitable for quality control by the individual worker.
Requirements: Must be an elderly or handicapped resident of Brooklyn.
Provisions: Training and supplies are provided. Pick up and delivery of supplies and finished work are provided on a weekly basis. Pays piece rates. Has advocate on staff to insure SSI and disability insurance benefits are protected.

A.G. BUSCH & COMPANY, INC., 6060 Northwest Highway, Chicago, IL 60631.
Positions: Light asembly of small plastic and metal parts. Currently has 18 home workers.
Requirements: Must be local resident. Must obtain home worker certificate from Illinois State Department of Labor.

Provisions: Pays piece rates.

BUTACO CORPORATION, 6051 South Knox, Chicago, IL 60629.
Positions: Butaco is a producer of advertising specialties. Home workers assemble metal pins into lithographic buttons. Currently has 20 home workers.
Requirements: Must be local resident. Must obtain home worker certificate from Illinois State Department of Labor.
Provisions: Pays piece rates.

CADIE PRODUCTS CORPORATION, 100 Sixth Avenue, Paterson, NJ 07524.
Positions: Packaging small items produced by the company.
Requirements: Must be local resident. No machinery or experience needed.
Provisions: Pays piece rates.

CARDINAL SHOE CORPORATION, 468 Canal Street, P.O. Box 1349, Lawrence MA 01842.
Positions: Pressing and benchwork. Currently has about 30 home workers.
Requirements: Must own machinery as prescribed by the employer and must be experienced. Local residents.
Provisions: Materials supplied. Pays piece rates equal to about $6.50 an hour (considerably higher than for the same work done in-house).

CAROL SHOES COMPANY, Division of Shaer Shoe Corporation, Lowell, MA 01852.
Positions: Stitching of shoe uppers.
Requirements: Experience is required. Must be local resident.
Provisions: Pick up and delivery provided. Machinery provided. Pays piece rates equal to $3.35 an hour.

CARTRIDGE ACTUATED DEVICES, INC., 123 Clinton Road, Fairfield, NJ 07006.
Positions: Soldering and some bridgewiring of explosive devices.
Requirements: Must be local resident in order to pick up and deliver supplies and finished work. Must own a microscope as prescribed by the company.
Provisions: Training is provided. Pays piece rates, but workers are full employees with basic benefits provided by law. Inquiries welcome.

CENTRAL ASSEMBLY COMPANY, INC., 1110 West National Avenue, Addison, IL 60101.
Positions: Light assembly of small products.
Requirements: Must be local resident. Must obtain home worker certificate from Illinois State Department of Labor.
Provisions: Pays piece rates. Work availability fluctuates according to availability of contracts.

CENTRAL-SHIPPEE, INC., 46 Star Lake Avenue, Bloomington, NJ 07403.
Positions: Manual assembly of color cards, swatching, inserting and mailing.. Central-Shippee is a swatch manufacturer. Home workers put together the swatch cards from provided samples.
Requirements: Must be local resident.
Provisions: Training is provided. Pick up and delivery also provided. Pays piece rates.

CONSOLIDATED INDUSTRIES OF GREATER SYRACUSE, INC., 541 Seymour Street, Syracuse, NY 13204.
Positions: Electrical and electronic assembly of small parts. Also collating and packing of other products. Currently has 11 home working participants; anyone qualified is welcome to apply.
Requirements: Applicant must go through an extensive evaluation process, since all the home work is issued to disabled workers only.
Provisions: "Homebound Program" provides complete and ongoing training, plus as much counseling as is needed for each individual. Pick-up and delivery of supplies and finished work is provided weekly. Pays piece rates.

CORD CRAFTS, INC., 244 Bergen Boulevard, West Paterson, NJ 07424.
Positions: Hand assembly of plant hangers. Currently has over 70 home workers.
Requirements: Must be local resident in order to pick up and deliver supplies and finished products.
Provisions: Training is provided. Pays piece rates.

COTTAGE INDUSTRIES, 1308 Old County Road, Belmont, CA 94002.
Positions: Electronic asembly of PC boards and harnesses. There is no soldering; only stuffing of boards and harness pulling.
Requirements: Workers are independent contractors and must have business licenses. Must supply own tools, pick up and delivery, etc. Local residents only. Experience is also required.
Provisions: Pays piece rates. Current number of home workers is small. Company has had more in the past, but orders at this time are mostly too big to handle outside the plant on time schedules provided by contracts.

COVENTRY MANUFACTURING COMPANY, INC., 5152 Commerce Drive, Baldwin Park, CA 91706.
Positions: Hand assembly of specialty cleaning swabs for the electronic and medical industries. Most of the work is overflow, therefore the work is not steady.
Requirements: Must be local resident.
Provisions: Training is provided. A specially designed device that aids in the assembly of the product is also supplied. $3.85 and hour is paid during the training period. "It takes two to three weeks to come up to speed." After reaching that 'quota', piece rates are paid equaling about $6 to $7 and hour. The number of home workers is dependent on the marketplace; it comes and goes. Generally about 20 home workers are used at a time.

DATAMETRICS, DRESS INDUSTRIES, INC., 340 Fordham Road, Wilmington, MA 01887.
Positions: Hand assembly of PC boards, stuffing only.
Requirements: Experience necessary. Must be local resident.
Provisions: Electrical and hand tools are provided as necessary. Pays piece rates averaging $6 and hour.

DAVCO, INC., 42 Walnut Street, Haverhill, MA 01830.
Positions: Hand assembly of shoe findings.
Requirements: Must be local resident.
Provisions: Pick up and delivery provided. Pays piece rates equal to minimum wage.

DIECRAFTER'S INC., 832 West Erie Street, Chicago, IL 60622.
Positions: Folding and glueing involved in the business of paper diecutting and finishing.
Requirements: Must be local resident. Must obtain a home worker certificate from Illinois State Department of Labor. Prefers referrals from current employees.
Provisions: Pays piece rates.

EASTER SEAL SOCIETY OF METROPOLITAN CHICAGO, INC., 220 South State Street, Room 312, Chicago, IL 60604.
Positions: This is a not-for-profit program for handicapped Chicago residents. 31 home workers handle small packaging, light assembly, collating, and hand-addressing.
Requirements: Must be handicapped and live in Chicago.
Provisions: Training is provided. Pick up and delivery is provided. Pays piece rates.

> "We have lots of work coming up. In addition to our established line, we are open to any new ideas."
> --Rocking Horse

FEDERATION OF THE HANDICAPPED, 211 West 14th Street, 2nd Floor, New York, NY 10011.
Positions: The Home Employment Program (HEP) is a workshop program which consists of industrial bench assembly (manual assembly work).
Requirements: All workers must live in New York City and have a disability. Requires evaluation through lengthy interviews and personal counseling before participating.
Provisions: The workshop provides training plus any extra help necessary to overcome any unusual problems an individual might have. Pick up and delivery of supplies and finished work is provided regularly. Pays piece rates. Disability insurance counseling is provided. Number of home workers fluctuates, but over 1000 have participated in the program since the early 60s and there are currently several hundred participants.

FENWICK WOODSTREAM (F.P., INC.,), 14799 Chestnut Street, Westminster, CA 92683.
Positions: Hand wrapping of guides onto fishing rods. Number of home workers fluctuates seasonally—up to 27.
Requirements: Prefers experienced workers. Must be local resident.
Provisions: Training is provided in the plant. A special wrapping table and all supplies are provided. Pick up and delivery of supplies and finished work is provided once a week. Home workers are given the same status and benefits as in-house employees with paid vacations, holidays, and sick leave plus group medical and dental insurance. Pays piece rates equal to or better than in-house salary.

FINEST FASHIONS, INC., 3650 North Cicero Avenue, Chicago, IL 60644.
Positions: Product packaging.

Requirements: Must be local resident. Must obtain home worker certificate from Illinois State Department of Labor.

FOUR WORD INDUSTRIES CORPORATION, 9462 Franklin Avenue, Franklin Park, IL 60131.
Positions: Hand assemblers insert pins into the backs of metal buttons for this producer of advertising specialties. Currently has 23 home workers.
Requirements: Must be local resident. Must obtain a home worker certificate from Illinois State Department of Labor.
Provisions: Pays piece rates.

HOMER

BY RICH TENNANT

FULLER BOX COMPANIES, 150 Chestnut Street, North Attleboro, MA 02760.
Positions: Manual assembly involved in the production of steel set-up boxes and jewelry display boxes. Work consists of rimming, padding, tipping, wiring, and other assembly functions.
Requirements: Must be local resident.
Provisions: Pick up and delivery of supplies and finished products is provided. Pays piece rates equal to about $4 and hour.

GERSON INDUSTRIES, 4501 Dell Avenue, North Bergen, NJ 07047.
Positions: Sewing covers for mattresses and boxsprings.
Requirements: Must be local resident and own industrial sewing machine. Production level experience is required.
Provisions: Training is provided. Pick up and delivery of supplies and finished work is provided.

GORDON BRUSH MANUFACTURING COMPANY, INC., 2150 Sacramento Street, Los Angeles, CA 90021.
Positions: Hand assembly of brush parts.
Requirements: Must live nearby.
Provisions: Training is provided. Pays by the piece. There is a long waiting list.

GREENWOOD ENTERPRISES, INC., 9834 South Kedzie Avenue, Evergreen Park, Chicago, IL 60642.
Positions: Company manufactures novelty and custom design buttons. Hand assemblers insert pins into the backs of the buttons. Currently has 28 home workers.
Requirements: Must be local resident. Must obtain home worker certificate from Illinois State Department of Labor.
Provisions: Pays piece rates.

HARPER LEATHER GOODS MANUFACTURING COMPANY, 2133 West Pershing Road, Chicago, IL 60609.
Positions: Light industrial work involved in the manufacture of pet supplies; packaging rawhide "bones", sewing cat and dog toys, and sewing cat collars.
Requirements: Must be local resident. Must obtain home worker certificate from Illinois State Department of Labor.

HARVARD LABS, INC., 98 Pratts Junction Raod, Sterling Junction, MA 01565.
Positions: Hand assembly of plastic disposable medical goods.
Requirements: Must be local resident in order to pick up and deliver supplies and finished work.
Provisions: Training is provided. Pays piece rates equal to a minimum of $4 and hour.

HYGIENOL COMPANY, INC., 73 Crescent Avenue, New Rochelle, NY 10801.
Positions: Hand assembly involved in the manufacture of powder puffs.
Requirements: Local residents only.
Provisions: Home work force is extremely small now, but at one time (before 1950) there were over 400. Company is considering revitalizing home work program.

JACKSON SPRING & MANUFACTURING COMPANY, INC., 2680 American Lane, Elk Grove, IL 60007.
Positions: Packing parts.
Requirements: Must be local resident. Must obtain home worker certificate from Illinois State Department of Labor.
Provisions: Pays piece rates.

I. KASSOY, INC., 30 West 47th Avenue, New York, NY 10036.
Positions: Assembly work involved in the manufacture of diamond papers.
Requirements: Must live nearby.
Provisions: Pays piece rates.

L. G. IMPORT & MANUFACTURING COMPANY, 8121 Central Park Avenue, Skokie, IL 60076.
Positions: Hand assembly of jewelry for jewelry manufacturer. Currently has 26 home workers.
Requirements: Must be local resident. Must obtain home worker certificate from Illinois State Department of Labor.
Provisions: Training is provided. Pays piece rates.

LEE WRAPPING COMPANY, 18474 Amistad, #G, Fountain Valley, CA 92708.
Positions: Hand wrapping of fishing rods. Currently has 12 home workers.

Requirements: Must have experience and be local resident. Prefers to hire through referrals.
Provisions: Pays piece rates bi-wekly. Workers are full employees with the same benefits as in-house workers.

LESANDE SHOE COMPANY, 81-87 Washington Street, Haverhill, MA 01830.
Positions: Stitching shoe parts. Currently has about two dozen home workers.
Requirements: Experience is required. Must be local resident.
Provisions: Machinery is provided. Pays piece rates equal to about $5 and hour.

LIMALDI & ASSOCIATES, 165 Vanderpool Street, Newark, NJ 07114.
Positions: Hand inserting pins into metal buttons. Current number of home workers is 10, but that number fluctuates.
Requirements: Must be local resident.
Provisions: Pick up and delivery of supplies and finished work is provided. Home workers are salaried employees.

LORINA EMBROIDERIES, INC., 6900 Park Avenue, Guttenberg, NJ 07093.
Positions: Hand packaging of embroidered products.
Requirements: Must be local resident.
Provisions: Pays piece rates.

Z. A. MACABEE GOPHER TRAP COMPANY, INC., 110 Loma Alta Avenue, Los Gatos, CA 95030.
Positions: Hand assembly of components for traps that are manufactured at the factory.
Requirements: Must live nearby.
Provisions: Pays piece rates.

MADISON COUNTY CHAPTER, NEW YORK STATE ASSOCIATION FOR RETARDED CHILDREN, Alternatives, Inc., 588 Broad Street, Oneida, NY 13421.
Positions: Hand assembly of various kinds, including stuffing envelopes, packaging, and silver polishing. Some machine sewing is being introduced. All home work is part of the Sheltered Workshop program for homebound disabled residents of Oneida. Currently has 200 participants. "Previously, we were able to accept applications from disabled people only. Now, anyone in Oneida can sign up."
Requirements: Must go through extensive evaluation.
Provisions: Pays piece rates. Training is provided. Pick up and delivery of supplies and finished work is provided twice a week.

ROSS MATTHEWS CORPORATION, DeValles Street, Fall River, MA 02722.
Positions: Hand assembly tasks for manufacturer of narrow fabrics.
Requirements: Must be local resident.
Provisions: Pays piece rates equal to $3.75 and hour.

MONTGOMERY COUNTY ASSOCIATION FOR RETARDED CHILDREN, Liberty Enterprises, P. O. Box 639, Amsterdam, NY 12010.
Positions: Hand assembly of various products.
Requirements: Must have verifiable disability that requires work at home. Must be local resident.
Provisions: Training is provided. Pick-up and delivery of supplies and finished work

is provided. Pays piece rates.

NATIONAL STAY COMPANY, INC., 680 Lynnway, Lynn, MA 01905.
Positions: Hand assembly of bows and vamps for shoes. Work is seasonal.
Requirements: Local residents only.
Provisions: Pays hourly rate of $3.50.

NORTH AMERICAN PLASTICS CORPORATION, 9 Water Street, Leicester, MA 01524.
Positions: Hand assembly work involved in the manufacture of plastic sleeves.
Currently has 60 home workers.
Requirements: Must live within 25 mile radius of factory.
Provisions: Pays minimum wage.

> "A good freelancer can make $50,000 a year."
>
> —CCA, Inc.

NOVA MEDICAL SPECIALTIES, INC., R.D. 2, Jackson Road, Indian Mills, NJ 08088.
Positions: Heat molding of PVC tubing.
Requirements: Must be local resident. Workers are required to pick up and deliver supplies and finished work.
Provisions: Training and any necessary equipment is provided. Home workers are salaried employees with the same benefits as in-house employees.

OUR WAY ENTERPRISES, INC., 1552 West 6th Drive, Mesa, AZ 85202.
Positions: Assembly of various products such as wall clocks and small lamps. All work is performed by handicapped workers.
Requirements: Must be disabled resident of Mesa.
Provisions: Complete training is provided, since the objective of Our Way is "to train handicapped persons in a marketable skill, and then help to place these persons in industry where they could make as much money in wages as anyone else."

PENT HOUSE SALES CORPORATION, 860 West Central Street, Franklin, MA 02038.
Positions: Hand assembly of shoe parts and accessories.
Requirements: Must be local resident.
Provisions: Pays minimum wage.

PHILLIPS MANUFACTURING COMPANY, INC., 190 Emmet Street, Newark, NJ 07114.
Positions: Company manufactures buttons.
Requirements: Home work is only distributed to contractors with valid state permit for redistribution.

SCRIPTURE PRESS PUBLICATIONS, 1825 College Avenue, Wheaton, IL 60187.
Positions: Proofreading and packet assembly for religious publisher.
Requirements: Must be local resident. Good English skills required. Must obtain home worker certificate from Illinois State Department of Labor.

SKILLS UNLIMITED, INC., 405 Locust Avenue, Oakdale, NY 11769.
Positions: Hand assembly of various items. Currently has 15 home workers in program.
Requirements: Only people with catastrophic disabilities may apply. One to four weeks evaluation and state certification is required. Must live within 15 mile radius of headquarters.
Provisions: Training is provided, as well as ongoing help and support. Skills Unlimited will set up the home work station, provide transportation to the central facilities for training as needed, and pick up and deliver supplies and finished work regularly. Pays piece rates.

"We use almost completely independent, very diversified types of people. . . we're always open to inquiries."

—Clear Star International

SMC PRODUCTION SERVICE, 6548 West 26 Place, Berwyn, IL 60402.
Positions: Various tasks involved in packaging small plastic samples for manufacturer.
Requirements: Local residents only. Illinois State Department of Labor requires home worker certificate.
Provisions: Pays piece rates.

STUART SPORTS SPECIALTIES, P.O.Box 13, Indian Orchard, MA 01151.
Positions: Hand assembly of fishing tackle components.
Requirements: Experience preferred. Must be local resident.
Provisions: Pays $4 an hour.

SWIB INDUSTRIES, 4810 Venture, Lisle, IL 60532.
Positions: Hand assembly; attaching jewelry to plastic cards and other packaging of jewelry. Currently has 30 home workers.
Requirements: Must be local resident. Must obtain home worker certificate from Ilinois State Department of Labor.

TELEDYNE ISOTAPES, 50 Van Buren Avenue, Westwood, NJ 07675.
Positions: Two Types of work are performed at home. One is the assembly of badge cases and the other is slicing of ultrathin discs.
Requirements: Must be local resident. Prefers referrals.
Provisions: Equipment is provided as necessary.

TOMORROW TODAY CORPORATION, P. O. Box 612, Westfield, MA 01086.
Positions: Hand work consists of tying bows and working with flowers to make decorations.
Requirements: Must be local.
Provisions: Pays minimum wage.

UNITED CEREBRAL PALSY ASSOCIATION OF WESTCHESTER COUNTY, INC., King Street and Lincoln Avenue in the Town of Rye, NY; mailing address P.O. Box 555, Purchase, NY 10577.
Positions: Hand assembly of various items on subcontract basis. Program is for homebound disabled workers only.
Requirements: All home workers must be approved by the U.S. Dept. of Labor which generally requires a doctor's statement. Local residents only.
Provisions: The screening is tight, but once the program is there, there is a lot of support available. Each participant is assigned a vocational trainer and a counselor that meet with the worker at least once a month after the initial training is completed. Pick up and delivery of supplies and finished work is provided. Any tools and/or equipment necessary for the work are provided. Pays piece rates. Inquiries are welcome from Westchester County and from throughout Connecticut. Some work is opening up in the computer field,too.

WEST COAST BRUSH COMPANY, 3814 East Medford Street, Los Angeles, CA 90022.
Positions: Assembly of stainless steel wire brushes.
Requirements: Must live nearby.
Provisions: Training is provided. Home workers are reqular employees and are paid a salary plus basic benefits.

YORK SPRING COMPANY, 1551 North La Fox Street, South Elgin, IL 60177.
Positions: Assembly and packaging springs for manufacturer. Currently has 41 home workers.
Requirements: Must be local resident. Must obtain home worker certificate from Illinois State Department of Labor.
Provisions: Pays piece rates.

Closeup: Village of the Smoky Hills

Village of the Smoky Hills is an award-winning cottage industry center in Osage, Minnesota. Fifteen buildings nestled amid 67 acres of pine forest showcase every imaginable type of handcraft.

Founder Lorelei Kraft came up with the idea in 1984 as a way to employ her neighbors without forfeiting the clear air and natural beauty of the area. At that time, unemployment was over 20%; the area was the poorest in the state. Kraft says she was inspired by Rockefeller's Appalachian quilting project, but rather than send the handcrafted products away to be sold, she gave the plan a whole new twist. She envisioned a village so unique it would not only attract customers, but would charge admissions to covver the cost of personal appearances by the craftspeople.

It took two months to develop the original business plan, during which time Kraft and 11 other social activists formed The Founding Mothers, Inc. From that point, it took only five months to locate the land, apply for a loan, get a zoning variance, build the complex, interview and train employees to run it, and open to the public.

Over 350 local artisans bring their products from home to be displayed and sold. The Village takes care of inventory, staffing clerks, advertising, etc. Everything is of high quality; nothing "plastic" is accepted.

Each building houses something different; Woodworking, Stenciling, Pottery, Indian Arts, Mrs. Santa's House, Bake Shoppe, Candle-Dipping, Quilting, Stained Glass, "Country", Old-Tyme Photo, and Ice Cream Parlor.

If this sounds like just another cutesy shopping center, it's far from it. In addition to displaying the crafts, the group demonstrates how they are made. The Pavilion in the center of The Commons features special demonstrations throughout the summer. There's soap-making, birchbark weaving, making tea from common plants, spinning and weaving, chainsaw sculptures, tole painting, basketmaking, silver-smithing, and more.

Visitors are invited to get involved, too. Want a souvenir T-shirt? Stencil your own! Or dip your own candles, or grind your own flour at the Bake Shoppe. The biggest project so far has been the erection of an authentic log cabin.

The key to the Village's success is participation. 20,000 visitors were expected the first year, but 100,000 came from all over to get involved in all the fun activities. For that, the Village won the State Travel Marketing of the Year Award, swept the top awards at the 1984 Minnesota Tourism Conference, and won the Regional Development Award for outstanding tourism

Chapter 9
Opportunities in Sales

The field of sales has long been a traditional from-home opportunity. Today, most salespeople have offices at home and some even conduct all their business from home.

Sales may be the only true opportunity to earn an executive level income with literally no educational requirements or experience. It is particularly good for women, who often report doubling or tripling their income after leaving other types of jobs. It also allows for a maximum amount of flexibility in terms of time spent and when it is spent.

What does it take to be a good salesperson? Good communication skills are at the top of the list. You must truly enjoy talking to people to make it in sales. You must be careful to listen to them as well. Assertiveness is also important. This does not mean you must be aggressive or go for the "hard sell," but shrinking violets aren't likely to make it in this field. The toughest part of this job is handling rejection. Nobody likes rejection; some people are traumatized by it. But, it goes with the territory. The professional salesperson knows that with each rejection, he/she is one step closer to a successfully-closed sale.

Sales is a profession with its own set of rules, just like any other profession. The job basically consists of prospecting for customers, qualifying the prospect to make sure the potential customer is a viable prospect, making the presentation, overcoming objections, closing the sale, and getting referrals. A good company will teach you all you need to know about each of these steps. You can also find classes in salesmanship for both beginners and advanced students at community colleges and adult learning centers.

Many of the opportunities listed in this section have interesting ways of introducing the product. Home parties are especially fun and easy. Many home parties now seem more like classes than sales pitches with hands-on demonstrations in cooking, baking, needlework, and crafts. If you think you might be interested in a particular company, you can check it out first by hosting your own party. You'll not only be able to check out the company first hand, but you'll earn a bonus gift at the same time.

For those who want to be home all the time, telemarketing is the best bet. It is a marketing method that is mushrooming because it is more efficient and cheaper than face-to-face methods of selling. Telemarketing jobs rarely exceed four hours a day, but the pay can equal a full-time salary for a good communicator. For additional opportunities in telemarketing, look in your local newspaper "help wanted" ads.

ACCENTS INTERNATIONAL, 909 Commerce Circle, P. O. Drawer 11047, Charleston, SC 29411.
Positions: Direct sales of decorative accessories for the home. Most reps sell the products at exclusive showings in customers' homes.
Provisions: Pays commission. Training is provided.

ALCAS CUTLER CORPORATION, 1116 East State Street, P.O. Box 810, Olean, NY 147600-0810.
Positions: Alcas make cutlery, cookware, and tableware. The products are sold with the aid of mail order catalogs.
Provisions: Catalogs and other supplies are provided. Pays commission.

ALFA METALCRAFT CORPORATION OF AMERICA, 7970 Bayberry Road, Suite 10, Jacksonville, FL 32216.
Positions: Direct sales of cookware. Reps can use any direct sales methods. Some reps have incorporated the sales of Alfa cookware into cooking classes in their homes.
Provisions: Pays commission.

ALOE CHARM, INC., 741 Third Aveneu, King of Prussia, PA 19406.
Positions: Direct sales of aloe-based cosmetics.
Provisions: Pays commission.

ALOE MAGIC, Division of Exalo Tech, 2828 East 55 Place, P.O. Box 20423, Indianapolis, IN 46220.
Positions: ALoe Magic has an extensive line of aloe-based cosmetics and health and skin care products. Reps use a variety of direct sales methods.
Provisions: Pays commission.

AMERICAN MILLIONAIRES CLUB, 1100 Glendon Avenue, Suite 2045, Westwood, CA 90303.
Positions: Telemarketers provide research services for a singles social club.
Requirements: Must have good phone voice and be able to communicate effectively. Self-discipline is very important.
Provisions: Training is provided. Work is available throughout Southern California plus some other urban areas of the country. Hours can be very flexible. Pays commission averaging $100 a day.

AMERICA'S BUYERS, INC., 339 East 16 Street, Holland, MI 49423.
Positions: America's Buyers is one of many new buying clubs springing up around the nation. The line includes a wide array of products available to the customers at discount prices. Positions are not available in every state due to some legislative restrictions.
Requirements: A small start-up investment is required.
Provisions: Pays commission and override plus buying discounts on personal purchases.

AMWAY CORPORATION, 7575 East Fulton Road, Ada, MI 49355.
Positions: Amway is well known as the original multilevel organization. There are now five different divisions which include not only products but many services as well, such as MTI Long DIstance.

ANDREWS TELEMARKETING, INC., 35 South Grady Way, #250, Renton, WA

98056.
Positions: Telemarketing in various projects.
Requirements: Must live in either Seattle or Renton.. No experience required.
Provisions: Pays commissions only. "This is a new and growing company. Opportunities exist for many new telemarketers."

ARBONNE INTERNATIONAL, INC., 530 West 9460 South, Sandy, UT 84070.
Positions: Direct sales of European cosmetics and skin care products. Reps build customer bases using any direct sales methods that work for them.
Provisions: Training and ongoing managerial support is provided. Pays commission.

AUBREY MCDONALD CREATIONS, INC., 565 Wolf Ledges Parkway, Akron, OH 44311.
Positions: Direct sale of costume jewelry, primarily through the use of catalogs.
Provisions: Pays high commission. No territories.

AVACARE, INC., 9200 Carpenter Freeway, Dallas, TX 75247.
Positions: Direct sales of "natural" cosmetics and skin, hair and health care products.
Provisions: Pays commission.

AVON PRODUCTS, INC., Nine West 57 Street, New York, NY 10019.
Positions: Avon, which is known for door-to-door sales, rarely uses this method anymore. Instead, its huge number of reps use telemarketing methods to arrange home parties and make appointments for exclusive showings.
Requirements: Reps are required to buy samples, hostess thank-you gifts, and necessary paperwork.
Provisions: Pays commission. Management opportunities are available.

BEAUTICONTROL, INC., 2101 Midway Road, P.O. Box 345189, Dallas, TX 75234.
Positions: BeautiControl primarily markets a cosmetic line that is tied into the "seasonal" method of color coordination. A secondary line of women's apparel is marketed in the same way. In 1985, the company topped $30 million in gross sales. BeautiControl does not use the party plan method of direct sales, but rather focuses on one-on-one sales. This is accomplished through intensive training, personal development, and corporate support of the consultants, A free color analysis is offered to potential customers; this has proven to be the company's most powerful marketing tool.
Requirements: A one-time investment of $500 is required.
Provisions: Personal earnings are reported in the company's monthly in-house publication, "Achiever", and typically range from $12,000 down to $3,700 per month after being in the company for about two years. It is not unusual for new Consultants to earn $100 to $200 per day.

BEL KRAFT INTERNATIONAL, LTD., 32431 Schoolcraft Road, Livonia, MI 48150.
Positions: Bel Kraft manufactures cookware, china, crystal, flatware, and cutlery. Reps sell the products at home shows.
Provisions: Training is provided. Pays commission.

BETTER LIVING PRODUCTS, INC., 600 Busse Road, ELk Grove Village, IL 60007.
Positions: Direct sales of household, nutritional and personal care products.

Requirements: Start-up kit of samples and supplies requires an investment.
Provisions: Pays commissions.

BIT O'LOVE, 236 Cochituate Road, Framinham, MA 01701.
Positions: DIrect sales of clothing line. Biggest seller is pantyhose.
Provisions: Pays commission.

BON DEL CORPORATION, 3716 East Main Street, Mesa, AZ 85205.
Positions: Bon Del manufactures household bacteriostatic water treatment units. Independent reps sell the units direct by placing ads in local papers, through telemarketing, and sometimes with company provided leads.
Provisions: Training is provided. Pays commission.

CALICO SUBSCRIPTIONS, P.O. Box 11, Milpitas, CA 95035.
Positions: Telemarketing for periodical subscription renewals.
Requirements: Must be in the Bay area or Silicon Valley.
Provisions: Pays commission only. "Our telemarketers make very good money. We're always looking for good phone people."

CAMEO COUTURES, INC., 9004 Ambassador Row, P.O. Box 47390, Dallas, TX 75247.
Positions: Home party sales of lingerie, cosmetics, and food supplements.
Provisions: Training is provided. Pays commission.

CAMEO PRODUCTS, INC., P.O. Box 13388-A, Orlando, FL 32959.
Positions: Cameo has been offering quality products and services for over 17 years now. The products are typically craft kits such as needlepunch, fabric painting, bow art, iron-on transfers, etc. Product demonstrators act as craft instructors in a home party style "class".
Provisions: Minimum 25% commission for instructors. Commission plus override for managers.

CARE FREE INTERNATIONAL, INC., 1725 Hurd Drive, Irving, TX 75062.
Positions: Direct sales of food supplements, personal care, household, and safety products. Company uses multilevel marketing techniques.
Requirements: There is a small start-up investment required.
Provisions: Pays commission and bonuses.

CATTANI OF CALIFORNIA, 11842 Hamden Place, Santa Fe Springs, CA 90670.
Positions: Direct sales of lingerie and loungewear through home parties.
Provisions: Training and ongoing support is provided. Pays commission and bonuses.

CERES COSMETICS, INC., 201 College Avenue, Salem, VA 24153.
Positions: Direct sales of "glamour" cosmetics and other skin care products. Reps use any sales methods they wish.
Provisions: Catalog and some samples are provided. Pays commission.

CHAMBRE COSMETIC CORPORATION, P.O. Box 7777, Chatsworth, CA 91311.
Positions: Direct sales of cosmetics and food supplements. Pays commission.

Sue Rusch
The Pampered Chef

"Working at home has lent tremendous flexibility to my family life. I can be a full time mother first, but a very successful business person as well. And best of all, I call the shots. I decide when to work, how much to work, and I can still be on the PTA and sit down on the floor to play with my kids. I used to be a personnel manager, but hour for hour, the rate of pay can't even come close to what I make now."

CHRISTMAS AROUND THE WORLD, P.O. Box 9999, Kansas City, MO 64134-9999.
Positions: Home party demonstrators and supervisors. Company markets an upscale line of gifts and ornaments. All work is transferred via UPS. No investment requirements of any kind.
Provisions: Full training is provided. Pays commission plus override.

CONCEPT NOW COSMETICS BY RITA GROSS, 14000 Anson Street, Santa Fe Springs, CA 90670.
Positions: This 17 year old company has been selling an extensive line of skin care products primarily though party plan sales.
Requirements: A start-up kit with $325 requires a $65 investment.
Provisions: No set territories. Training is available and includes tapes, manual, presentation outline and company support. Car allowance is provided along with specified promotions. Pays commission only for reps and override for managers.

CON-STAN INDUSTRIES, INC., 19501 Walnut Drive, City of Industry, CA 91748.
Positions: Direct sales of cosmetics and food supplements.
Provisions: Pays commission.

CONSUMER EXPRESS, One Lakeshore Drive, Suite 1580, Lake Charles, LA 70629.
Positions: Consumer Express offers a wide vriety of products including food, cleaning products, cosmetics, and health care. It also offers services such as the Legal Services Plan. Direct distributors are free to market these products and services any way they wish with no set territories or methods.
Requirements: A one time $12 start-up fee is required.
Provisions: Pays commission plus bonus plan. This is a multilevel marketing plan so extra bonus plans for enrollments are available, but it is not the primary thrust of the program. Complete training is available.

COPPERSMITH COMPANY, 7500 Bluewater, N.W., Albuquerque, NM 87105.
Positions: Coppersmith is a manufacturer of decorative home accessories including tableware and wall decor, all made out of copper. Reps use a variety of means to market the products: home parties, exclusive showings, one-on-one consultations, and catalog sales.
Provisions: Strong company support is provided. Pays commission.

> "This is a new and growing company. Opportunities exist for many new telemarketers."
> —Andrews Telemarketing, Inc.

COPY MAT, 1475 Polk Street, San Francisco, CA 94108.
Positions: Telemarketing to set up appointment for sales staff for business-to-business sales.
Requirements: Must be San Francisco resident. Experience required. Must be available to work part-time, two to four hours a day.
Provisions: Pays hourly wage.

CORNET PRODUCING CORPORATION, 4738 North Harlem, Schiller Park, IL 60141.
Positions: Inside sales of entertainment events to businesses. 20 hours a week.
Requirements: Experience in business-to-business sales is necessary.

THE CREATIVE CIRCLE, 9243 Cody Street, Overland Park, KS 66214.
Positions: Party plan sales of needlework kits. Work involves conducting classes in needlework.
Requirements: $40 investment buys $90 worth of merchandise and paperwork supplies for three classes.
Provisions: Pays 25% commission plus incentives. Also provides thank-you gifts for hostesses and premiums used during parties. Managerial opportunities available. "The beauty of our company is we have no quotas, set territories, or anyone looking over our shoulders."

CREATIVE EXPRESSIONS, East Meadow Avenue, Robesonia, PA 19551.
Positions: Direct sales of craft products, kits, and supplies. Most of the reps conduct "classes" in how to use the products.
Provisions: Pays commission plus incentive bonuses.

CREATIVE TREASURES, 6836 Duckling Way, Sacramento, CA 95842.
Positions: Creative Treasures is a home party business that markets quality handcrafts of all kinds. Home party demonstrators and their supervisors are home-based. Items are ordered from a sample that is provided by each crafter.
Requirements: Write a letter of interest.

DEBBIE HOWELL COSMETICS, 8650 South Lafayette, Chicago, IL 60620.

Positions: Direct sales of extensive cosmetics line. Reps act as makeup artists and skin care consultants building a permanent clientele in a variety of ways.
Provisions: Pays commission. Management opportunitites exist.

DELUXE BUILDING MAINTENANCE, 760 Market Street, San Francisco, CA 94140.
Positions: Telemarketing. Cold calls only.
Requirements: Experience is required. Must be resident of San Francisco.
Provisions: Pays commission only.

DIAMITE CORPORATION, 131-D ALbright Way, Los Gatos, CA 95030.
Positions: Now 13 years old, Diamite still offers groundfloor opportunities nationwide. Manufacturer of skin care and nutritional products with the latest technology for anti-aging and life extension. Innovative marketing plan through networking part-time or full-time. Product line has 100% customer money back guarantee.
Provisions: Training is provided in the form of literature and video tapes.

DISCOVERY TOYS, INC., P.O. Box, 232008, Pleasant Hill, CA 94523.
Positions: DIscovery Toys was started as a home-based business in 1982. The company markets a line of educationally sound toys and accessories through home parties. Home party demonstrators and their supervisors are all home-based.
Requirements: Send letter of interest.
Provisions: Complete training is provided. Pays commission and override. Can live anywhere.

DIVERSIFIED MARKETING, LTD., 655-125 Deep Valley Drive, P. O. Box 2512, Rolling Hills Estates, CA 90274.
Positions: DIrect sales, utilizing multilevel techniques, of several different product lines: clothing and lingerie, automotive products, and household products.
Requirements: An initial purchase of products is required to start.
Provisions: Pays commission. Commission percentages increase with the level of sales production.

DONCASTER, Box 1159, Rutherfordton, NC 28139.
Positions: Doncaster trains women to be fashion consultants, "Selling the art of dressing well." Fashion Consultants present the Doncaster collection in private showing in their own homes four times a year. These fashions are considered to be investment quality and are designed primarily for career women.
Provisions: Training is provided. Pays commission. Management opportunitiesd are available.

DUDLEY PRODUCTS COMPANY, 50 East 26 Street, Chicago, IL 60616.
Positions: Direct sales of cosmetics using home parties as primary sales method.
Provisions: Training is provided. Pays commission and override for managers.

DUSKIN-CALIFORNIA, INC., 108E Star of India Lane, Carson, CA 90746.
Positions: Direct sales of household products. Primary focus is on dust control products. Reps use any method of sales they choose.
Provisions: Pays commission.

ELECTRIC MOBILITY CORPORATION, Number 1 Mobility Plaza, Sewell, NJ 08080.
Positions: This manufacturer of electric mobility three-wheelers uses a national network of independent reps to demonstrate and sell their products. All reps are home-based, but must travel to demonstrate the products to interested buyers because they are either elderly or handicapped.
Requirements: This is not hard sell; reps must be easy going, caring, efficient and very

---

"Our top typists average $15 an hour."
—The Office Connection

---

organized. Apply with resume.
Provisions: Leads are generated through national advertising and are prequalified by telmarketers before being sent to reps. Territories are assigned by zip codes. Commission are about $300 per sale.

ELEGANT COSMETICS, INC., 202 West McNeese Street, Lake Charles, LA 70605.
Positions: An extensive line of cosmetics is marketed by independent distributors by any method they chose.
Requirements: A small start-up investment is required.

EMMELINE COSMETICS CORPORATION, 3939 Washington Avenue, Kansas CIty, MO 64111.
Positions: Direct sales of commissions.
Provisions: Pays commission.

ENCYCLOPAEDIA BRITTANICA, INC., Brittanica Centre, 310 South Michigan Ave, Chicago, IL 60604.
Positions: This is the largest company of its kind in the world. It also has a reputation for having the highest paid direct sales reps of any industry. Britannica is now sold thgough a variety of means, very little door-to-door effort is used.
Provisions: A two week training session is provided. In most areas, write-in leads are provided. Pays highest commission in the industry,. plus override for managers.

E.S.A., P. O. Box 94141, San Francisco, CA 94141.
Positions: Telemarketers for nationwide education network. E.S.A. is a software company that develops coursewear. ALso uses outside sales reps and counselor/advisors.
Requirements: College degree and three years of experience required for any position. Must live in the Bay area.
Provisions: Salary plus commission.

FASHION DYNAMICS, 1155 Triton Drive, Suite D, Foster City, CA 94404.
Positions: Direct sales of cosmetics and skin care products.

Provisions: Pays commission.

FASHION TWO TWENTY, INC., 1263 South Chillicothe Road, Aurora, OH 44202.
Positions: Direct sales of extensive line of quality cosmetics. Reps start by conducting home parties. After building an established clientele, home parties are usually replaced with prearranged personal consultations.
Provisions: Pays commission. Management opportunities exist.

FINANCIAL ASSOCIATES, 5439 Madison Avenue, Carmichael, CA 95608.
Positions: Telemarketing; prospecting for new accounts. Work consists of obtaining credit collection accounts from businesses only, no consumer collections or sales involved.
Provisions: Will train anyone with the right voice and attitude. Pays commission only. Pay may not acrue for at least 60 days. "If you have the patience, you can make several thousand dollars a month."

FIRST RATE ENTERPRISES, INC., 413 Elmwood, Troy, MI 48084.
Positions: Direct sales of food, particularly sugar-free candy.
Provisions: Pays commission.

FIVE STAR COMMUNICATIONS, 888 Saratoga Avenue, San Jose, CA 95129.
Positions: Telemarketers. Work consists of generating leads and setting appointments for sales force, two hours a day. Product is cellular phone.
Requirements: Must live in the Greater Bay Area.
Provisions: A two-day training session is provided. Pays commissions "with good potential."

FORTUNATE CORPORATION, P.O. Box 5064, Charlottesville, VA 22905.
Positions: A wide variety of products including pet care, personal care, vitamins, and home cleaning products are sold direct using catalogs.
Provisions: Pays commission.

FULLER BRUSH COMPANY, 2800 Rockcreek Parkway, Suite 400, Kansas City, MO 64117.
Positions: Telemarketing program replaces old door-to-door method.
Requirements: $29 fee to start. There are set production requirements.
Provisions: Leads are provided. Pays commissions of 25% to 50% plus many incentives. Extends $900 credit line after joining firm. Can live anywhere.

GARMENT PRINTERS, 2920 Arden Way, Sacramento, CA 95825.
Positions: Telemarketing in local business-to-business marketing program.
Requirements: Must live in Sacramento.
Provisions: Offers choice of part-time or full-time work.

JAY GAUMAN ENTERPRISES, 1735 South Main #13, Salt Lake City, UT 84115.
Positions: Telemarketers generate leads and conduct call-backs for soft water rental company.
Requirements: Must be local resident. Self-discipline is extremely important.
Provisions: Training is provided. Hours are part-time in the evening only. Pays $6 per lead. "A self-disciplined telemarketer averages two leads per hour."

GRACE UNLIMITED, INCORPORATED, 14430 East Valley Boulevard, City of Industry, CA 91746.
Positions: Direct sales of cosmetics, skin care, and jewelry.
Provisions: Pays commission.

GROLIER INCORPORATED, Sherman Turnpike, Danbury, CT 06816.
Positions: Grolier is best known for publishing Encyclopedia Americana and has expanded into other educational publishing (such as the Disney series and Mr. Light).
Provisions: Training is provided in one-week classroom sessions. No leads, no territories. Sales are direct and usually accomplished

THE HANOVER SHOE, INC., 111 North Forney Avenue, Hanover, PA 17331.
Positions: Hanover is over 50 years old and still markets its shoes primarily through the use of independent reps. Reps sell direct through any method they chose, usually by starting with friends and neighbors and building up an established pool of customers through referrals.
Provisions: A portion of the retail price is returned to the rep.

HEALTH-GLO, INC., 6689 Peachtree Industrial Boulevard, Suite P, Norcross, GA 30092.
Positions: Direct sales of "natural" cosmetics. Reps use a variety of sales methods, but mostly home parties.
Provisions: Training is provided. Pays commission.

HEALTH-MOR, INC., 35 East Wacker Drive, Chicago, IL 60601.
Positions: Health-Mor is a manufacturer of vacuum cleaners, specifically Filter Queen. Company provides advertising and reps follow up on specific leads.
Provisions: Training is provided. Pays commission.

HEREFORD COMPANY, 1664 South Grand Avenue, Los Angeles, CA 90017.
Positions: Telemarketing for advertising firm. Work consists of developing leads for sales force.
Requirements: Must live in Los Angeles.
Provisions: Pays commission.

HERITAGE CORPORATION OF AMERICA, P.O. Box 401209, Dallas, TX 75240.
Positions: Catalog sales of food supplements.
Requirements: An initial purchase of the products is required.
Provisions: Pays commission.

HIGHLIGHTS FOR CHILDREN, INC., Parent and Child Resource Center, Inc., Representative Sales Dept., P. O. Box 810, Columbus, OH 43216.
Positions: Highlights for Children is an educational book for children ages 2 through 12. It is available by enrollment only. It is not sold on any newstand, contains no advertising and is created primarily for family use.
It is sold through authorized independent representatives directly to families, teachers, preschools, daycare centers, doctors' offices, etc. Exclusive territories are given so there may not be openings in some areas.
Requirements: Must be located where there exists an opening.
Provisions: Exclusive leads are provided. Hours are totally flexible. No investment is

Homeworker Profile: Nancy Maynard

Nancy Maynard's work has changed in ways she never expected since graduating from Berkeley with two degrees. Her work life started in the corporate world of Xerox.

"If found there was pressure to slow down, to do just what you're supposed to do. There was no encouragement to do more to earn more. Raises were the same for everyone; they came along once a year no matter what. After six years, I asked myself why I should work hard for another $10 a week—especially since I'd get it regardless of my accomplishments."

Shortly before leaving Xerox, Nancy started working with Oriflame, selling their European skin care system. The initial intent was to make a little extra cash. Much to her surprise, she matched her corporate salary within six months. In another six months she became assistant manager and was well on her way to earning her present $40,000 a year salary, plus bonus gifts.

"My whole way of thinking has changed. The corporate atmosphere fosters short-term thinking. Back then, if I wanted a new car, I'd have to wait and see what kind of a raise I got to decide if I could afford it. In direct sales, a person is in control. I can say, 'I need a car. I'll buy it and work an extra four hours a week to pay for it.'" She adds, "Of course, I don't need to do that. I've earned a gold Mercedes through Oriflame's incentive bonus plan!"

Nancy believes direct sales is an ideal choice for women who want to combine working and homemaking. It gives them control over their earning power and greater flexibility in their daily schedules.

For Nancy, that means spending time with her husband, who also works at home, and with their five year old daughter. "We both like to take time out of the day when we want to go to the park, have lunch together, or maybe just go for a walk. It allows us to give our daughter a better sense of us as people. What could be better than that?"

required. Training and ongoing support is provided. Pays commission, bonus plan, and incentive gifts.

HOME INTERIORS & GIFTS, INC., 4550 Spring Valley Road, Dallas, TX 75234.
Positions: Direct sales of pictures, figurines, shelves, foliage, and other home accents. Reps set up exclusive shows that include about 35 pieces of merchandise. After the show, the rep offers individual service and decorating advice to the customers.
Requirements: Reps must order, deliver, and collect.
Provisions: Training is provided in the form of ongoing sales classes, weekly meetings and monthly decorating workshops. The average rep presents about three shows a week and works about 25 hours a week.

HOUSE OF LLOYD, 11901 Grandview, MO 64030.
Positions: Home party sales reps and supervisors. Product line includes toys and gitfts.
Provisions: Training and start-up supplies are provided with no investment. Commission equals approximately $9 an hour. Can live anywhere.

HY CITE CORPORATION, 340 Coyier Lane, Madison, WI 53713.
Positions: Home party sales of cookware, china, crystal, tableware, stoneware, and cutler.
Provisions: Training is provided. Pays commission.

INSTANT PHOTO CORPORATION, 20280 Governors Highway, Olympia Fields, IL 60461.
Positions: Sales management poitions are available in protected territories nationwide with this special events photography business.
Requirements: A successful track record in sales and management. Write for complete instructions.

JAFRA COSMETICS, INC., P.O. Box 5026, Westlake Village, CA 91359.
Positions: Jafra makes high quality, "natural" cosmetics and skin care products. Reps sell the products through the party plan and by offering free facials to participants.
Provisions: Pays commission.

THE KIRBY CORPORATON, 14600 Detroit Avenue, Cleveland, OH 44107.
Positions: Kirby has been selling its vacuum cleaners door-to-door for many years. Now, reps use telemarketing methods to prearrange demonstrations.
Provisions: Some write-in leads are provided. Pays commissions.

KITCHEN FAIR, 1090 Redmond Road, P.O. Box 100, Jacksonville, AR 72076.
Positions: Kitchen Fair is a 60 year old maker of cookware, kitchen accessories, and home decorative items. All products are sold in home demonstrations. There is no ordering, packing, or shipping merchandise and no collection by the consultants.
Provisions: Training is provided. Regional advertising is provided by the company and the resulting inquires are passed along to the area consultants. The initial kit is free. Pays commission to consultants and up to 7% override to managers.

LADY FINNELLE COSMETICS, 1376 River Street, P.O. Box 1726, Haverhill, MA 01831.
Positions: Home party sales of cosmetics and skin care products.
Provisions: Training is provided. Pays commission plus incentive bonuses.

LADY LOVE COSMETICS, INC., 4503 Salt Lake Road, P.O. Box 1043, Addison, TX 75001.
Positions: Direct sales of cosmetics and skin care products. Most reps conduct home parties, but they can use any methods they choose.
Provisions: Training is provided. Pays commission.

LASTING IMPRESSIONS, 3683 Enochs Street, Santa Clara, CA 95051
Positions: Lasting Impressions sells specialty chocolates via hotels, florists, card shops, gift shops, etc. The company is expanding nationwide and is looking for wholesale reps in every state.
Requirements: Send letter of interest.
Provisions: Training is provided along with necessary literature, samples, etc. Pays commission.

LAURA LYNN COSMETICS, INC., 5456 McConnell Avenue, Suite 189, Los Angeles, CA 90066.
Positions: Direct sales of cosmetics and skin care products. Reps are trained in color by season consultation as a method of gaining a regular clientele.
Provisions: Training is provided. Pays commission.

LEARNEX LTD., INC., Saugatuck Station, P.O. Box 2043, Westport, CT 06980.
Positions: Learnex produces educational toys, children's books and cassettes. Reps use a variety of direct sales methods.
Provisions: Training is provided. Pays commission.

LIFE PRODUCTS CORPORATION, 2340 South El Casino Real, Suite 18, San Clemente, CA 92672.
Positions: Direct sales of food supplements and cosmetics.
Provisions: Pays commission.

LUCKY HEART COSMETICS, INC., 138 Hurling Avenue, Memphis, TN 38103.
Positions: Lucky Heart is a line of cosmetics for black women. The products are sold direct by independent distributors in any way they choose.
Requirements: A one-time $10 start-up fee is required.
Provision: Color catalogs, samples and testers are provided. Pays commission plus bonuses. Management opportunities exist.

MARLEY INGRID USA, INC., 3601 North Skokie Highway, North Chicago, IL 60064.
Positions: Home party sales of plastic housewares.
Provisions: Training is provided. Pays commission plus override for managers.

JOE MARTHA TELEMARKETING, 1615 Republic Street, Cincinnati, OH 45210.
Positions: Telemarketing of Catholic publications.
Provisions: Training is provided. Good repeat business. Can be located anywhere in the U.S. Pays good commission.

MARY KAY COSMETICS, INC., 8787 Stemmons Freeway, Dallas, TX 75247.
Positions: Beauty consultants and sales directors. Mary Kay started this cosmetics

empire on her kitchen table in 1963. In 1984 there were 151,615 consultants and 4,500 sales directors producing over $300 million in sales. All of these people worked from their homes.
Requirements: An investment of $100 is required to start.
Provisions: Pays commission up to 12%. Offers incentives such as jewelry, furs, cars and trips through special promotions and contests. Consultants can earn over $30,000 annually, generally averaging over $10 an hour after taxes. Directors average over $100,000 a year. Can live anywhere.

MASON SHOE MANUFACTURING COMPANY, 1251 First Avenue, Chippewa Falls, WI 54729.
Positions: Mason is a 35-year-old family business with an extensive line of American-made, quality shoes. All shoes are guarenteed for quality and fit and can be easily exchanged or refunded.
Provisions: Reps are provided with catalogs and all necessary supplies. Incentive bonus plans several times a year. Portion of the retail price is taken out by the rep before placing the order with the company.

MIRACLE MAID, P.O. Box C-50, Redmond, WA 98052.
Positions: Miracle Maid cookware is sold through pre-arranged product demonstrations in customers' homes.
Provisions: Training is provided. Pays commission.

MONITOR BUILDERS, 135 East 9th Avenue, Homestead, PA 15120.
Positions: Telemarketers set appointments for outside sales force. Work is available within local calling area; no set territories.
Provisions: Method and rate of payment is worked out with individual workers.

MULTIWAY ASSOCIATES, 633 Lawrence Street. P.O. Box 2796, Batesville, AR 72501.
Positions: Multiway sells its line of health products through independent contractors who are free to sell the products in any manner they wish. Although the company has suggested retail prices and the reps deduct the wholesale prices to deduct their commissions, the reps are free to set any prices they want.
Requirements: A one-time fee of $39 is required for a starter kit which includes all necessary instructions, paperwork and samples. No product inventory is required. No set territories.

NATIONAL MARKETING SERVICES, 2140 Sutter Street, San Francisco, CA 94115.
Positions: Work is available for various telemarketing projects; most involve selling tickets to charity events. Projects are available nationally as well as locally.
Requirements: Experience is required.
Provisions: Pays commission which varies with each project, but is typically in the $6 to $15 an hour range. Hours can be part-time or full-time, days or evenings. Script is provided.

NATIONAL TELEMARKETING ASSOCIATION, 908 Palmer Road, Walnut Creek, CA 94596.
Positions: Telemarketing on a variety of projects.
Requirements: Experience is preferred, but not required.

Provisions: Work is available anywhere in the country. Training is provided. Pay varies.

NATURAL ACCENTS BY PHILLIPINE IMPORTS, 8 B Street, Hyde Park, MA 02136.
Positions: Handcrafted decorative accents for the home are sold primarily through home party sales and also with the aid of catalogs.
Provisions: Catalogs are provided. Pays commission plus bonus plan.

> "We have turned competition into cooperation and we all have more work because of it."
> --L.A. Professional Typists

NATURAL IMPRESSIONS CORPORATION, 182 Liberty Street, Painesville, OH 44077.
Positions: Direct sales of jewelry.
Provisions: Pays commission. Catalogs are provided.

NEO-LIFE COMPANY OF AMERICA, P.O. Box 5015, Hayward, CA 94540.
Positions: DIrect sales of household products, vitamins, minerals, and some food products. Multilevel techniques are used.
Requirements: A small investment is required.
Provisions: Pays commission on a sliding scale.

NUTRIENT COSMETIC, LTD., 309 Old York Road, Jenkintown, PA 19046.
Positions: Home party sales of "natural" cosmetics.
Requirements: To get started with this company, you must first book a home party and be the hostess.
Provisions: Pays commission and bonuses.

OLDE WORLDE, INC., 401 Fraley Road, High Point, NC 27263.
Positions: Direct sales of household and personal care products and vitamins.
Provisions: Pays commission.

OMNI CREATIONS, 28651 Darrow Avenue, Saugus, CA 91350.
Positions: Direct sales of extensive jewelry line. Reps sell through home parties, fashion shows, wholesale, and any other method they choose. Company is now 11 years old.
Requirements: No investment is required. The company is expanding nationwide, but for now it is mostly operating in New York, New Jersey, California, Illinois, and Florida.
Provisions: There is a start-up program available for anyone interested in management opportunities in states not mentioned above. Work is part-time and reps average $30,000 a year.

KENNETH OLSON & ASSOCIATES, 399 Main Street, Los Altos, CA 94022.

Positions: Telemarketers for business-to-business insurance sales.
Requirements: Must be local resident. Prefers experience in business-to-business dealings.
Provisions: Specific training is provided. Leads are also provided. No high pressure selling involved. Part-time hours only. Pays salary plus "substantial" commission.

ORIFLAME INTERNATIONAL, 76 Treble Cove Road, North Billerica, MA 01862.
Positions: Direct sales reps for European cosmetics line. Oriflame International is a high-quality cosmetic line that has gained a reputation for being "the largest, most prestigious direct sales company in Europe." Company has been expanding throughout the U.S. for about five years. Advisors are trained as skin consultants. Business does not usually consist of door-to-door or party style sales. More often, advisors act as make-up artists and customers come to their home offices by appointment only. Opportunity also for part-time sales leadership positions. Significant "groundfloor" opportunity for Group Directors.
Provisions: Complete training is provided. Commissions are reportedly the highest in the U.S. for a direct sales company.

PACIFIC SECURITY SYSTEMS OF AMERICA, INC., 11924 N.E. Summer, Portland, OR 97024.
Positions: Telemarketers set appointments for salespeople.
Requirements: Must live in Portland. Experience in telemarketing required.
Provisions: Can work any hours. Pays commission weekly plus monthly bonus.

PAMPERED CHEF, 9913 Kell Avenue South, Bloomington, MN 55437.
Positions: Consultants and their supervisors conduct gourmet cooking demonstrations in order to show the Pampered Chef line of kitchen tools.
Provisions: Training is provided. Pays commission plus override for supervisors.

PARTYLITE GIFTS, Building 16, Cordage Park, Plymouth, MA 02360.
Positions: Home party sales of decorative accessories and giftware for the home.
Provisions: Pays commission plus bonuses. Management opportunities available.

PERFUME ORIGINALS, INC., 45 West 34 Street, New York, NY 10001.
Positions: Perfumes, oils, and Ultramink skin care systems are marketed in the home by skin consultants.
Requirements: To become an independent product representative you must first place an order for yourself.
Provisions: Upon placing your personal order, all future orders are 30% off. That is your commission. After $145 in retail sales, a sales kit is forwarded free; the kits contains a sales manual, necessary order forms and paperwork, and a vial box containing samples of the complete line of fragrances. Commissions climb with volume and go as high as 50%.

DAVID PHELPS INSURANCE, 7844 Madison Avenue, Suite N111, Fair Oaks, CA 95628.
Positions: Insurance sales for special program offered by National Association of Self Employed (NASE).
Requirements: Must live in Northern California to work for this particular agency.
Provisions: All leads are supplied by the association. Pays commission. Training is provided.

PLANTMINDER, INC., 22582 Shanon Circle, Lake Forest, CA 92630.
Positions: Direct sales of self-watering plant containers. Reps sell the product in a variety of ways, usually starting by placing ads.
Provisions: Pays commission.

POINT OUT PUBLISHING, 26 Homestead Street, San Francisco, CA 94114.
Positions: This European publisher of maps and guides uses home-baed telemarketers to make appointments for salespeople. Work is not permanent; it comes and goes all the time.
Requirements: Good phone manner and experience is required. San Francisco residents only.
Provisions: Pays $8 an hour.

POLA, U.S.A., INC., 250 East Victoria Avenue, Carson, CA 90746.
Positions: Home party sales of cosmetics.
Requirements: A start-up kit requires an investment.
Provisions: Pays commission.

PRINCESS HOUSE, INC., 455 Somerset Avenue, North Dighton, MA 02764.
Positions: Home party sales of crystal products.
Provisions: Pays commission plus override for managers. Training is provided.

PROFESSIONAL ACCOUNTANCY PRACTICE, 14111 Buckner Drive, San Jose, CA 95127.
Positions: Telemarketing of professional services to businesses only.
Requirements: Must be local resident. Experience is required.
Provisions: Specific training is provided.

QUEEN'S WAY TO FASHION, INC., 2500 Crawford Avenue, Evanston, IL 60201.
Positions: Direct sales of women's fashions mostly, but not necessarily, through home parties.
Requirements: There is a deposit required for the start-up kit.
Provisions: Training is provided. Pays commission "on a higher level than any other direct sales apparel company in the U.S." Management opportunities are available.

RAMA ENTERPRISES, P.O. Box 6010, New Philadelphia, OH 44663.
Positions: Rama is a Christian-oriented direct sales company using multilevel techniques to market personal care products such as perfume, shampoo, bath oil, skin care products, and home cleaning items.
Requirements: A $35 fee is required to register with the company. There is a quota of $25 a month in sales to continue as a rep. Pays 7% commission. Matches your 10% tithing to the ministry of your choice out of company profits.

THE W. T. RAWLEIGH COMPANY, 223 East Main Street, Freeport, IL 61032.
Positions: Direct sales of household products, food, cleaning products, medicine, and pet supplies. Reps use any sales methods they choose.
Provisions: Pays commissions.

REGAL WARE, INC., Kewaskum, WI 53040.
Positions: Direct sales of cookware, usually through home parties.

Provisions: Training is provided. Pays commission.

RENA-WARE COSMETICS, INC., P.O. Box C-50, Redmond, WA 98052.
Positions: Cookware is sold by independent reps in any manner they choose.
Provisions: Pays commission.

RICHLINE COSMETICS, INC., 2000 Richline Way, P.O. Box 3279, Zanesville, OH 43701.
Positions: Direct sales of cosmetics. Reps usually start out by conducting home parties and then develop a regular clientele.
Provisions: Training is provided. Pays commision.

ROSE JOYCE COSMETICS, 13037 Dorothy Drive, Philadelphia, PA 19116.
Positions: Home party sales of cosmetics.
Provisions: Pays commission and bonuses.

ROYAL AMERICAN AMERICAN FOOD COMPANY, 24307 East 40 Highway, P.O. Box 1000, Blue Springs, MO 64015.
Positions: Whey-based and dehydrated food products are sold direct using multilevel techniques.
Requirements: A minimum sales quota is required to remain in the sales program.
Provisions: Pays commission. Offers discounts on personal purchases.

S.T.A., 900 North 400 West, Building 6, North Salt Lake City, UT 84054.
Positions: Direct sales of automotive lubricants and fuel conditioners.
Provisions: Training and samples to get started are provided. Pays commission.

SALADMASTER, INC., 131 Howell Street, Dallas, TX 75207.
Positions: Home party sales of cookware and tableware.
Provisions: Training is available. Pays commission plus bonus plan.

SAMANTHA JEWELS, INC., 162-27 99 Street, P.O. Box 477, Station B, Howard Beach, NY 11414.
Positions: A line of more than 2,000 kinds of jewelry (mostly gold and diamond) are sold direct with the aid of mail order catalogs.
Requirements: A $4 fee for a sales package including the catalog with wholesale price instructions, sales instructions and paperwork supplies.
Provisions: Pays commission of a minimum 55%.

SAN FRANCISCO CHRONICLE, Circulation Department, 925 Mission, San Francisco, CA 94103.
Positions: Telemarketers sell subscriptions. Work is part-time.
Requirements: Some previous telemarketing experience is required.
Provisions: Can live anywhere in Northern California. Training is provided. Some leads are supplied. Pays commission and bonuses.

SASCO COSMETICS, INC., 2151 Hutton Drive, Carrollton, TX 75006.
Positions: Home party sales of cosmetics and personal care products, mostly based on aloe vera.
Provisions: Training is provided. Pays commissions. Management opportunities

available in most areas.

SCHOOL CALENDAR, P.O. Box 280, Morristown, TN 37815.
Positions: Account executives sell advertising space. Company is a 30 year old publishing firm.
Requirements: Must be bondable.
Provisions: A protected territory is assigned. Training and accounts are provided. Pays commission and bonuses.

"There is no question that working at home is better for productivity, especially for creative work. . . Professionals have always done it."

—Rising Star Industries

SHAKLEE CORPORATON, Shaklee Terraces, 444 Market Street, San Francisco, CA 94111.
Positions: Shaklee's line of products includes "natural" cosmetics, health care products, household products, and now some services as well. All of Shaklee's products are sold by independent distributors.
Requirements: Distributors must stock inventory in all basic products. Does require a cash investment.
Provisions: Pays commission.

SILVAN EVE, 560 Oakbrook Parkway, Suite 170, Norcross, GA 30093.
Positions: High quality silver and gold jewelry is sold by independent reps through a variety of methods.
Requirements: A refundable deposit is required for start-up sample case.
Provisions: Provides new catalogs as they come out. Training is provided. Pays substantial commission.

SOCIETY CORPORATION, 1609 Kilgore Avenue, Muncie, IN 47304.
Positions: This is a manufacturer of cookware, china and crystal. The product line is sold through independent reps with assigned exclusive territories.

THE SOUTHWESTERN COMPANY, P.O. Box 820, Nashville, TN 37202.
Positions: Southwestern is a well established publisher of educational books and cassettes. Independent reps sell the products, mostly with the aid of company provided leads. Exclusive territoties are assigned and many are taken by long-time reps so there may not be anything available in your area.
Provisions: Pays commission plus bonus plan.

STANHOME, INC., 333 Western Avenue, Westfield, MA 01085.
Positions: Direct sales of household cleaning products and personal grooming aids. Reps can used any method for marketing the products.
Provisions: Pays commission.

STEINHAUS AUTO ELECTRIC SERVICE, 3717 2nd Avenue, Sacramento, CA 95816.
Positions: Telemarketers set appointments for alarm systems salespeople.
Requirements: Must live in Sacramento. Experience preferred.
Provisions: Training provided. Pays guaranteed hourly rate.

THE STUART MCGUIRE COMPANY, INC., 115 Brand Road, Salem, VA 24156.
Positions: Direct sales of shoes and clothing for both men and women through the use of catalogs.
Provisions: Catalogs are provided. Pays commission on a sliding scale.

SUBSCRIPTION PLUS, 228-35 Edgewood Avenue, Rosedale, NY 11422.
Positions: Subscription agents for several hundred major consumer magazines.
Provisions: Some training is provided. Can be located anywhere in U.S. Pays commission up to 50%.

SUITCASE BOUTIQUE, 12228 Spring Place Court, Maryland Heights, MO, 63043.
Positions: Suitcase Boutique is a home party business. Home party demonstrators sell hand crafted items like stuffed animals, wood crafts, toys, soft sculpture, framed pictures, and cross-stitch.
Requirements: Investment is required for start-up kit, but kit will be bought back upon request.
Provisions: Pays commission. Training is provided. Work is part-time; average income for demonstrators is $9,000 a year. Can live anywhere.

THE SUNRIDER CORPORATION, 452 West 1260 North, Orem, UT 84057.
Positions: Direct sales of food products and personal care items using the multilevel techniques.
Requirements: A small investment in inventory is required.
Provisions: Pays commission on a sliding scale plus bonus incentives.

SUNSETS UNLIMITED TRAVEL CLUB, INC., 3007 South West Temple, Suite L, P.O. Box 15100, Salt Lake City, UT 84115.
Positions: Travel services are sold by independent reps mostly through telemarketing.
Provisions: Pays commission.

SYBIL'S, 9034 Natural Bridge Road, St. Louis, MO 63121.
Positions: Direct sales of jewelry and fragrances. Reps mostly use home parties, but it is not required.
Requirements: A refundable investment in start-up kit is required.
Provisions: Pays commission plus bonuses.

TELEMARKETING ASSOCIATES, 2924 North River Road, River Grove, IL 60171.
Positions: Telemarketing in various fund raising projects. Some projects are nationwide so home workers can live anywhere. Most projects, however, are in Illinois only.
Provisions: Training is provided. Pays hourly wage or high commission.
"One of our projects pays $500 and up per week in commission."

TIARA EXCLUSIVES, Dunkirk, IN 47336.

Positions: Home party sales of decorative home accessories mostly consisting of glassware.
Provisions: Training is provided. Pays commission plus override for managers.

TOMORROW'S TREASURES, INC., 111 North Glassboro Road, Woodbury Heights, NJ 08097.
Positions: Direct sales of photo albums, cameras, and other photographic equipment. Reps mostly use direct mail.
Provisions: Pays commission.

TOTAL SUCCESS, INC., 7975 North Hayden Road, Suite A-201, Scottsdale, AZ 85258.
Positions: Cosmetics and health related items are sold through multilevel sales techniques.
Requirements: A start-up kit requires an investment.
Provisions: Pays commission plus bonus plan.

TOWN & COUNTRY, 5060 Gardenville Road, Pittsburgh, PA 15236.
Positions: Telemarketing for carpet cleaning company.
Requirements: Must live in the greater Pittsburgh area.
Provisions: Training is provided. Each telemarketer is assigned a territory. Pays commission.

TRI-CHEM, INC., One Cape May Street, Harrison, NJ 07029.
Positions: Tri-Chem manufactures craft products. The leading product in their line is a liquid embroidery paint. Reps conduct craft classes to show potential customers how to use the products.
Provisions: Training is provided. Pays commission.

U.S. SAFETY & ENGINEERING CORPORATION, 2365 El Camino Avenue, Sacramento, CA 95821.
Positions: Direct sales of security systems including fire and burgular alarms. Reps have exclusive territories and are free to use any sales methds they choose. Most use telemarketing to set appointments for personal consultations.
Provisions: Pays commission.

UNDERCOVERWEAR, INC., 66 Concord Street, North Reading, MA 01864.
Positions: Home party sales of clothing, mostly lingerie.
Requirements: Rep is required to host a home party first.
Provisions: Pays commission. Training is provided.

UNION TRIBUNE, 4069 - 30th Street, Suite 9, San Diego, CA 92104-2631.
Positions: Telemarketers sell subscriptions.
Requirements: Must live in the San Diego area. Self-discipline is important.
Provisions: Training is provided. Some leads are supplied. Pays commission plus bonus.

UNIQUE DECOR, P.O. Box 491, Mansfield, MA 02048.
Positions: Decorative home accessories are sold by independent reps in exclusive showings.
Provisions: Training in both sales and some interior decorating techniques is provided.

Pays commissions.

UNITED LABORATORIES OF AMERICA, INC., 1526 Fort Worth Avenue, P.O. Box 4499, Station A, Dallas, TX 75208.
Positions: Direct sales of photo albums, photo enlargements, books and Bibles.
Provisions: Pays commission.

UNITED MARKETING GROUPS, 411 Borel Avenue, Suite 430, San Mateo, CA 94402.
Positions: Telemarketers work on a variety of projects throughout the Bay area.
Requirements: Experience is required in some kind of phone work. Must live in the Bay area.
Provisions: Training is provided. Leads are supplied. Pays commisison.

USA TODAY, P.O. Box 500, Sixth Floor—Circulation, Washington D.C. 20044.
Positions: Telemarketers solicit subscriptions. Work is distributed to home workers on a local basis only through USA Today's distributors. Distributors can be found in the phone book, or you can contact the main office to locate the distributor in your area.

VITA CRAFT CORPORATION, 11100 West 58 Street, Shawnee, KS 66203.
Positions: Home party sales of cookware, china, crystal, tableware and cutlery.
Provisions: Pays commission and bonuses. Training is provided.

VORWERK USA, INC., 700 Northlake Boulevard, Altmonte Springs, FL 32701.
Positions: Independent sales advisors (over 11,000 of them) sell products directly to consumers for the maintenance and cleaning of floor textiles.
Provisions: Complete training is provided.

WATKINS INCORPORATED, 150 Liberty Street, Winona, MN 55987.
Positions: Watkins is a well established company that uses independent reps to sell its extensive line of household goods including food, health products, and cleaning items.
Requirements: A small start-up investment is required.
Provisions: Pays commission.

WELCOME WAGON, P.O Box 177, Auburn, CA 95604.
Positions: Welcome Wagon is a personalized advertising service. Individuals in all areas work from home to represent local businesses in the homes of brides-to-be, new parents, and newcomers.
Requirements: Outgoing personality is most important. Car is a necessity.
Provisions: Training is provided. Flexible scheduling, part-time or full-time. Pays commission.

WESTERN HOME SYSTEMS, 3270 Orange Grove Avenue, North Highlands, CA 95660.
Positions: Telemarketers set appointments for sales force.
Requirements: Must live in the Central Valley.
Provisions: Training is provided. Some leads are supplied. Pays commission.

WORLD BOOK, INC., 510 Merchandise Mart Plaza, Chicago, IL 60654.
Positions: World Book, the encyclopedia publisher, sells its products through the use of direct sales reps.

Provisions: Training is provided. Some leads are provided. Pays commission. Sales kit is provided without cost. Managment opportunities are available.

WORLD WIDE SYSTEMS, 222 Madison Avenue, New York, NY 10031.
Positions: Sales reps and managers sell large line of imports from home.
Requirements: Territorial managers need five years experience.
Provisions: Specific training is provided. Pays commission. Part-time hours for reps, full-time for managers. Commission equals about $200 for reps; $500 a week for managers.

ZONDERVAN BOOK OF LIFE, P.O. Box 6130, Grand Rapids, MI 49506.
Positions: The Book of Life is a set of books based on the parables of the Bible. The company was established in 1923 and has always used direct salespeople to market the product.
Requirements: A refundable $20 deposit is required.
Provisions: The deposit buys a sales kit which includes all necessary training materials. Pays commission on a sliding scale which increases with volume. Cash bonuses and promotions are available. Also available are credit union membership, company-paid insurance, and a deferred retirement compensation plan.

Resource Guide

Periodicals

THE WHOLE WORK CATALOG.* Offers an unusually good selection of books, tapes and other materials on working from home, home businesses, alternative careers, etc. A trial subscription is $1.

THE WORKSTEADER NEWS.* Edited and published by the author of this book, "The Worksteader News" gives news and tips on working at home. Ideas are given on how to start and operate a successful home-based business, where and how to get a home-based job, and how to move your present work situation home. Each issue there's a pull-out section listing home jobs and business opportunities. Subscriptions are $24/year (6 issues).

EXTRA INCOME, Box 2688 Boulder, CO 80322. Each issue of this magazine tells how to begin and build a business at home, with examples of home-based businesses you can start for $100 or less. A 1-year subscription (6 issues) is $8.95.

NATIONAL HOME BUSINESS REPORT.* One way home-based business owners avoid feeling isolated is by plugging into networks of others in the same situation. A great deal of sharing and networking takes place in each issue of this highly personal newsletter, which is now in its sixth year of publication. Readers pass along ideas and marketing information which is often hard to find anywhere else. Subscriptions are $18/year (4 issues).

TELECOMMUTING REVIEW: THE GORDON REPORT, TeleSpan Publishing, 50A West Palm Street, Altadena, CA 91001. Organizations using or thinking about telecommuting should investigate this monthly newsletter produced by a management consultant who is a leading authority in the field.

FAMILY AND HOME OFFICE COMPUTING, Box 2511, Boulder, CO 80302. This magazine for personal computer enthusiasts, published by Scholastic, Inc., is the only magazine on the newsstands directed at home workers. Contains very practical information on how to get started making money with your personal computer. A 1-year subscription is $19.95.

Items with an asterisk are available from The New Careers Center, P.O. Box 297-SB, Boulder CO 80306

Books

WORKING AT HOME: IS IT FOR YOU? by William Atkinson. This is probably the most comprehensive guide to deciding whether you will enjoy working at home. From Dow Jones-Irwin, Homewood, IL 60430.

EXTRA CASH FOR WOMEN* by Susan Gillenwater and Virginia Dennis. Very well-written guide to making money from home with a very small investment. $10.95 postpaid.

THE HOME OFFICE: HOW TO SET IT UP, OPERATE IT, AND MAKE IT PAY OFF! by Peg Contrucci. This guide to starting a home business is nicely organized and comprehensive, but expensive. $24.95 from Prentice-Hall, Inc., Englewood Cliffs, NJ 07632

HOW TO START AND RUN A SUCCESSFUL HOME TYPING BUSI-NESS* and WORD PROCESSING PROFITS AT HOME,* both by Peggy Glenn. These are excellent books covering personal considerations, planning, advertising, pricing, equipment, marketing and more. Highly recommended. Each book is $17.95 postpaid.

HOW TO QUALIFY FOR THE HOME OFFICE DEDUCTION by Katherine M. Klotzburger, Ph.D. Discusses what constitutes a bona fide home office, how to maximize your deductions, etc. $8.95 from Betterway Publications, Inc., White Hall, VA 22987

HOMEMADE MONEY: THE DEFINITIVE GUIDE TO SUCCESS IN A HOME BUSINESS* by Barbara Brabec. One of the foremost authorities on the boom in home businesses gives expert advice on getting started, selecting the right home business (and avoiding the wrong ones), planning for profits, diversifying, expanding and more. $15.95 postpaid.

MOONLIGHTING WITH YOUR PERSONAL COMPUTER* by Robert J. Waxman. If you have a home computer and know how to operate it, you can turn a relatively small investment into a profitable source of income with this book. Step-by-step advice and inspiring ideas. $10.95 postpaid.

Items with an asterisk are available from The New Careers Center, P.O. Box 297-SB, Boulder CO 80306

TELECOMMUTING: HOW TO MAKE IT WORK FOR YOU AND YOUR COMPANY by Gil Gordon and Marcia Kelly. This is the definitive book on telecommuting. How your company can benefit by moving your employees out of the office and into remote locations—either the home or a satellite office— through using computer terminals linked to telephone systems. Prentice-Hall, Inc., Englewood Cliffs, New Jersey.

CREATIVE CASH: HOW TO SELL YOUR CRAFTS, NEEDLEWORK, DESIGNS & KNOW-HOW* by Barbara Brabec. There's a good reason why over 70,000 copies of this book are in print: it is truly outstanding. Very comprehensive information with step-by-step how-to's for every aspect of a crafts business. $15.95 postpaid.

KIDS MEAN BUSINESS: HOW TO TURN YOUR LOVE OF CHILDREN INTO A PROFITABLE AND WONDERFULLY SATISFYING BUSINESS* by Barbralu Manning. This book covers a very wide range of child-related business opportunities, including day care and other businesses that can be operated from home. $10.95 postpaid.

THE WORK-AT-HOME SOURCEBOOK. Additional copies of this book may be ordered directly from the publisher for $13.95 postpaid. Live Oak Publications, P.O. Box 2193, Boulder, CO 80306.

WORKING FROM HOME* by Paul and Sarah Edwards. In 488 pages the Edwards cover all aspects of home businesses including presenting a business image at home, dealing with zoning, licenses and legal obligations and setting up an efficient home office. The emphasis throughout is on computer-related businesses. $14.95 postpaid.

Organizations

NATIONAL ALLIANCE OF HOMEBASED BUSINESSWOMEN, Box 306, Midland Park, NJ 07432. Open to men as well as women, this network is active in all 50 states and has many local chapters. Conducts seminars and workshops, provides life insurance and group discounts, monitors legal issues affecting home workers, etc.

* Items with an asterisk are available from The New Careers Center, P.O. Box 297-SB, Boulder CO 80306

MOTHERS' HOME BUSINESS NETWORK is a membership organization offering support and information for those already operating home businesses and those actively considering the idea. Publications include a newsletter, annual directory of members, fact sheets and guides to starting home typing businesses and home mail-order businesses. MHBN, Box 423, East Meadow, NY 11554.

ASSOCIATION OF ELECTRONIC COTTAGERS, 677 Canyon Crest Drive, Sierra Madre, CA 91024. If you work from home using a computer, this group can be a helpful contact.

For a very comprehensive listing of other organizations of interest to home businesses, write to the Center for Home-Based Businesses at Truman College, 1145 West Wilson, Chicago, IL 60640 and ask for their "Organizations for Home-Based Businesses."

ALPHABETICAL INDEX

Location Index

National and/or Multi-Regional

Opportunities For the Disabled